PASSION AND PERSISTENCE

Rick + Dianne
Please enjoy!
Diane Pind
19/09/19

PASSION &

Fifty Years of the Sierra Club in British Columbia

PERSISTENCE

DIANE PINCH

Harbour Publishing Co. Ltd.
P.O. Box 219, Madeira Park, BC, VON 2H0
www.harbourpublishing.com

Chapter 14 is an abridged version of *The Future Is Here*, used by permission of Sierra Club of
    BC Foundation
Edited by Pam Robertson
Indexed by Michelle Chiang
Text design by Brianna Cerkiewicz
Printed and bound in Canada

Canadä

Harbour Publishing acknowledges the support of the Canada Council for the Arts, which last
year invested $153 million to bring the arts to Canadians throughout the country.

*Nous remercions le Conseil des arts du Canada de son soutien. L'an dernier, le Conseil a investi 153
millions de dollars pour mettre de l'art dans la vie des Canadiennes et des Canadiens de tout le pays.*

We also gratefully acknowledge financial support from the Government of Canada and from
the Province of British Columbia through the BC Arts Council and the Book Publishing Tax
Credit.

Library and Archives Canada Cataloguing in Publication

Title: Passion and persistence : fifty years of the Sierra Club in British Columbia, 1969-2019 /
    Diane Pinch.
Names: Pinch, Diane, 1955- author.
Description: Includes bibliographical references and index.
Identifiers: Canadiana (print) 20190128402 | Canadiana (ebook) 20190128461 | ISBN
    9781550178814 (hardcover) | ISBN 9781550178821 (HTML)
Subjects: LCSH: Sierra Club of British Columbia—History. | LCSH: Environmentalism—British
    Columbia—History.
Classification: LCC QH77.C3 P575 2019 | DDC 333.95/1609711—dc23

To Brian, my husband and best friend,
who introduced me to the Sierra Club

Contents

Foreword

READING THROUGH THIS VOLUME, I WAS DRAWN INTO A FRANK Capra moment. Imagine a version of It's a Wonderful Life, all about Sierra Club BC. Just as George Bailey got to see how the world would have been altered if he had never been born, it is worth considering how much worse everything would be had Sierra Club British Columbia never existed.

The scenes would evoke similar emotions. Pottersville's depressing and seedy dystopic future never came to pass thanks to our hero's slow and steady work to protect Bedford Falls. For a British Columbia without Sierra Club, we can imagine walking through bad development after bad development in a dark place where legions of volunteers had never been engaged to make a difference. What if the late Pete Dixon had never fought to save forested lands near Victoria to stop inappropriate housing sprawl? Or if Vicky Husband had never saved the Khutzeymateen or critical ancient forests on Vancouver Island? Or Rosemary Fox had not continually acted to preserve habitat in and around Smithers?

Those early days needed to be chronicled. Back then it was the Sierra Club of Western Canada and one lone staff person carried the load. The long hours put in by Sharon Chow, aided by key volunteers, could have faded away without this book. I recall the amazing Geraldine Irby, who worked so steadfastly in preparing annual reports and many other often thankless tasks over the years!

Diane Pinch has contributed significantly to a critical piece of Canadian history by documenting the decades of work by different generations of leadership, staff and volunteers. Her kind comments about my time as the first executive director of the Sierra Club of Canada are appreciated. The seventeen years I worked to first establish a Sierra Club of Canada and then build a coast to coast to coast organization is one of my proudest accomplishments.

From its beginnings in the Sierra Nevada in 1892, under the prophetic leadership of John Muir, Sierra Club has always been ahead of its time. One of the hallmarks of its work over more than a century has been to empower volunteers. It is a remarkable level of trust that allows a large organization to encourage volunteers to act in its name. For a long time, the Sierra Club of British Columbia not only trusted volunteers to act in its name, but the name of one outstanding volunteer leader was synonymous with the organization itself. When I think of the major conservation successes of the Sierra Club of BC, it is impossible to think of them without being grateful to Vicky Husband.

For eighteen years, Vicky worked day and night to build Sierra Club BC. Another prominent part of the movement, who should be included in this history, Toronto philanthropist Glen Davis, once phoned Vicky's home. Her partner, Patrick, answered the phone with a frustrated, "You have reached the office of Save the World. She's not home."

Vicky also donated generously to the organization. And thanks to her prominence in the legions of movers and shakers in BC, she was able to open doors that had traditionally remained closed to environmentalists.

One aspect of Sierra Club BC's leadership in the national environmental movement was the early adoption of GIS mapping to clearly demonstrate loss of old-growth. It was thanks to Vicky, identifying the need and then raising the funds to make it possible, that the club started GIS mapping. A brilliant young mapper, David Leversee, joined the club's growing staff. Mapping the disappearance of old-growth forests on Vancouver Island and then the fragmentation of large forested watersheds for all of British Columbia was groundbreaking work. So too was the investment in aerial photography so that images reflected a landscape-wide view of impacts.

When I think of the many successes of the Sierra Club in the United States and Canada, I think of the philosophy of John Muir.

Over one hundred years ago he wrote, "When we try to pick out anything by itself, we find it hitched to everything else in the Universe."

We usually absorb that thought as applying to the natural world: that we cannot pick out a spider without snagging a forest. But I increasingly think it means more. Our universe is hitched together through relationships. It is humans as activists, woven together through years of work and knitted together in an unbroken web of love and trust, that is most needed to save the world. The irony, of course, is that we must save ourselves and the natural world from the thoughtless greed of a small minority of humanity.

That human ecosystem is reflected in the history of the Sierra Club of British Columbia. We never want to find out where we would be without it.

—Elizabeth May

Preface

I MARRIED AN ENVIRONMENTALIST. I DID NOT THINK ABOUT IT much in the early days of our marriage. I was busy, first with university and later with my career in health care. We sometimes laughed about it, saying that he would take care of the environment and I would look after the people.

Brian has been a member of the Sierra Club almost from its early beginnings in BC in 1969—not quite that long but close. Certainly, it was before we met in 1975 at university. He is a lover of nature, a keen backpacker, and he introduced me to this love of his, this passion. Later, I met others who were involved with the club and watched from the periphery as they attempted to save the areas of nature that they loved. Vancouver Island, in particular, had suffered over the years from logging and other encroachments, and I saw some of the devastation when I hiked with Brian. I sometimes went to slide shows and talks put on by speakers advocating for a particular area or issue. Sometimes there were board meetings at our home. These were people with a mission, and their passion about protecting wilderness impressed me.

I also learned about John Muir, the driving force behind the formation of the Sierra Club in the US in 1892. He wanted to protect the Sierra Nevada area of California, especially Yosemite Valley and Hetch Hetchy. Muir spent many years exploring the mountains of the region, with their magnificent waterfalls and gigantic trees, and he worked diligently to protect this sanctuary. I visited Yosemite National Park—established in 1890 thanks to his efforts—for the first time in 2013 and finally understood why he had been so concerned about preserving that spectacular area. We are indeed fortunate that his efforts were successful.

Since the days of John Muir, the Sierra Club has gradually grown across North America. However, it was not until 1969 that a Sierra Club group was formed in Vancouver, British Columbia—the first one outside the United States. I thought I knew the story about how this happened. But there was a lot more to it than I thought, and I found that through researching the beginnings of Sierra Club BC for this book. I also met some fascinating people. These people had accomplished some very ambitious and challenging goals and I got to listen to their stories, which was a rewarding and enlightening experience for me. I only wish I could have included stories from more people.

I have not been able to describe each and every campaign, landmark accomplishment, or leadership initiative, so some may notice gaps here and there, for which I apologize. Also, I would like to point out that the environmental achievements described in this book were frequently due to not just the work of Sierra Club BC but also to efforts by many other organizations and individuals not affiliated with the club. I have attempted to point out the many instances in which a campaign was successful because of coalitions, alliances, and partnerships that were formed at the time.

I would also like to acknowledge and celebrate how much our province owes to dedicated individuals, many of whom are either unpaid or give far more of their time and energy than the hours for which they are paid. It is not by chance that British Columbians can boast about the many parks and protected wilderness areas now available to us, nor is it by chance that there is a significant rise in environmental awareness about the need for sustainable use of our natural resources. It is only because we, the public, have insisted. We must continue to do so.

Sierra Club BC's official name has gone through various iterations over the last fifty years.[1] For most of this time there were two entities as well: the "club," a lobbying and activist arm, and the "foundation," a charitable arm able to issue tax receipts for donations when appropriate. For the purposes of this account, I will use the name Sierra Club BC or the acronym SCBC throughout.

To accomplish great things, we must not only act,
but also dream; not only plan, but also believe.
—Anatole France

1

The Origins of Sierra Club BC

American Roots

THE SIERRA CLUB WAS ONE OF THE FIRST LARGE-SCALE CONSERVA-tion groups in the world. It began in the United States in the late nineteenth century and continues to play a vital role in the global environmental movement. The club deserves credit for many of the most iconic parks and wilderness areas in the United States as well as a wealth of environmental legislation and regulations that have reshaped modern human activity.

The club's roots go back to the Sierra Nevada Mountains of California, home of the giant redwood forests and the scenic granite peaks of what is now Yosemite National Park. John Muir, a native of Scotland, has been credited with founding the Sierra Club, though, in truth, many were involved. Muir left Scotland at the age of eleven when his family moved to Wisconsin. His lifelong interest in the natural environment inspired him to travel widely, often on foot—those travels included a thousand-mile walk from Kentucky to Florida in 1867 as a young man of twenty-nine.[2] Muir eventually settled in Martinez, northeast of San Francisco, but spent a great deal of time in Yosemite; it was here that he gained renown as a writer and a naturalist. He described the flora, geology, watersheds, glacial pathways,

In 2013, the author visited Yosemite Valley. She is pictured here with El Capitan in the left foreground and Half Dome by the clouds in the centre. *Photo by Brian Pinch*

and ecology of the area; he extolled the region's beauty and promoted the idea that the area should be preserved.

Although a core tract of land within the Yosemite Valley had been set aside and granted to the state in 1864 by President Lincoln and Congress, it provided only limited protection. Encouraged by his friend Robert Underwood Johnson, associate editor of *The Century* magazine, in 1889 John Muir published a set of articles[3] outlining his plan to protect Yosemite from the effects of grazing by establishing a national park modelled after Yellowstone. Congress passed a bill in 1890 that essentially followed Muir's recommendations to protect portions of Yosemite; however, the bill unfortunately left Yosemite Valley and Mariposa Grove under state control and vulnerable to logging and over-grazing.

Around this time, Muir, Johnson, and others held meetings to establish a local alpine club along the lines of the Appalachian Mountain Club, which had formed in 1867. The idea came from a Berkeley professor, Henry Senger, who with a group of other young professors proposed that Muir take a leading role. The Sierra Club was formed in 1892 and Muir remained its president until his death twenty-two years later in 1914. The association's goals were to assist with the campaign to expand the national park as well as provide a means for recreation and education about the Sierra Nevada area. The members actively promoted the benefits of hiking and encouraged people to participate in day hikes and camps in the high country. Along the way, the club learned a lesson that environmentalists continue to learn: "no environmental war is ever finally won, though any battle when lost, is lost forever."[4]

Sierra Club BC's logo commemorates its beginnings in the Sierra Nevada mountains with an image of a sequoia and the cliff face of Half Dome, found in Yosemite National Park. *SCBC Photo Files*

A seminal and famed event occurred in 1903 when John Muir convinced President Teddy Roosevelt to accompany him on a three-day camping trip to the alpine area of the Sierra Nevada mountains. Anne Rowthorn, in *The Wisdom of John Muir*, described this event as a turning point for the conservation movement. As a result of his experience, Roosevelt designated 148 million acres as national forest and created five national parks and twenty-three national monuments.[5]

The Sierra Club remained primarily a Californian organization until 1950, although it was involved with opposition to the building of a dam in Yellowstone Park, a campaign to enlarge Grand Teton National Monument in Wyoming, and lobbying to protect Olympic National Park in Washington. In 1950, the Atlantic Chapter—made up of eighteen eastern states and the District of Columbia—was formed, becoming the first Sierra Club organization outside of California. Not long after, the Pacific Northwest Chapter was established in 1954. The club continued to grow across the US with the establishment of many local groups and chapters. The Sierra Club is somewhat unique in having an administrative structure that allows for units known as "local groups," regional entities known as chapters, and a national level in its organization. In the US, chapter boundaries often coincide with state borders and a local group might be associated with a county or a city. It currently has sixty-four chapters nationwide, with 2.4 million members and supporters.

For most of its early history, the Sierra Club was involved in conserving wilderness areas and advocating for protected park status. It was due to the Sierra Club's promotion of the locales' unique wildlife, recreational opportunities, and remarkable natural features that Glacier National Park and Mount Rainier National Park were established. As well, it launched successful crusades against proposed dams in Dinosaur National Monument in Utah (1950s) and in the Grand Canyon (1960s).

Members differed in their ideas concerning the definition of "wilderness" and the activities that should be allowed in wilderness areas, and these views evolved over the years. A number of major conferences held in the 1950s and 1960s helped to shape these understandings. Diverse perspectives were melded to develop a more formal definition and a wilderness bill was presented to Congress in 1957 (although it was not passed until 1964, after many drafts).

The 1960s were a period of great social change. Young people were often at the forefront of campaigns advocating for reforms on civil rights, drug use, gender roles, and the acceptance of homosexuality. The first non-violent sit-in took place in 1960 at a Woolworth's luncheon counter in Greensboro, North Carolina, where black protesters voiced their opposition to racial segregation; in 1963, Martin Luther King Jr. gave his famous speech following the March on Washington, which led to the signing of the Civil Rights Act by President Johnson in 1964. In 1960, the birth control pill was approved; 1966 saw the founding of the National Organization for Women, dedicated to promoting equality for all women.[6]

The rock and roll of the 1950s transformed into the rock music of the Beatles and the Rolling Stones. Folk music took on the great social issues of the day with the iconic lyrics of musicians such as Bob Dylan, Joan Baez, and Pete Seeger. Large open-air concerts became widespread, culminating in 1969 with the celebrated Woodstock, which some say signified the end of a simpler time of free love and psychedelic drugs.[7] In the background, the Vietnam War raged on despite rising public opposition and eruptions of mass anti-war protests. The space race between the US and the Soviet Union was well underway, climaxing with the moon landing by the Americans in July 1969. By the 1960s, most homes had televisions and people were able to follow the protests, engage with the issues, enjoy variety programs introducing new entertainers, and watch the lunar spacewalk unfold.

During this time, people also became concerned about detrimental changes to the environment. Rachel Carson published *Silent Spring* in 1962, which brought to light the indiscriminate use of pesticides. Paul Ehrlich published *The Population Bomb* in 1968, raising concerns about the alarming potential effects of overpopulation.

Prior to the 1960s, most campaigns by groups such as the Sierra Club focused on preserving wilderness areas, protecting endangered wildlife species, and conserving resources such as timber. A shift occurred during the 1960s as people began to understand the significant effects humans had on their environment. They began to worry about air and water pollution, solid waste disposal, dwindling energy resources, and noise pollution. There was a growing suspicion that government and industry were colluding and that the public was not being protected from the devastating effects of industrial growth. Perhaps the landing of Apollo 11 on the moon was a pivotal event. Tom Turner, in his history of the US Sierra Club, suggested that when it sent back a photo of the earth from space, "The sight of the fragile, vulnerable blue ball floating in black space—the only living thing we know for certain exists in the universe—made millions of people stop and think about what humanity was doing to its home."[8]

What followed was a remarkable outpouring of federal legislation, including the Clean Air Act and the National Environmental Policy Act in 1970 and the Water Pollution Control Act in 1972. The Sierra Club, through its lobbying and grassroots support, played a strong role in passing these pieces of legislation.

Sierra Club Comes to Canada

CANADIANS WERE ALSO UNDERGOING SOCIAL CHANGES THROUGH-
out the 1960s, although perhaps not with the same degree of intensity
that Americans were. Despite the border between Canada and the US,
Canadian youth participated in the same "counter" culture as their
American neighbours, avidly listening to new styles of rock music,
opposing the war, supporting civil rights, and being transformed by
the idea of women's liberation.

On the Canadian political front, the 1960s saw a strong resurgence of the separatist movement in Quebec with the founding of
a violent radical fringe group, the FLQ (Front de libération du Qué-
bec). As well, Canadians were beginning to take a hard look at their
own history of mistreating First Peoples, perhaps stimulated to some
extent by the civil rights movement; the residential school system
was only beginning to be challenged.

A 1963 federal commission on Indigenous people's social conditions led to Prime Minister Pierre Trudeau's trial balloon, the White
Paper of 1969 (formally called *The Statement of the Government of
Canada on Indian Policy*). This document resulted in one of the first
moments of open resistance and a coalescing of several First Nations
organizations around a number of issues (including rights, title,
and status)—the beginnings of a nascent activism that did not really
gather momentum until the 1970s.

The Canadian Bill of Rights was approved in 1960 and the Maple
Leaf flag was adopted in 1965—two years later, Montreal hosted the
World's Fair, Expo '67, which coincided with Canada's hundredth
birthday. Medicare, a key part of Canada's national publicly funded
healthcare system, was enacted in 1966. Pierre Trudeau proposed
amendments to the Criminal Code, which were passed in 1969 and
resulted in, among other things, the decriminalization of contracep-
tion, abortion, and "homosexual acts." On these matters, Trudeau
famously told the press: "there's no place for the state in the bed-
rooms of the nation."

It also happened that in 1969—at the end of an iconic decade,
with its social upheaval and its rise in political, social, and

environmental awareness—the Sierra Club arrived in Vancouver.

Michael Doherty, a member of Sierra Club BC at the time, later discussed the club's origins in his master's thesis[9] and attributed its success to three factors. First was the timing. The environmental movement was clearly gaining momentum across North America. Second, a number of people in Canada were already Sierra Club members. Many Americans had kept their membership active when they moved north to Canada—often because they were opposed to the war in Vietnam. Others were Canadians who had joined to participate in outings offered by the US Sierra Club, many of which took place in British Columbia and Alberta. The third factor was the north-south geography of the west coast. Environmental issues that concerned people in California, Oregon, and Washington were also of interest to people in British Columbia.

Terry Simmons, a new American graduate student at Simon Fraser University, had spent a summer working as a research assistant at the Sierra Club's national office in San Francisco. Looking around BC, he did not see any environmental groups with similar depth and experience. In May 1969, he wrote a letter to Brock Evans, a Sierra Club organizer in Seattle, telling him that there was great potential in Vancouver and that somebody should do something. Brock pragmatically wrote back, "You're right. Why don't you do it?"—thus providing Simmons with the impetus to start the club.

The Sierra Club sent Simmons its mailing list of members living in BC, which was essentially the subscription list for its magazine, known at that time as the *Sierra Club Bulletin*. There were forty to fifty names on it. In July 1969, Simmons arranged a meeting of members at Simon Fraser University in Vancouver. About fifteen people came including Katy Madsen, Ken Farquharson, Irving Stowe, Jim Bohlen, Ian Bain, Bill Darnell, and Bill Chalmers.

There was strong agreement among the attendees that more could be accomplished by working together and joining an organization with name recognition, resources, and international contacts. Simmons had been in contact with Sierra Club members on the other side of the border in Washington who were very supportive of the club expanding into Canada. Consequently, on November 28, 1969, the Sierra Club of BC was incorporated as a society under the BC Societies Act. This allowed the group to receive tax-deductible (charitable) donations and apply for grants and other funding. It also meant that, legally, Sierra Club BC was an independent organization, separate from the US Sierra Club.

Several leaders within the Pacific Northwest Chapter of the Sierra Club were aware of the need for the BC group to incorporate as they had attended some preliminary meetings where it had been discussed. Nevertheless, when word reached the national office in San Francisco, especially the legal department, it led to some consternation and discussions, with Simmons having to explain the rationale for the group's autonomy at one of the board meetings in San Francisco. Ultimately, after a committee had been formed and had researched the issue, it was agreed that despite being a separate legal entity the Sierra Club BC would function as a "local group" of the Pacific Northwest Chapter, which was made up of the groups within Washington, Oregon, Idaho, and Montana. As such, it fit into the administrative framework of the American parent organization.

Sierra Club BC's first job was to write a constitution. The members decided the society's purpose was to "explore, enjoy and preserve the scenic resources of British Columbia, in particular, its forests, waters, and wilderness." The group would research and publish scientific, literary, and educational studies about these resources, which would help to educate people and enlist their cooperation in advocating for wilderness protection.

The new Sierra Club BC quickly became entangled in the existing campaigns of its members and initiated new campaigns as well. Three endeavours in particular soon established the club as a force to be reckoned with: Cypress Mountain, the Skagit Valley and the West Coast Trail.

Cypress Mountain

CYPRESS BOWL WAS A POPULAR LOCAL SKI AREA NESTLED AMONG three mountains behind West Vancouver. The area had been used by skiers willing to hike up into the mountains since the 1920s. In the mid-1960s, a group of Vancouver businessmen purchased the land and proposed a multi-purpose outdoor recreation resort. After four years of negotiations between the developer, the municipality, and the province, logging began and, with it, public controversy. Some thought the development was being used as a cover for simply clear-cutting the land.

In 1968, a Save Cypress Bowl Committee was established, made up of members from the BC Mountaineers, the Alpine Club, and the Federation of BC Naturalists. However, Ken Farquharson recalled that the group had very little success in lobbying the government and raising the profile of the issue.

It was not until Sierra Club BC was established and joined them as an ally that the coalition became effective on this file. After further controversy—including the revelation that the development's new owners were mixed up with casinos in the Bahamas—the newly elected New Democratic Party (NDP) government stepped in and designated the entire area as Cypress Provincial Park in 1972. The coalition of groups, including Sierra Club BC, continued to exert pressure to limit commercial development and contribute to the master plan (eventually completed in 1997).

The Skagit Valley

IT WAS REALLY THE CONTROVERSY ABOUT THE SKAGIT VALLEY THAT became Sierra Club BC's inaugural issue. The Skagit River starts in Manning Park, east of Vancouver, and flows south across the US border to Puget Sound in Washington state. In 1967, the BC government and Washington's Seattle City Light, the city's public utility,[10] concluded decades of on-again, off-again negotiations and quietly came to an agreement to construct a fourth-stage dam on the Skagit River to meet peak period electrical demands in Seattle. Known as the High Ross Dam, the project would raise the level of the Skagit, flooding portions of the Ross Lake National Recreational Area in Washington and the Skagit Valley southeast of Vancouver. The BC government did not have any significant concerns about the location of the dam. The agreement involved an annual rental payment from the public utility that would compensate the province for the timber and any other losses.

In April 1969, some members of the Save Cypress Bowl Committee, including Ken Farquharson, found out about the agreement. They were concerned about the loss of the scenic valley bordered by majestic mountains and enjoyed by many fly-fishing enthusiasts and hikers, which had the additional benefit of not being far from the urban centre of Vancouver. They thought the government had not considered the valley's significant recreational value when it made the agreement. In July, when Simmons proposed starting a Sierra Club group, this issue was at the top of people's minds as a reason why the club was needed. The opponents needed more clout behind them than what they had when they first attempted to lobby about the Cypress Bowl issue.

On the other side of the border, an American coalition was equally concerned: the North Cascades Conservation Council, with members from the Washington Sierra Club group making up part of the coalition. The council had started in 1957 and one of its major goals was to achieve a national park in the Cascade Mountains. The coalition had recently celebrated success when the North Cascades National Park was formed in October 1968, and now council members were concerned that portions of the park would be affected by flooding from the dam construction. When the Americans learned that Simmons was considering forming a Sierra Club in Vancouver, they saw it as a means of strengthening their campaign and were on board with the idea.

The BC opponents to the dam project, along with the newly formed Sierra Club BC, started a coalition known as Run Out Skagit Spoilers (ROSS). Various organizations, including the Society Promoting Environmental Conservation, the Alpine Club of Canada, and the BC Wildlife Federation, made up the coalition. As both coalitions, north and south of the border, hoped, Sierra Club BC's involvement helped raise the profile of the issue and facilitated cross-border collaboration.

Ultimately, the dispute was referred to the International Joint Commission, which exists to manage boundary water disputes between the us and Canada. The commission held public hearings in Bellingham and Vancouver in June 1971. John Massey, president of the ROSS coalition, and Ken Farquharson, its secretary, provided testimony, while John Fraser presented a legal brief for the ROSS committee.[11] Although the joint commission did not fully endorse the dam project, it nevertheless assumed that it would go through. However, its conclusions recommended that "social preservation values" should be taken into account and left the us government with several questions to consider: Was there was an immediate need for the power, and were there alternative sources that could be used? If so, were they more expensive? And if they were, would the benefits of preserving the Skagit Valley be worth the expense?

Despite the disappointing outcome, the members of the coalition did not give up. Little did Sierra Club BC realize that the fight would continue for fourteen years. Geraldine Irby, long-time editor of the Sierra Club BC newsletter, recalls Ken Farquharson's "tough Scot's advice" as "grab on to their balls and hang on like a mastiff."[12]

Farquharson, a civil engineer who had worked on several of BC Hydro's dams, contributed to the resolution. He had learned that BC Hydro, because of the dispute with Seattle City Light on the Skagit, was reluctant to raise the level of its proposed Seven Mile Dam on the Pend d'Oreille River. Flooding a small stretch of the narrow canyon between the head of the Seven Mile Reservoir and the Boundary Dam upstream in Washington would actually provide Seattle with much of the power anticipated from High Ross. He advised the BC cabinet of this fact and BC Hydro was instructed to build to the higher level.

An agreement was reached between BC and Seattle in 1983 and, as a formality because it was a cross-border issue, the Canadian and us federal governments became involved to sign the Skagit River Treaty (also known as the High Ross Treaty) in 1984. The treaty required British Columbia to deliver to Seattle an amount of energy and capacity that would approximate what was expected from the output of the proposed High Ross facility and established the Skagit Environmental Endowment Commission to manage the endowment fund that was provided to ensure the preservation of the wilderness and the fish and wildlife habitat until 2065.[13, 14] The Skagit was saved!

Continued lobbying led the BC government to establish the Skagit Valley Recreation Area and in 1995 it was upgraded to a Class A provincial park.

The West Coast Trail

IN 1969, THE ORIGINAL PLAN FOR THE PACIFIC RIM NATIONAL PARK Reserve included Long Beach, the Effingham Islands portion of the Broken Islands in Barkley Sound, and the life-saving trail between Bamfield and Port Renfrew—used from the 1800s to rescue survivors of the many shipwrecks that occurred on the coast over the years. However, rumours were circulating that the provincial government was having second thoughts about including the life-saving trail (which would eventually be known as the West Coast Trail). There was considerable public concern, including from the new Sierra Club BC members. David Anderson, Liberal MP for Esquimalt–Saanich at the time, was described in a *Victoria Times* article in December 1969 as "alarmed," pointing out that the plan would violate the joint federal-provincial agreement. Finally, in 1970, the provincial government relented and all three sections were included to form the new park.

The newly formed Sierra Club group decided that the original boundaries were not enough, writing that "a substantial buffer strip of forest is required along the Trail to preserve its wilderness quality."[15] That buffer included the lakes and forest of the Nitinat area. Farquharson joined forces with Hugh Murray, who knew Vancouver Island well, and together they produced a softcover book with photos and maps, called *West Coast National Park Life-Saving Trail: A Plea for Wider Boundaries*, in 1971. A copy of this publication was sent to all Members of Parliament.

Sierra Club BC also obtained Opportunities for Youth grants to hire students to explore the area, identify appropriate campsites, and appraise access trails for the purpose of encouraging visitors. The club promoted the hiring of First Nations youth, particularly from among the Ditidaht First Nation who lived in that area, to help with trail building. Their work was incorporated into a guidebook written by John Twigg and Ken Farquharson, and published in 1972: *The West Coast Trail and Nitinat Lakes: A Trail Guide by the Sierra Club of British Columbia.* In local terms, it was a bestseller, selling over 30,000 copies and benefitting the Sierra Club from its royalties until it went out of print. Today this iconic trail is so popular that access is carefully managed through a reservation system and it is often rated as one of the world's most popular backpacking trips.

The fight for widening the boundaries of the West Coast Trail led to the formation of a second Sierra Club group on Vancouver Island.

Terry Simmons, Initiator of SCBC

Terry Simmons, who resides in Vancouver, found the location of our interview—at the office of Greenpeace—fitting, especially as the room had a large photo on display of the *Phyllis Cormack*, the ship on which Simmons had sailed towards Amchitka in 1971. Simmons was a founding member of not only Sierra Club BC but also Greenpeace.

This came about because several members of the fledgling Sierra Club group were concerned about the US underground nuclear testing near Amchitka Island, one of the Aleutian Islands in Alaska. Under the auspices of the SCBC, they formed the Don't Make a Wave Committee, which included Irving and Dorothy Stowe, Jim and Marie Bohlen, and Terry Simmons, among others. Although Sierra Club BC was concerned about the prospect of geological destruction and the potential for a tidal wave, there was a sense that the issue and the strategy—sailing a boat into the test zone to confront the action—did not fit with the mandate of the newly formed Sierra Club. As a result, the Don't Make a Wave Committee separated from Sierra Club BC and, by 1971, had renamed itself Greenpeace.

The *Phyllis Cormack* set off for Amchitka in September of 1971, only to be intercepted by the US Navy before reaching the testing site. Nonetheless, five months later, the US put a halt to the nuclear testing program and the island was eventually declared a bird sanctuary. Even though Sierra Club BC and the US Sierra Club provided funding for the initial endeavour, Greenpeace's tactics were not in keeping with the ethos of the Sierra Club. Though individuals could be members of both and the two groups have been allies in many campaigns, the organizations remained quite separate from each other.

Simmons recalled that when he was volunteering in the main office in San Francisco, it was a difficult time for the US Sierra Club; there were clashes between the board of directors and its then executive director, Dave Brower, over a variety of issues, including whether the club should launch itself into the international arena.[16] Brower was put on leave and later fired. Simmons pointed out that, in many respects, he was involved in what Brower was fired for: "I went international with a lot of help of co-conspirators in Seattle, who also for the most part turned out to be Brower's allies in the broader sense."

Simmons attributed much of the early success of Sierra Club BC to the fact that talented volunteers were attracted to the club from the very beginning. Many of them were well educated and able to contribute meaningfully to the research reports and background information required for oral and written submissions to hearings, legal actions, and other lobbying efforts.

Simmons recalled that John Fraser—a Vancouver lawyer who became a Conservative MP in the 1970s and 1980s, Speaker of the House of Commons, and for a short time minister of the environment—was very helpful in providing behind-the-scenes support to him and Sierra Club BC. Fraser was involved in several environmental matters, including the Skagit River issue, the establishment of a US–Canada agreement on acid rain abatement, the rehabilitation and conservation of Pacific salmon stocks and habitat through the Pacific Salmon Treaty, and the preservation of the South Moresby archipelago as a national park reserve.

Simmons recounted how he learned how to intervene in a public hearing. "At the time, these hearings were rather closed; a person had to work hard to find out, first, that a hearing was happening, and then what was going on and what to do." In the summer of 1973, Simmons was invited by Andy Thompson, a UBC law professor, to participate in a hearing on the status and pricing of natural gas. Simmons attended the three-month-long hearing over the summer

Terry Simmons (fourth from left) on his way to Amchitka Island on the *Phyllis Cormack. Photo ©Greenpeace/Robert Keziere*

as an intervenor for Sierra Club BC and spent many long, not-well-paid-for hours preparing, reading huge submissions and learning the specialized vocabulary, and then many more hours at the actual hearings.

After finishing his degree in geography in 1974—and his master's thesis, "The Damnation of a Dam: The High Ross Dam Controversy"—Simmons moved to Thunder Bay where he taught at Lakehead University for a year. When he returned to Vancouver the next year, he was no longer involved with Sierra Club BC or Greenpeace. Instead, he had become a member of the Sierra Club International Committee, affiliated with the United Nations, which had grown out of the UN's 1972 Stockholm Conference on the Human Environment. Simmons was a committee member from 1973 to 1976. In May and June of 1976, Vancouver hosted Habitat, the UN Conference on Human Settlements, a sequel environmental conference. Simmons was the organizer of the side event, known as Habitat Forum, which was attended by fifteen thousand people and featured a collection of organizations, events, speakers, and seminars.

Simmons went on to obtain a PhD in geography from the University of Minnesota followed by a JD from the University of California, Berkeley, and became a member of the bar in California and Nevada with an interest in natural resources and environmental law, management, and policy.

He is now retired but still enjoys acting "independently and being available to help quietly" without much fanfare. ♠

Ken Farquharson, Formidable Campaigner

Ken Farquharson, born in Nairobi in 1935 to Scottish parents, spent his formative years in Kenya, Tanzania, and Scotland. There is a trace of a Scottish accent still present when he speaks. After obtaining a master's degree in mechanical sciences from the University of Cambridge, he worked as an engineer and consultant. Nearly eighty at the time of our interview, he remains fit and appears younger than his age. No doubt this is partly due to his love of hiking, climbing, and skiing, prospects that attracted him to BC in the first place and later motivated him to become involved in environmental activism.

In addition to his volunteer campaign work, Farquharson also worked as an independent consulting engineer. He remembers it as a stressful time but found that his love of hiking and nature kept him going. He later branched into environmental consulting and was able to obtain contracts with various government agencies, including BC Hydro. His activism did not make him popular with government, his main source for contract work, and at one point, he was essentially blacklisted. Fortunately, he was able to find other clients to tide him over until the political regime changed.

Beyond his work on the West Coast Trail, Cypress Bowl, and Skagit Valley campaigns, Farquharson was also involved in Sierra Club BC's campaign to protect the area from Cultus Lake through to Manning Park, which was threatened by intensive logging. He expressed disappointment that, despite their efforts, only the area around Chilliwack Lake itself, now known as Chilliwack Lake Provincial Park, was protected in 1973.

Farquharson received several awards for his advocacy, including a Community Service Award from the Association of Professional Engineers, the BC Wildlife Federation's Roderick Haig-Brown Conservation Award, the Sierra Club of Western Canada Conservation Award, and the Lieutenant Governor's Conservation Award.

Farquharson became less active in the club in the late 1970s and early 1980s as his business required more of his time. Around 1985, he and his wife moved back

Ken Farquharson. *Photo by Diane Pinch*

to Scotland to help his aging parents and they did not return to BC until 1996. Subsequently, Farquharson volunteered with other organizations, but eventually returned to work with Sierra Club BC in 2013. He is currently working on a number of projects, including a review of the Columbia River Treaty and a public education initiative concerning the plan by FortisBC to build a 540-foot hydroelectric dam on the Similkameen River. He is also helping to remediate the old mine site at Jordan River to allow the return of salmon thirty years after its contamination by the old Sunro Copper Mine. For that project, Farquharson had help from a student at the University of Victoria Environmental Law Centre, who identified the company responsible as Cominco, which is now owned by Teck Resources.

Farquharson plans to continue in this way until it is "no longer fun." 🌲

The Victoria Connection

THE 1960S AND '70S SAW MASSIVE EXPANSION OF THE FOREST INDUSTRY on Vancouver Island, accompanied by enormous clearcuts and overwhelming degradation of streams and rivers. The effects were apparent to any who enjoyed hiking the mountains, forests, and beaches of the Island.

In 1971, a Sierra Club BC group was established in Victoria. This came about through the efforts of Ric Careless, Gordon Price, and a handful of students from the University of Victoria Outdoors Club, many of whom had been inspired by Ken Farquharson's account of Sierra Club BC's efforts to protect areas along the west coast of Vancouver Island. Many were already familiar with the wilderness trails in this part of Vancouver Island and were committed to the proposal that the Nitinat Triangle—a series of three lakes deep within unlogged forests adjoining the West Coast Trail—should also be included in the recently created Pacific Rim National Park. The first meetings were held at UVic a couple of times a month, starting in the spring of 1971, and were popular, often generating attendance of up to a hundred people.

Whereas SCBC founders broke Sierra Club protocol by incorporating when they formed, in Victoria, no protocol was followed at all! The Victoria group simply used Letraset to replace the name on some letterhead received from the US Sierra Club with "Victoria" and photocopied enough for newsletters and mailings. Careless explained, "we never thought about remitting money to San Francisco or that there might have been legal implications. We were just too young to understand that. And later on, it did create problems."

Careless described the group's first lobbying attempt. They found out that there was to be an inauguration ceremony for the recently established Pacific Rim National Park in Tofino at Green Point with Jean Chrétien—at the time, the minister of Indian affairs and northern development—along with Princess Anne. The group organized a rally with banners that said "Save the Nitinat Triangle." The students, holding their banners, stood behind the large group of dignitaries. The police, who were there for security, were obviously curious about the banners, which were kept rolled up until after the ceremony. When Careless gave the signal for them to be unrolled, Chrétien and Princess Anne glanced behind and saw what they said. Careless then lined up with other well-wishers and when he had a chance, encouraged Chrétien to complete the job by including the Nitinat. Princess

Anne told Careless, "If you keep going the way you are, I'm sure you will be successful."

The group decided that it was important to encourage people to see the place for themselves. Groups of twenty to thirty university students travelled there to work on the trails, flagging the route, clearing the brush, and prepping the trail. John Willow, who had been a faller, cut the bigger deadfall logs. After two weekends, they were able to complete the first portage between Tsusiat and Hobiton, although many agreed that it was a particularly tough trek, especially when carrying a canoe and packs.

The group worked hard for over a year and a half, backed by groups such as the BC Wilderness Federation, the Society Promoting Environmental Conservation, and the BC Federation of Naturalists, with lots of articles in the media, mall displays, petitions, and presentations spreading the word about the project. A research paper even explained the rationale for the area's protection, including a detailed analysis of recreational demand for canoeing and opportunities available to the residents of southern Vancouver Island and nearby Vancouver.

Careless and the small core group were not working on their own. Resources from the US Sierra Club were behind them. Brock Evans, the Pacific Northwest coordinator based in Seattle, went to see the Nitinat in the fall of 1971. He was so impressed with the area that he arranged for three high-quality filmmakers to make a documentary. This film was aired nationally on CBC television.

In March 1972, the group held a major rally in the Nootka Theatre in the Royal BC Museum and there was an overflow crowd. Jean Chrétien was an invited speaker and they showed a film clip along with a slide show. Several important elected officials appeared on stage and one official said to Careless, "That thing was like a religious revival in there."

During his speech, Chrétien deviated from his prepared remarks and surprised everybody, including his staff, by saying that he was committed to preserving the Nitinat. In 1972, Ray Williston, the BC minister of lands, forests and water resources, in the lead-up to the election that the Social Credit Party lost to the NDP, made the final announcement that the area would not be logged. Careless notes that "this was a really big deal because it meant the province had to compensate the company, BC Forest Products, for it."

The group had initiated the campaign in 1971, and just eighteen months later it had succeeded. Careless described the campaign as one of the first broad-based populist environmental campaigns in Canada, with methodology that became a model for subsequent campaigns across the country. As well, he said that the relatively quick achievement of their goal, "the first environmental victory for wilderness in Canada," made it difficult for the US Sierra Club to dismiss the young Canadian upstarts.

Expansion across Canada

AT FIRST, THERE WAS SOME CONCERN AT THE NATIONAL LEVEL OF the US Sierra Club, particularly in the legal section, about the new Canadian offshoots usurping the Sierra Club name and possibly damaging its image. A Committee on International Relations was formed to look into the matter. The committee found that concerns about the club's name being tarnished were unfounded and that the activities and the public image projected by the various groups fit well with club policies. Indeed, their initiatives were a credit to the Sierra Club. No doubt the SCBC's remarkable success in protecting the Nitinat Triangle was an important consideration in these findings. The committee recommended that formation of more Canadian local groups should be encouraged and that the groups should be allowed to set and collect their own membership fees.

By 1972 there were multiple groups across the country, with five hundred paying members in BC and Alberta alone. Having 250 members was sufficient to establish a chapter so the US Sierra Club determined that two Canadian chapters should be formed, an eastern one and a western one. The Sierra Club of Western Canada included British Columbia, the prairie provinces, the Yukon, and the Northwest Territories. The eastern chapter covered the rest of Canada.

The Sierra Club of British Columbia, which was the legal

incorporation under the BC Societies Act, continued its operation and later would act as the charitable arm of the organization as the foundation.

Ric Careless, Protector of Wild Places

Ric Careless grew up in Toronto and his first experience with the outdoors was at a summer camp in Algonquin Park, where he learned to canoe. Ever since he was a young boy, he was captivated with mountains. His father, head of the history department at the University of Toronto, was invited to be a visiting professor at the University of Victoria in the summer of 1966. Careless and his parents travelled by train and upon approaching the mountains, Ric experienced a thrill and the feeling that he had come home. In 1968, his father returned for another year at UVic. Careless again joined him and began university, remaining in Victoria after his father returned to Ontario. He started off studying science but soon changed to geography, which better suited him. One of his professors, Bret Wallach, from Berkeley, introduced him to the US Sierra Club and the wilderness movement.

Careless recalled that the core people involved with the Nitinat Triangle campaign included Karen McNaught—his girlfriend, who later became his first wife—Gordon Price, John Willow, Pepper McLeod, and Eve Howden. They turned McNaught's mother's house "into a war room. When we were working on things, we had stuff plastered all over her house." McNaught was the secretary and Willow the vice president of the Victoria group. Careless found Willow, a marine architect in his forties, helpful for his strategic insight. Howden was in her sixties and had been involved with outdoors clubs in the past. Careless recollected that Price had "a natural understanding of the media and he really taught me how to relate to the media and how to frame an issue."

The group wrote a brief outlining the ecological and recreational features of the Nitinat Triangle area and the potential benefit of protecting it within the National Park system. After sending it to various government officials, both federal and provincial, Careless, McNaught, and Price decided to explore the Nitinat Triangle by canoe. Only First Nations people and some foresters who were inventorying the area tended to go there. Due to the thick brush with tall, barely penetrable salal bushes and big log jams, they had to use the Hobiton River as an access route. "We were three kids in university and this was just unbelievably magical. We were wandering up to our waists and necks up this river." It was September when the salmon swim upstream to spawn. Careless recalled the thrill of having "big salmon literally exploding between our legs." It was raining heavily while they paddled across Nitinat Lake and as they turned the corner into the Hobiton, "the whole thing cleared. It was just this remarkable light that was over Hobiton Ridge, which became the whole focus of the battle because it was very dominant and it was all old-growth . . . It was spiritual. It was very, very intense."

This campaign was Careless's first attempt at lobbying and provided a valuable learning experience for him. Being in Victoria had the advantage of being close to the legislature and, in those days, it was possible to meet legislative members fairly easily. Careless became acquainted with some high-level civil servants who were able to provide him with tips on how to deal with politicians.

The campaign also taught Careless a lot about getting his message out through the media. He relates an experience he had talking about the Nitinat Triangle on Jack Webster's radio program. Scottish-born Webster was a well-known radio and television host, active from the mid-1950s through much of the 1980s. He had a gruff, confrontational style and a reputation for asking tough questions. Careless was only twenty at the time and Webster tore him to shreds on the air. However, whenever there was a break, Webster explained to Careless—off air—how to do better. Webster told him, "First of all, if you are going to campaign you get three points you hit again and again and again." The long interview continued, with Webster persisting with his attack-style interview on air, while advising Careless off air on how to improve his presentation technique.

Early in the Nitinat campaign, the group members produced their own film about the Nitinat Triangle to use as a lobbying tool. Careless

Ric Careless overlooks a glacier in Tatshenshini-Alsek Provincial Park, one of the areas he played a significant role in protecting.
Photo by Dona-lyn Reel

recalled their attempt to show the three-minute clip to a group of ten cabinet ministers. When the projector's lens cover was accidentally tripped, they did not know how to reopen it, leaving the cabinet ministers in darkness, laughing at the group's lack of technological know-how. "Talk about a total blown interview. But we learned."

They also showed the film to various logging crews that were intending to log the area. Careless said that the loggers listened really respectfully and that although they "might see things a little differently . . . a lot of them were really supportive. It was such a different time and as a conservationist it was in some ways one of my most satisfying times because we were really appreciated and really regarded well for what we were doing."

Later, Careless obtained some funding from a couple of Alberta-based philanthropists to look at preserving wilderness areas in both Alberta and BC. "I was technically working on behalf of Sierra Club BC and the Alberta Wilderness Association so I was called the Western Canada conservation representative. I think that's what I called myself and I printed up letterhead. As I say, I was pretty good at printing up letterhead! I've learned a lot over the years about the amount you can get with good letterhead and a good business card."

While touring around the province investigating places that should be preserved, he met Art Twomey, who was trying to protect a beautiful section of the Purcell Mountains. In 1974, when he started working for the Environmental Land Use Committee Secretariat (ELUCS), Careless helped write legislation that shepherded this area through cabinet and established the Purcell Wilderness Conservancy.

Careless received multiple awards for his achievements, including a 1991 Equinox Magazine Citation for Environmental Achievement, the American Rivers Group's River Conservationist of the Year award, the 1994 Sierra Club Special Achievement Award for saving Tatshenshini-Alsek, as well as the Order of BC, the Wilburforce Foundation Conservation Leadership Award, and, in 2013, the J.B. Harkin Conservation Award from the Canadian Parks and Wilderness Society.

Careless has been an environmentalist throughout his career, and may, in fact, have been the first paid environmentalist in BC. He was involved not only with the beginning of the Sierra Club group on Vancouver Island but with the formation and expansion of multiple parks in BC including Tatshenshini-Alsek, Spatsizi Plateau, Stikine River, and Height of the Rockies.

He ended his 1997 book, *To Save the Wild Earth*, with the words, "Wilderness British Columbia is my passion, my life. It is my place on the most precious of planets. Here is home where along with dear friends and courageous companions I have campaigned to pass Nature onward, to save the wild earth. How fortunate I have been to be blessed with this work. How privileged and grateful I feel."[17] 🌲

Gordon Price, Media Whiz

Like Ric Careless, Gordon Price became involved with the Victoria Sierra Club in the early 1970s as one of its founding members. Price eventually moved to Vancouver, where he continued his activism by working to protect the city's West End.

Price hiked the West Coast Trail in its early days, when it was not developed to the same degree it is now. He and his companions had intended to only hike the southern quarter of it, but it was so "brutal" they thought it would be better just to keep going and ended up doing the whole trail. They ran out of food and the weather deteriorated. He said that this "engagement with the environment" helped him develop an "intimate relationship" with BC's wilderness.

Price was involved with the Nitinat Triangle campaign and as part of their reconnaissance, he canoed into the area. "One time we were canoeing down the lake and there was this incredible [crash], it sounded like an explosion. And what it was, was just a tree that had just reached its natural age. It wasn't windy or anything. It just fell. It must have been huge. There's the cycle of life. It could have been a thousand years old."

Price discussed the importance of having a name for the campaign and he believed that it was Careless who had created the Nitinat Triangle name. Having an identity and photographs were vital for selling the idea to the public. They put together a slide show of photos set to music: "We did what would now be a You-Tube video."

Price emphasized the necessity of having an overall vision in order to make a concept graspable for the public and the media. He suggested that the Nitinat Triangle campaign's success was likely a combination of the times and the emergence of the environmental movement, as well as the special makeup of Vancouver Island and its beautiful natural spaces. But it was important to have "that vision of a park, this watershed . . . we always said It was the last low-level old-growth watershed in this environment. You come out of the Hobiton River; there's a small little bay there and you come into the lake. So, you have this very distinct sense that you're in a lost world, a special place. I think that was so critical. How do you convey that to people? And we did!"

Price also thought the fact that the campaign coincided with the creation of Pacific Rim National Park was crucial. "This discrete piece was easy at the bureaucratic level to be included. I think again

Ric Careless and Gordon Price (on the right) explore the Nitinat Triangle to gather further evidence of the need to protect this area. *Courtesy of Ric Careless*

it was the astuteness—Ric was a great strategist. But I think it was just fortuitous as well in the sense that the timing was right. Everything had to line up."

Since moving to Vancouver in 1978, Price, an openly gay man, has been a champion of the West End, a focal area for Vancouver's LGBTQ community. He served six terms as councillor for the City of Vancouver, from 1986 to 2002. He was also on the boards for the Greater Vancouver Regional District (now Metro Vancouver) and TransLink, the regional transportation authority. From 2005 to 2016, when he retired, he was the director of the City Program at Simon Fraser University. As a result of his community and university work, Price has received a number of accolades including the Plan Canada Award for Article of the Year, The Smarty (People Category) from Smart Growth BC, the Simon Fraser University President's Award for service to the university through public affairs and media relations, and, in 2013, the Canadian Institute of Planners President's Award for outstanding lifetime contribution to education and professional planning in Canada. 🌲

Not blind opposition to progress, but opposition to blind progress.

—John Muir

2

Sierra Club BC Comes of Age

Key Beliefs

IF YOU ASK TEN MEMBERS WHAT SIERRA CLUB BC STANDS FOR, YOU will get ten different answers. Nevertheless, ask enough members and three key themes come out.

First, Sierra Club BC has been consistent over the years in being willing to work *with* all levels of government, including First Nations. The club strives to work *within* the system to ensure that goals related to conservation and sustainability are actively highlighted and considered in decision-making and policy development. The guiding principle is that change is best achieved by moral persuasion.

Second, the Sierra Club does *not* endorse nor engage in civil disobedience—sit-ins or blockades[18]—or any form of violence or harassment. However, it does encourage peaceful demonstrations and rallies as a valuable method for spreading the word about a particular issue and displaying the extent of its public support.

Third, Sierra Club BC is committed to credibility, which it considers fundamental to its ability to persuade the public and decision makers to support whatever case it is making. Credibility is hard to gain and easy to lose. Therefore, the club is committed to getting its facts straight through careful research and the use of correct science.

During the past fifty years, Sierra Club BC has undertaken many studies and reviews on a variety of topics, including sustainable forestry practices, aquaculture, hydrology initiatives, stream inventories, fish habitat, and wildlife diversity, to name just a few. This research has been the basis for Sierra Club BC's legal actions and its many submissions at public hearings.

A final point is that the SCBC has always been willing to work with other environmental groups, even if it sometimes loses public profile while doing so. Indeed, Sierra Club BC has rarely confronted a major environmental issue without taking part in a coalition or alliance with other organizations. Even the early campaigns concerning Cypress Bowl and the Skagit River Valley involved alliances.

Although alliances always bring with them the risk of differing opinions that have to be mediated, the risk is generally offset by being able to demonstrate a broad base of public support. Sierra Club BC's alliances initially involved like-minded groups with a vested interest in the areas in question—outdoor associations, hunters, naturalists, and so on—and later came to include more diverse ones such as First Nations, social justice groups, credit unions, stream stewardship organizations, organic growers, and non-profit groups fighting cancer, to name a few.

A Sierra Club representative once said, when asked where the organization sits along the spectrum of environmental groups, "we're often described as the most radical of the mainstream groups. I like both halves of that, 'radical' and 'mainstream.'"[19]

Organizational Growth and the Transition to Professional Staffing

THE 1980S AND '90S BROUGHT MEMBERSHIP GROWTH, THE FORMATION of new groups, and increasing campaign activity. Sierra Club BC's first paid professional, Bob Nixon, was hired in late 1970s. The position lasted only two years due to loss of funding. In an interview with Peter Grant,[20] Nixon identified his role as providing grassroots groups with professional and technical assistance: "The geographical diversity of BC creates a great problem of isolation. It's difficult to communicate effectively where it counts—with the senior public servants who formulate policy and legislative initiatives, under the direction of their ministers. My job is to give people a clear and continuing voice in Victoria. We're seeking to break down what is perceived as a distinction between urban and hinterland populations."

Nixon also explained what he thought made the Sierra Club different from other environmental groups: "First, it is a policy-oriented, advocacy-type organization, dealing largely with government and related industries. That's also called lobbying; we provide the best possible information on a subject, say a land use situation, and point to the policy we believe ought to be followed. Second, the Sierra Club is committed to looking at the whole picture of environmental issues, which means the economics and social and labour aspects."

In order to keep the membership informed, the Sierra Club BC had a newsletter, the *Sierra Report*, which came into being in 1973 and was produced about four times a year by editor Geraldine Irby—who remained at the helm for over twenty-five years and ensured its consistently high quality. Many of the local groups also produced newsletters that they distributed to members.

Geraldine Irby, Exemplary Editor

Geraldine Irby was born in Montreal, but lived much of her early adult life in California. There, she joined the Sierra Club due to her concern about the environmental destruction of some of her favourite hiking places. After moving to Vancouver in the early 1970s, she joined Sierra Club BC and was immediately appointed by Jim Bohlen as the club's newsletter editor. Ken Farquharson recalled Irby as "the one person who was totally consistent from the beginning . . . I don't think that the club would have really got off the ground without her support in terms of newsletters and getting the information out and about."

The original two-page typed newsletter eventually morphed into a multi-page printed newspaper with photos. Her partner, John Condit, a journalist, helped Irby edit submissions. She had never

Geraldine Irby in her garden. *Photo by Diane Pinch*

learned to type; she handwrote everything and then took it to a typist, after which she pasted it up, did the layouts, and took it to a printer. The end result was a very professional-looking newspaper with articles about the club and current environmental issues. She died a year after our interview in the summer of 2016, having lived healthily until her mid-nineties. The Geraldine Irby Award for Volunteerism recognizes those who work behind the scenes and lay the groundwork for the organization's success. ▲

Recipients of Geraldine Irby Award for Volunteerism

2006	Judy Leicester
2007	Janet Brazier
2008	Gordon Hawkins
2009	Diane Pinch
2010	Jamie Biggar
2011	Martin Golder
2012	Meaghan Dinney
2013	Carla Stein
2014	Dana Peng & Andre Holdrinet
2016	Morag Keegan-Henry
2017	Karli Mann
2018	Lola Rabinovitch

Ric Careless returned to the Sierra Club BC board in 1986–87, the same year that Vicky Husband joined. Together they undertook to leverage SCBC's excellent reputation into receiving funding from foundations, in particular big American ones that understood the global importance of the work that Sierra Club BC was doing to protect the temperate rainforest and other special areas of BC. They were highly successful in this endeavour and, over a number of years, many new staff members were hired. The SCBC Chapter office slowly transitioned from a fully volunteer organization into one where the main work was done by professional staff. The local groups, on the other hand, continued to be entirely volunteer-run.

Major foundations contributing to Sierra Club BC included the Wilburforce Foundation, the McConnell Foundation, and the Brainerd Foundation. The Tides Canada Foundation also provided significant assistance. In addition to financial support, the foundations provided training opportunities geared to non-profit organizations. For example, the Wilburforce Foundation supports a leadership training organization, Training Resources for the Environmental Community (TREC), which runs workshops that have benefitted many Sierra Club BC staff members. The McConnell Foundation helped Sierra Club BC to develop an education program that provides meaningful and effective programs for teachers and students, and the Tides Canada Foundation helped to fund the Great Bear Rainforest campaign.

Sierra Club BC was also supported by numerous members of the business community. For example, Happy Planet Foods featured caps on their juices that revealed messages when opened, such as "Stop the Chop" and "Save the Great Bear Rainforest," which included an image of a grizzly bear claw along with the premier's phone number. Denman Island Chocolate made special edition chocolate bars with labels promoting the Great Bear Rainforest and the Flathead causes, promising a donation to Sierra Club BC as part of each purchase.

Sierra Club of Western Canada continued to grow, and by 1994 there was a sufficient number of members in BC to form a separate provincial chapter. The name Sierra Club of British Columbia was restored, and the Alberta group formed its own chapter.

Bill Wareham became the first executive director of Sierra Club BC in 1998 and held that position for four years. This was a period of transition that saw Sierra Club BC grow from a seven-person organization with a $700,000 budget to an organization with twenty-seven staff members and a budget of $2 million. Growth was not without tension, however, as the executive director, the staff and the volunteer-run board struggled to adjust.

Sierra Club BC attracted considerable criticism from its opponents, both for having an American parent and for receiving extensive funding from US foundations. Bill Wareham wrote a

Bill Wareham, SCBC's first executive director. *University of Victoria Archives*

counter-argument in the *Sierra Report*. He pointed out that Sierra Club BC was Canadian-based and therefore accountable to its Canadian members and supporters. Also, it received considerable funding from many Canadian foundations and individuals in addition to the American sources.

He argued that "markets for BC wood products are international in scope" and drew attention to the fact that foreign capital was being used to augment the forest industry, and several forest companies were owned by foreign investors. "So why, I ask of our detractors, is a US dollar used to pay wages and build logging roads clean and acceptable, while a US dollar directed at conservation initiatives is taboo?"

The legal incorporation of the Sierra Club of British Columbia under the BC Societies Act continued its operation as the club's foundation arm. By this point, it also had its own board of directors. This separation was important to maintain because in Canada charities were restricted in their ability to engage in political activities. Thus, the foundation was considered to be a charitable organization with the ability to offer tax receipts to donors, whereas any political lobbying or related activities occurred under the umbrella of the chapter and its board.

The foundation's mission statement directed it to "motivate and financially support groups involved in research and education towards conservation of the earth's ecosystems thereby fostering a commitment to protect and restore the quality of the natural and human environment." Over the years the foundation financed and supported not only Sierra Club endeavours but also a host of other environmental groups and projects throughout the province. For example, Tybring Hemphill, chair of the foundation board, noted in his annual report in 2000 that the foundation had provided funds for "habitat conservation in the Fraser headwaters; a watchdog program in the Cassiar area; a conservation project in Robson Valley; a campaign to protect the South Chilcotin Wilderness area; and the conservation of threatened salmon stocks in the Shuswap area of BC." It also worked closely with "the East Kootenay Environmental Society, the Transboundary Watershed Alliance, the Environmental Mining Council of BC, Earth Witness Media, Cassiar Watch, and the Hesquiaht Rediscovery Society to name a few."[21]

Jack Hemphill: Exceptional Volunteer

Jack Hemphill, originally from New York state, joined the US Sierra Club in the late 1960s. After his move to Victoria in the early 1970s, he was recruited to be the Sierra Club BC Foundation's treasurer because of his financial expertise. By this point, the BC Chapter office had moved to Victoria. He continued in this role for many years and was a Sierra Club BC volunteer for over three decades.

His memory is honoured by the Jack Hemphill Exceptional Volunteer Award, which recognizes individuals for their valuable contributions and commitment as volunteers.

Involvement with the Sierra Club has been a family affair for the Hemphills, with Jack's wife, Wenche, and son, Tybring, also contributing for many years. Wenche was one of the BC Chapter's first office staff in the late 1970s and Tybring followed in his

Recipients of the Jack Hemphill Exceptional Volunteer Service Award	
2008	Jack Hemphill
2009	Brian Pinch
2010	Betty Zaikow
2011	Ruth Zenger
2012	Judy Leicester
2013	Esther Dyck, Myrtle Creek Stewards & Sierra Malaspina
2014	Caspar Davis
2016	Terry Dance-Bennink
2017	Rolling Justice Bus
2018	Finn Kreischer

Jack and Wenche Hemphill. *Courtesy of Tybring Hemphill*

father's footsteps as a member of the foundation board, acting as chair for ten years (1994–2004). ♠

Sierra Club BC has sometimes employed litigation to encourage change, although often as a last resort. The US Sierra Club resorted to legal action for the first time in the late 1960s, when the Walt Disney Company's proposal to build a ski resort at Mineral King required construction of a highway and power lines through Sequoia National Park. The US club set up the independent Sierra Club Legal Defense Fund (SCLDF)[22] in 1971 and proceeded to sue the US Secretary of the Interior in an effort to block the development, ultimately unsuccessfully.[23] The SCLDF, now known as Earthjustice, has since launched thousands of successful lawsuits in the US dealing with a variety of environmental issues.

Sierra Club BC has often been helped in Canada by a similar organization, the Sierra Legal Defence Fund (SLDF), known as Ecojustice since 2007. It was established in Vancouver in 1990 with Stewart Elgie as a founding board member. Elgie was a lawyer who had worked with the American SCLDF, taking on the high-profile legal battle with Exxon in Alaska. The Canadian SLDF opened an office in Toronto in 1996 with Greg McDade as its executive director. Later, offices were opened in Ottawa, Calgary, and Halifax.

Over the years, Ecojustice has won countless precedent-setting cases, which helped force various levels of government to live up to their responsibilities in ensuring the protection of our environment.[24] Sierra Club BC was involved with some of these cases and examples are described later in the book.

Sierra Club BC has also received legal advice and support on a number of occasions from West Coast Environmental Law (WCEL), which was established in Vancouver in 1974 to promote environmental law reform. WCEL also has an Environmental Dispute Resolution Fund, which has enabled the club to hire a lawyer at a legal aid rate for legal advice as well as help with appearances before government tribunals and court challenges to government decisions.

The Sierra Club of Canada and SCBC

DISCUSSIONS BEGAN IN 1982 ABOUT SETTING UP A NATIONAL-LEVEL organization in Canada. With the support of the US club, a Canadian National Committee was established, with Jim Bonfonti as its first chair. This venue allowed delegates from the various groups across Canada to work on matters in common and begin to lobby the federal government more effectively.

By 1986 an agreement between the Canadian entities and the US club was signed and in 1992, Sierra Club of Canada (SCC) was incorporated. From this point forward, the various Sierra Club chapters in Canada were legally sub-entities of the Sierra Club of Canada. However, the two foundations, the Sierra Club of BC Foundation and the Sierra Club of Canada Foundation, could not be subsumed as they were separate legal entities. They remain so to this day, and there has been tension at times between the foundations, which value their independence (and require it under the income tax act), and the SCC, which sometimes wishes to direct them.

From the beginning, members of the SCC were considered members of the US Sierra Club as well and received its magazine, originally entitled *Sierra Club Bulletin* (now known simply as *Sierra*). A small portion of the dues of Canadian members was remitted to San

Francisco to cover the cost. In 2003 the board of the SCC decided that it wanted to sever this relationship and become fully independent. Separate licensing agreements were negotiated between the US Sierra Club and the Sierra Club of Canada and the two Canadian foundations, which allowed them to continue using the name "Sierra Club" and its brand logos. However, Canadian members were no longer US members as well.

Elizabeth May, environmental activist, was appointed as the national representative in September 1989 and a Sierra Club office was established in Ottawa in 1990, headed by May and two volunteers. In 1992 May became the Sierra Club of Canada's first executive director, a role she continued to serve until 2006, at which time she assumed the office of leader of the Green Party of Canada.

During May's tenure, the SCC experienced rapid growth just as SCBC did, also growing from a small organization to one with a budget of over two million dollars and an extensive staff.

Following May's departure in 2006, a number of administrative and financial issues frayed the relationship between Sierra Club BC and the Sierra Club of Canada. Both organizations had lost important donors around the same time, which meant that budget constraints left them competing for funding and membership.

In 2011, after much consideration, the executive director of Sierra Club BC, George Heyman, recommended that it would be best to dissolve the board of the BC Chapter and move its activities into the Sierra Club of British Columbia Foundation, thereby ending its status as a chapter within the Sierra Club of Canada. The legal entity, the Sierra Club of British Columbia Foundation, would continue to exist. By 2013, the board had confirmed the decision and the paperwork was complete, along with the negotiation of a new licensing agreement with the US Sierra Club that acknowledged its legal status.

Elizabeth May, First Executive Director of the scc

Elizabeth May was born in Connecticut to an activist mother and a father working in the insurance business. After a holiday in tranquil

Cape Breton in 1972, the family decided to move there, away from the political upheaval and worries of the United States.[25] After reading Rachel Carson's *Silent Spring* as a young teenager, she joined the Friends of the Earth and the Sierra Club, and began her career of environmental activism with a campaign opposing aerial insecticide spraying in Cape Breton's forests. In the 1980s, May completed law school at Dalhousie University and after working as a lawyer in Halifax, she decided to move to Ottawa.

Elizabeth May. *Courtesy of Elizabeth May*

Between 1986 and 1989, May served as the senior policy advisor to Tom McMillan, environment minister for Brian Mulroney's Conservative government. She was instrumental in helping to resolve the controversial South Moresby conflict with logging interests on the Queen Charlotte Islands (now known as Haida Gwaii)—a process that led to the establishment of the Gwaii Haanas National Park. May was also involved in negotiating the international Montreal Protocol to protect the ozone layer in 1987. Two years later she resigned when McMillan approved the Rafferty-Alameda dam projects in Saskatchewan without an environmental impact assessment.

During her seventeen years with the Sierra Club of Canada, May received a number of awards and accolades for her contributions to environmental protection—including an award for Outstanding Achievement from the Sierra Club of Western Canada, the us Sierra Club's International Earthcare Award, the J.B. Harkin Conservation Award from the Canadian Parks and Wilderness Society, three honorary doctorate degrees, and an Order of Canada appointment. ♣

A true conservationist is a man who knows that the world is not given by his fathers, but borrowed from his children.

—John James Audubon

3

Education Programs

SIERRA CLUB BC HAS ALWAYS ENDEAVOURED TO CAPTURE THE PUB-lic's attention in a variety of ways, including bumper stickers, pamphlets, photo books, slide shows, and videos. But in the 1990s, the club came up with some other creative approaches to educate the public about BC's "lands, forests, parks, and other natural resources," one of its mandates in the original mission statement.

The Rainforest Bus was one of these—created in 1994 to help people learn about temperate rainforests. A walkway first took the visitor through a lush rainforest teeming with life—complete with arrangements of rare forest plants growing on moss-covered logs, models of small forest creatures, and a life-size replica of "Bella the grizzly bear" fishing for salmon—an experience permeated with birdsong and the sound of rushing water.

The passage then proceeded through a clearcut forest, and at the far end it featured examples of ecoforestry alternatives to clearcutting. There was also a display illustrating other sources of energy: geothermal, solar, and wind. The bus toured widely throughout BC over six years—including to Haida Gwaii and a number of resource-based towns where it received a mixed reception. Youth hired to travel with it went to various festivals and markets with some

Sierra Club BC hired youth to travel with the Rainforest Bus around the province. FRONT ROW, LEFT TO RIGHT: Kim Kobayashi, Michelle Johnson, Camila Cowan. BACK ROW, LEFT TO RIGHT: Jeff, Cori Yule, and unidentified person. *University of Victoria Archives*

musicians who helped encourage young people to visit. They eventually toured across Canada and south along the eastern seaboard of the US. Thousands of people toured through the bus and the exhibit generated a lot of media attention over the six years of its operation.

The School Education Program

JENN HOFFMAN, WHO WAS HIRED IN 1997 TO PROVIDE ENVIRONMENtal education to young children attending summer camp, made a pitch to Sierra Club BC's new executive director that it would be worthwhile to run a program year-round in the school system. She was correct in thinking there would be a strong demand as she found the teachers to be "wildly excited" about it. Since then, SCBC's Education Program, which continues to this day, has provided curriculum-based education programs about nature and environmental topics to over 125,000 BC students.

The J. W. McConnell Foundation, based in Montreal, helped the

Jenn Hoffman. *Photo by Stephen Legault Photography and Storytelling*

program become effective. This large Canadian foundation, known for its innovative initiatives, had started Green Streets, an umbrella structure for environmental education programs for youth, in 1999. SCBC's program had been in operation for a couple of years and was receiving good feedback from teachers when the McConnell Foundation decided to invite the program to be part of the Green Streets pilot along with a couple dozen other programs. The foundation wanted to invest in teaching methods that worked. With the foundation's help the program blossomed and developed into a well-run, professional component of the club.

Over time it expanded from one-off programs for very young children to visits from kindergarten to grade 7, twice every school year. As well, SCBC offered teacher training workshops and, for a period of time, it expanded to provide environmental education to high schools with its Sustainable High Schools program. The high school program later evolved into the Youth Environment Leadership Program (YELP), which fostered youth leadership skills and civic engagement through workshops, organized events, habitat restoration, and campouts. Eventually, after 2013, funding for high school programs was discontinued. By this time, many high schools were incorporating their own environmental education programs into the curriculum and SCBC involvement was no longer needed.

Hoffman, along with others, created a series of learning resources that matched the BC curriculum. Produced as bound books, they dealt with a variety of topics including temperate rainforests, watersheds, and sustainable technology. The package was sent to the teachers in advance with lesson plans, follow-up activities, and readings for their classes, all designed to be as easy as possible. Hoffman travelled around the province providing professional development for the teachers in how to use the materials even more effectively.

At its height, the educational team visited participating classrooms at least twice a year. The first visit was usually in the fall and the team left the class with an action challenge to work on over the winter months. This usually involved a tangible outcome such as cleaning up a watershed or revitalizing school grounds by replacing invasive plants with native ones. The second visit in the spring allowed the team to see how the students had made out with the challenge.

Kirsten Dallimore, an SCBC education staff person, reads one of the nature books developed by Sierra Club BC with a student. *SCBC Photo Files, photo by Brynne Morrice*

In 2006, following the announcement of the first Great Bear Rainforest agreements, central coast communities held workshops where discussions highlighted a desire to reconnect First Nations youth to traditional knowledge about forests, plants, and medicines in the temperate rainforest. This led to a collaborative project with the Coastal First Nations Turning Point Initiative, Sierra Club BC, and the Centre for Non-Timber Resources at Royal Roads University producing the 2009 guidebook for educators of grades 4 to 7, entitled *Going Wild: Teaching about Wild Products from BC's Coastal Rainforest.*

SCBC used this guidebook in schools on the central coast to teach children about their local ecosystem and the items that could be harvested. Early on, the program concentrated on how these resources could be used to develop small businesses. Over time, this focus became less pronounced and the emphasis shifted to the local plants and animals themselves, highlighting the ones that could be used for medicine, food, tools, technologies, or art. The roles of cedar, various berries, and plants like the Oregon grape were prominent.

After a few years, the SCBC education staff decided that similar guidebooks could be used more widely throughout the province. Gradually, modules were developed for other ecosystems. The education staff made sure to research the ethnobotany and the First Nations territories for each of the ecozones, whether it was the south Okanagan, the Cariboo or the northeast corner of the province.

In later years, as the club became more concerned about climate change and ways to educate the public about the need to address it, the education staff developed modules to help children understand the issue. One new program was entitled *Nature and Climate* and was piloted in classrooms in 2012. Subsequently, another module was developed based on the visionary document *The Future Is Here*, discussed in more detail later in this book. This document examines the urgent need to address climate change and suggests ten steps to help people shift to a more balanced, sustainable world with fewer carbon emissions.

Lisa Dumoulin was hired to coordinate the program in 2013 and she described some of the changes that occurred over the years. At its height, a team of four educators delivered the programs to schools across the province at both elementary and high school levels. During Dumoulin's tenure, there was funding for only one educator. That has since increased to two. Despite the reduction in capacity, the basic format of delivery remains similar. An educator visits a school for about an hour and a half, working in the classrooms or sometimes moving to a nearby forest to allow the children to have a hands-on experience in nature. Follow-up visits are no longer feasible and the assessments of the action challenges are now left to the teachers. However, for inspiration and advice, teachers can refer to a well-received e-newsletter and newly revised education website.[26]

The program continues to be available to communities throughout the province. There is also an adapted format for groups of homeschooled children. In 2018, the program began to offer French language workshops as well as a teacher mentorship program with monthly meetings. James Davis, the education manager hired in 2017, emphasizes the benefit of the workshops in providing children with experience outdoors in nature and information about the ecology of their particular environment.

The GAIA Project

IN 1993, A NOVEL PARTNERSHIP BEGAN THAT SPONSORED A PROGRAM known as the GAIA Project. Sandra Thomson, a volunteer with the project who started in 1997, became its first paid program manager the following year. She described the GAIA Project as "an amazing undertaking that was founded by a small group of inspired, globally minded people and ran for its first several years on goodwill alone." Over the years, it was "a place of deep commitment and positive global solutions."

Although not a core program within SCBC, the GAIA Project was affiliated with the organization. It was inspired by events in Central America. During the war in Guatemala, many Indigenous Guatemalans had fled to southern Mexico, and after the war, through an initiative known as Project Accompaniment, Canadians and other North Americans volunteered to accompany groups of these refugees back to Guatemala to resettle. Merran Smith and Mike Simpson were in El Salvador during the war working as filmmakers. They, along with Maeve Lydon, Lorenzo Mele, and Robin Hood, became involved in Project Accompaniment.

While doing so, they met Ricardo Navarro,[27] who was the head of CESTA (the Spanish acronym for the Salvadoran Center for Appropriate Technology) and an inspiring speaker about the work that CESTA was doing at the time. After Simpson and Smith returned to BC, they decided to create the GAIA Project and were able to convince SCBC to partner with CESTA. The name GAIA was thought to be appropriate as it is not only the name of the ancient Greek earth goddess but also a Spanish acronym for Grupo de Apoyo Internacional al Ambiente (International Environmental Support Group). One of the project's first ventures was to produce the inspirational video *Toilets, Trees and Transformation*,[28] narrated by Lorenzo Mele.

The GAIA Project's goal was twofold: to support the Salvadoran people in restoring and protecting their environment through education and hands-on activities, and to educate Canadians about sustainable technology successfully used in El Salvador that could also benefit Canadians. With funding from the Canadian International

Development Agency (CIDA), student interns from Canada were hired for nine-month periods to spend part of their time in El Salvador working with CESTA on various projects such as planting trees, building nurseries, developing solar technologies, and planning water treatment programs. The rest of the time, they travelled to various venues in BC with the Sustainable Living Bus.

Sandra Thomson's first task as a volunteer in 1997 was to write a funding proposal for the Sustainable Living Bus—Mike Simpson's idea for a travelling exhibit. The Sierra Club purchased a used school bus, gutted it, and fitted it out with sustainable methods appropriate for Canadians to consider, such as straw-bale technology, solar panels, wind generation, recycling strategies, composting toilets, and a vermiculture bin. Thomson pointed out that although recycling is very common these days, at that time there were no established recycling programs for paper, glass or metal. The idea was to display these technologies within the bus, along with an explanation of the GAIA Project and the north-south partnership between the Sierra Club and CESTA. The bus roved around BC and even travelled across Canada, dedicated to raising public awareness about renewable energy and sustainable resource use.

The first interns were Gail Hochachka, Jason Blanch, Chris Wilson, and Nola Sharp. These four landed in El Salvador with limited Spanish skills and ended up helping to replant forests on a mountain that had become a wasteland during the war due to landmines and deforestation. Thomson estimated that over the years, about twenty-five interns experienced this "amazing program where people would really have their worldview shifted." Although in some cases, the interns provided some technical knowledge to the El Salvadorans, the main goal was for Canadian youth to experience a different culture with alternate ways of doing things and to return to Canada to share what they had learned.

Thomson left the program in 2003, shortly after leading an eco-tour in El Salvador. During her stay, Lety Aparicio, the daughter of a CESTA employee, was murdered by gang members. Thomson had been out for dinner with her the night of her murder. Gang warfare was rampant in San Salvador and the city was dangerous at night.

The GAIA project outfitted the Sustainable Living Bus with solar panels and colourful murals and displayed it at various venues throughout the province and across the country. *SCBC Photo Files, photo by Paula Steele*

Aparicio was known to people in SCBC as she had been in Canada the year before, and news of her death was devastating. Thomson, who felt burnt out and had symptoms of post-traumatic stress disorder, believed that Aparicio's death had a significant impact on the GAIA Project and it never fully recovered.

Thomson decided to resign and, at the time, the program appeared to be in good shape financially. However, there were difficulties finding another program manager, and the program faltered and eventually ran out of funding. "I always felt like it was really unfortunate that it ended that way because for ten years it was vibrant, super inspiring, and quite a contrast to what was going on more broadly in the Sierra Club. It's just so challenging, the work that the Sierra Club does, but the GAIA Project was kind of this little bubble . . . That kind of youth energy was inspiring and the environmental education component was inspiring."

*The lesson is never give up even when the
situation seems hopeless.*

—Rosemary Fox

4

Campaigns in Northern BC

Talchako Lodge

EARLY ON, SIERRA CLUB BC HAD AN INTEREST IN NORTHERN BC, having inherited the operation of Talchako Lodge from the US Sierra Club. The lodge was situated in Tweedsmuir Provincial Park in the coastal mountains of BC, about sixty-five kilometres east of Bella Coola. The original lodge was built in 1931 by Canadian pioneer Tommy Walker, a guide and outfitter who ran a big game hunting and fishing operation along with his sister Molly, the first female guide licensed in BC.

It was advertised as "A Sportsman's Paradise,"[29] offering guided horseback expeditions into the nearby mountains. It was largely due to Walker's efforts that Tweedsmuir Provincial Park became established in 1938. Five years after the Walkers moved on in 1948, the original lodge was lost to fire but their home next door, Talchako Lodge, remained. Al Elsie, another guide, purchased Talchako Lodge, expanding and operating it as a big game hunting and fishing lodge for over ten years—with notable guests including Cary Grant and Clark Gable. After hunters depleted the grizzly population in the area, the lodge closed and it was eventually donated to the US Sierra Club in the late 1960s.

The newly formed Vancouver group became involved with overseeing the lodge, although it was not until 1978 that Sierra Club BC took over ownership. It had been left empty for a number of years, and during that time it had been vandalized and required significant repairs. Eventually, it was renovated enough to be listed in the BC approved tourist directory and was used by various organizations, including Canadian Nature Tours, for outings. With the help of long-term caretakers, Sierra Club BC managed the lodge until the undertaking became too onerous and costly. After much discussion, the board decided in

The Talchako Lodge, owned and operated by Sierra Club BC in the 1970s, is nestled in the coastal mountains of northern BC about 65 kilometres east of Bella Coola. *University of Victoria Archives*

1982 to sell it to the caretakers with a "trust" legally attached to the land title restricting the property to be used as a base for low-impact, human-powered wilderness trips and outdoor education.

Talchako Lodge provided Sierra Club BC members access to the northern parts of the province and served to increase their awareness about issues in the north. About 500 kilometres north of Tweedsmuir Park lies the Spatsizi Plateau—often described as the "Serengeti of Canada" for its size, beauty, and wide assortment of wildlife. The area supports large populations of woodland caribou, Stone sheep, mountain goats, moose, grizzlies, black bears, wolverines, beaver, hoary marmots, and ground squirrels. There had been previous attempts to encourage the government to protect the area; first by the above-mentioned guide outfitter Tommy Walker, and then by Vladimir Krajina, a professor and ecologist who convinced the BC government to establish the ecological reserves system in 1971. Both of these men inspired Ric Careless to begin the campaign to protect the Spatsizi in the spring of 1975.

Careless convinced Bristol Foster—head of the BC government's Ecological Reserves program—to help him, and in his book,[30] Careless describes how their efforts successfully resulted in convincing the NDP government to announce the establishment of the Spatsizi Plateau Wilderness Provincial Park—and the Gladys Lake Ecological Reserve contained within it—in December 1975, just prior to the provincial election. It was the first large protected area in Canada specifically established to safeguard wildlife. Careless recalled drafting the order-in-council that created the park, incorporating language from the US Wilderness Bill along with a draft management directive that indicated that there should be no hunting in at least part of the park. He lamented that the latter was disregarded following the election, which the NDP lost. Rosemary Fox, a stalwart northern member of Sierra Club BC, participated significantly in negotiations and lobbied to protect the integrity of the park.

The prospect of an ecological reserve provoked many hunters who had had a long history of using the Spatsizi region. In fact, when the Walkers left Tweedsmuir in 1948, they established a big-game hunting outfit at Cold Fish Lake in the heart of the park, northwest of the current Gladys Lake reserve. The intent of the protected zone was to preserve BC's Stone sheep as well as the largest remaining population of caribou in BC. There were some hunting outfits in the area that were taking as many as seventy caribou in a single season. Sierra Club BC called for a moratorium on hunting in the newly established Spatsizi Park while studies were undertaken to determine whether hunting was sustainable or whether, and to what extent, it would ultimately jeopardize the balance of the ecosystem.

In the end, Sierra Club BC decided it was best not to oppose hunting in the new park and so avoided a fight between hunters and non-hunters. Instead, SCBC promoted responsible wildlife management through an ecosystem-based management strategy—the first environmental organization to embrace this approach. As a result, hunting is not permitted in the Gladys Lake reserve but continues to be permitted in the rest of the wilderness park. Rosemary Fox indicated in a 1994 report that since establishing the reserve, "the sheep, which had been decimated, recovered and populations of the other large mammals are thriving (though grizzlies haven't recovered from heavy hunting in the 60s)."[31]

Rosemary Fox: Conservation Champion

Rosemary Fox and her husband, Irving (now deceased), have been long-time keen outdoorspeople and conservationists. Fox joined Sierra Club BC in the early 1970s and was an active member of the Lower Mainland group, serving as a director and later chair of the board. After moving to Smithers, she continued to play a vital role in Sierra Club BC throughout the 1980s and '90s, acting in various capacities including membership coordinator, group representative, and conservation chair of the SCBC Chapter board.

Fox was involved with many committees and working groups—some as the Sierra Club BC representative. A sampling includes the Lower Stikine Management Advisory Committee (Ministry of Forests); Babine River LRUP Steering Committee (MoF); Kispiox Resource Management Plan Advisory Group (MoF); Babine Recreational Area Master

Rosemary Fox. *University of Victoria Archives*

Recipients of the Rosemary Fox Conservation Achievement Award

2009	Judy Leicester
2010	Andrew Wright
2011	Patricia Molchan
2012	Douglas Channel Watch
2013	Geraldine Kenny & Sierra Quadra
2014	NorthWest Watch
2016	Tom Lane
2017	Ken Farquharson
2018	Eagle Eyes & FightC

Plan Study Team (BC Parks); Backcountry Commercial Recreation Policy (BC Lands); and BC Wolf Working Group (Wildlife Branch). The club's archives contain boxes of Rosemary Fox's correspondence[32] with many examples of her thoughtful, well-researched, detailed letters and reports on a variety of topics. She played a significant role in protecting the wildlife in the Spatsizi Plateau Wilderness Provincial Park and later in establishing the Stikine River Provincial Park and other key special areas.

She received a number of awards over the years including the US Sierra Club Special Achievement Award (1993), the Canadian Nature Federation Douglas H. Pimlott Award (1993), the BC Spaces Wild Earth Award (2001) and the BC Nature Elton Anderson Award (2013). ♠

Sierra Club BC developed an award in her name which recognizes individuals for significant achievement in protecting wildlife and wildlands.

Sierra Club BC also pushed for an ecosystem-based management scheme when it participated in the Wolf Working Group, formed in 1988 in response to increasing controversy over how to manage wolf populations in the province. BC has used a variety of strategies to try to eliminate wolves—including a bounty, beginning in 1870, and poisoning until 1961. Public opinion shifted in the 1960s when it became apparent that wolf populations were endangered in some areas of the province and concentrated in others. By 1979 the province had established management objectives in areas where ungulates had declined. In northern BC (e.g., the Muskwa-Kechika area), aerial culling was used, and on Vancouver Island (e.g., the Nimpkish Valley), wolves were trapped. Opposition to wolf control came to a head in 1988, spearheaded by the Northwest Wildlife Preservation Society. A well-received three-zone management strategy—preservation, control, and population management—was proposed to a number of interest groups and the Wolf Working Group was formed.[33] The idea was to collect information, advise, and (potentially) develop a management strategy. The ten-member team ranged from anti- to pro-wolf control, with Rosemary Fox participating on behalf of Sierra Club BC.

Sierra Club BC was also concerned about grizzly bear numbers. Both logging and hunting had taken a heavy toll on the grizzly population in British Columbia. In 1998 Sierra Club BC called on the BC government to legislate a moratorium on grizzly bear hunting and to undertake a comprehensive population survey and detailed analysis of all threats to BC's grizzly population.[34] When this did not come about, Sierra Club BC continued to advocate by asking the public to sign petitions and write letters against the hunting of grizzly bears. The club celebrated when, finally, in 2017, the new NDP government placed a moratorium on grizzly bear hunting.

Northern Rivers

BOTH INDUSTRY AND THE PROVINCIAL GOVERNMENT VIEWED northern BC's numerous large, powerful rivers as potential sources of hydroelectric power. The Nechako River—which has its headwaters in a vast chain of lakes in the interior plateau of British Columbia—flows east to Prince George to form a principal tributary of the Fraser River. The province invited Alcan to consider this area for a generating station because of its potential to meet an aluminum smelter's power-intensive requirements. In 1951, they came to a negotiated agreement with Alcan with respect to land and water rights. The Nechako was diverted through the Kitimat Range of the Coast Mountains to the Kemano Generating Station, which was completed in 1954 to provide hydroelectricity for Alcan's new smelter in Kitimat.

In 1979, Alcan decided to expand the capacity of the smelter, which would require more hydroelectric capacity. The company applied to the Utilities Commission for a certificate to begin Kemano II. The federal Fisheries and Oceans ministry raised concerns about how the project would affect migrating salmon in the Nechako River, and court action ensued. The issue was not resolved until 1987, when an agreement was signed between Alcan and both the BC and federal governments, resulting in a scaled-down version known as the Kemano Completion Project. Alcan gave up water rights to the Nanika and Cheslatta Rivers and agreed to set up a program to watch over fish habitat. Nevertheless, the scaled-down version still met with much opposition, resulting in an extensive public hearing held by the BC Utilities Commission between 1993 and 1994.

Pat Moss from Smithers joined the SCBC board in 1992, eventually becoming its chair for three years beginning in 1995. She had already been working on the Kemano issue since 1979 with the Rivers Defense Coalition and had received a conservation award from the Steelhead Society in 1991 for her contributions. She helped cultivate the relationship between the First Nations in the area and the environmentalists to provide a strengthened opposition to the project. Her presence on the board stirred Sierra Club BC to become more involved.

Sierra Club BC submitted a brief to the commission's public review, presenting concerns about the project's potentially devastating effect on the salmon in the Nechako River (a very important tributary of the Fraser River—one of the world's major salmon-producing rivers) and the ecosystems and people dependent upon the salmon.[35] As well, the brief discussed the likely significant social and economic hardship to the local community, Vanderhoof and the Cheslatta T'en (Cheslatta Carrier Nation), who would be affected by reduced flow of the Nechako. The club encouraged its membership and the public to sign petitions, write letters, and let their opposition be known. After a long, hard-fought campaign by the Cheslatta T'en, Greenpeace, and numerous other intervenors, including Sierra Club BC, Premier Harcourt cancelled the Kemano Completion Project in 1995. Pat Moss received the 1995 BC Minister of Environment Individual Award.

In 1978 BC Hydro also considered the feasibility of building two very large dams across the so-called "Grand Canyon" of the Stikine River. This prompted immediate opposition from environmental organizations, First Nations groups, and the general public, especially given the important salmon habitat at stake in the lower third of the river. In January 1980, Sierra Club BC held a workshop in Vancouver to organize public support from both northern and southern BC to protect the Stikine and to develop strategies to resist pressures to degrade it. One of the outcomes was the 1981 formation of the Friends of the Stikine Society. Ten years later Rosemary Fox wrote, "In those days, the dams seemed inevitable. While we cannot claim credit for stopping them (economic considerations did that), the concerted effort of people in Telegraph Creek and in southern BC delayed the construction of access roads until, finally, postponement of the dams made these roads unnecessary. The lesson is, never give up even when the situation seems hopeless!"[36]

Sierra Club BC continued to participate with the Friends of the Stikine in the campaign pushing for a management strategy to preserve the integrity of the watershed and proposing a park-managed recreation area, which eventually led to the creation of the Stikine River Provincial Park in 2001.

The Stikine became at risk again in 2004 when Shell Canada was awarded a 400,000-hectare tenure around what is known as the Sacred Headwaters, the origins of three major salmon-bearing rivers in northern BC—the Skeena, the Nass, and the Stikine—for developing coalbed methane. The project would result in a maze of wells, pipelines, and roads. There was massive opposition to this proposal and multiple First Nations and environmental groups, including Sierra Club BC, took up the cause. First Nations groups blockaded the main access road. Sierra Club BC helped spread the word to people in the urban centres not only in BC but also internationally. In 2008, the BC government declared a four-year moratorium on oil and gas development in the Sacred Headwaters and finally, in 2012, it issued a permanent ban.

Another controversial plan has been the Site C Dam proposal on the Peace River just southwest of Fort St. John, which first came to the attention of Sierra Club BC in the 1980s. Site C is the third of four major dams originally proposed for the Peace River in the mid-1950s. The three dams were designed to work together to generate power by reusing water from each dam as it moved downstream.[37] The first dam at Site A, the Bennett Dam, just west of Hudson's Hope, was completed in 1968 and created the Williston Lake Reservoir, considered the largest earth-filled structure ever built, and now the largest "lake" in British Columbia.[38] Site B, the Peace Canyon Dam, situated twenty-three kilometres downstream from the Bennett Dam, created Dinosaur Lake in 1980. Site C, eighty-three kilometres downstream from Site B, is intended to produce hydroelectricity for a third time, using water coming from the Peace Canyon Dam at Site B.

Leo Rutledge, a Sierra Club BC board member living in the Peace Valley, was central to the early campaign to oppose the construction of Site C. Rutledge established the Peace Valley Environmental Association in 1975 and worked with Sierra Club BC to lobby against the proposal. BC Utilities Commission hearings held in 1982, and again in 1989, provided conditional approval for the development but determined at the time that the extra electricity that would be generated was not necessary, so building the dam was deferred.

In 2010, BC Hydro resurrected the proposal when Premier Gordon Campbell included Site C in the government's Clean Energy Act. Building the dam became a priority for the government when Campbell resigned and Christy Clark took over in 2011. Sierra Club BC took a position against the Site C Dam when it learned that the BC government had exempted it from regulatory review by the BC Utilities Commission. From 2010 through 2013, senior campaign staff members Susan Howatt and Sarah Cox, working closely with Treaty 8 First Nations, brought the story of the Peace to southern British Columbians, many of whom were unaware of the environmental consequences of building the dam.

Ana Simeon took over as Sierra Club BC's Peace River campaigner in 2014. In order to educate the public and mobilize visible support for the Peace, Simeon toured the province with what she called the "Site C Show," which included speakers from the Peace Valley such as Julian Napoleon and Yvonne Tupper of the Saulteau First Nations, as well as Ken and Arlene Boon, third-generation Peace Valley farmers, showing images that Simeon said depicted a "beautiful, biodiverse valley." They raised a lot of support for saving the valley and the coalition grew to include other groups and organizations including church, interfaith, and food security groups. Meanwhile, the Treaty 8 First Nations connected with Amnesty International Canada, which made Site C one of its flagship campaigns for Indigenous rights—not just in Canada, but also internationally.

The proposed dam is expected to provide about 1,100 megawatts of power—enough electricity for approximately 400,000 homes—but there is much concern that the power would be used for other purposes instead, such as supporting future liquefied natural gas (LNG) projects. A dam at Site C would flood approximately 5,500 hectares of land, tripling the width of the river along eighty-three kilometres of the Peace River Valley and extending along thirty-five kilometres of tributary valleys (Halfway and Moberly Rivers and some smaller creeks).[39] Farmers in the area would lose their land and Treaty 8 First Nations (West Moberly and Prophet River) would lose traditional hunting and fishing grounds along with seventy-eight heritage sites, including burial grounds and places of cultural and spiritual significance. At the time of writing, a constitutional challenge by West Moberly and Prophet River First Nations was still before the courts.

At events and in media appearances, Ana Simeon argued that the $8 billion hydro project (the original estimated cost of the project, which has since grown to $10.7 billion, at the time of writing) was far from being a "clean energy" project. Instead it would end up as a net contributor to climate change. Not only would it enable fossil-fuel infrastructure (primarily LNG) but the flooding of boreal forests and the methane release from downstream wetlands affected by a changed hydrological regime would contribute to increased greenhouse gas emissions. She also pointed out that Site C would destroy carbon-sequestering wetlands that support large migratory bird flocks; farms and ranches passed down for generations; alluvial farmland capable of providing fruits and vegetables for one million people; fish habitat with methylmercury; and habitat for sensitive species such as wolverines, caribou, and grizzlies.

Sierra Club BC's executive director, Bob Peart, reached out to the Mikisew Cree First Nation in Alberta, whose territory in the Peace Athabasca Delta, a World Heritage Site wetland downstream from the Site C Dam location, would be severely impacted. Simeon explained, "That's a whole other aspect that was never included in the deliberations of the Joint Review Panel or the BC Utilities Commission—the downstream impacts on the Peace Athabasca Delta and the Wood Buffalo National Park, which is already experiencing serious drying caused by the other two dams on the Peace. The Mikisew Cree applied to UNESCO to send an investigative mission to Canada to look at the impacts on the Peace Athabasca Delta from Site C and tar sands development." Sierra Club BC helped publicize the investigation and the scientific research commissioned by the Mikisew Cree, which shows that Site C would be the "nail in the coffin of the Delta," exacerbating the drying process to the point where there is a serious risk of large-scale methane seepage from the wetlands; another contributor to climate change.

In the summer of 2015, BC Hydro began site preparation and construction in the Peace Valley. In the fall of 2016, Simeon was one of a group of activists and experts who met with the UNESCO mission in Edmonton to share their concerns about Site C's impact on the Peace Athabasca Delta. The mission had just finished a ten-day tour of the delta and Wood Buffalo National Park. Simeon, representing Sierra Club BC, gave an oral presentation, as did Candace Batycki, from the Yellowstone to Yukon (Y2Y)Conservation Initiative. As well, there were both oral and written submissions from other organizations,[40] including the Canadian Parks and Wilderness Society. The UNESCO committee released its report in March 2017, concluding that there were significant threats to the park from development and strongly criticizing Canada's failure to protect the area. It indicated that the park risked being listed as a World Heritage Site in Danger and provided seventeen recommendations to the Canadian government. If Canada failed to take steps to protect the park by the end of 2018, UNESCO would recommend that the park be listed as endangered.[41]

On February 1, 2019, Canada unveiled a ninety-six-page action plan to deal with concerns raised by the committee.[42] One of the recommended measures is a commitment to consider both specific and cumulative effects on the park in all future environmental assessments under federal jurisdiction. Although this recommendation is appreciated by Mikisew Cree First Nation, it does not address concerns related to projects already underway such as Site C, which did not include an assessment of cumulative effects. However, the federal government indicated it did not have the authority to launch a new study. The federal government also plans to increase the number of park staff and scientific monitoring of tailings from the oilsands. As well, it will allow increased flow in the spring from the controlled waterways to help restore the levels of the delta's lakes and streams.

A flotilla of boats participates in the twelfth annual Paddle for the Peace in 2017. *Photo by Louis Bockner, www.louisbockner.com*

The Site C coalition was able to make the campaign a provincial election issue in 2017 and when the NDP won the election, forming the government with the help of the Green Party, supporters were hopeful that the project would be cancelled despite the $2 billion the Liberal government had already spent on site preparation and construction. The new government called for a review by the BC Utilities Commission. The resulting report did not recommend what should be done but rather pointed out that all scenarios had associated economic risks. In the end, the NDP government decided to proceed with the project. Site C continues to face a great deal of opposition from First Nations, scholars, farmers, landowners, and environmental organizations, including Sierra Club BC.

Ana Simeon: Peace Keeper

When Ana Simeon, with a background in journalism, advocacy, and conflict resolution, learned about an upcoming job as communications coordinator at Sierra Club BC, she immediately applied and was hired in September 2005. Simeon loves getting her hands in the earth. At the Sierra Club BC office on Johnson Street, she often spent her breaks tending the container garden on the rooftop patio and dealing with the composting worms under the kitchen sink. With this background, it was not surprising that Simeon fell in love with the beautiful and fertile Peace River Valley when she participated in her first Paddle for the Peace in 2014. After nine years spent working in communications, she was ready for a change and asked to take on the Site C campaigner role.

She joined a loose coalition, some of whom had been fighting hard for the Peace since the 1980s: Treaty 8 First Nations, particularly the West Moberly and Prophet River nations, the Peace Valley Environmental Association (PVEA), and Peace Valley farmers and landowners. Simeon, too, found it an uphill battle. "It was clear that the BC government was deeply committed to Site C. Christy Clark [BC's premier at the time] had staked her political future on it and was not going to let anything stand in its way, certainly not pesky details like treaty rights, the cost to taxpayers, or the fact that the power wasn't needed." As well as the Peace Valley Environmental Association, the Yellowstone to Yukon Conservation Initiative and the Wilderness Committee (also known as the Western Canada Wilderness Committee) were fully committed to the campaign. The search for funding was difficult because of the widespread perception that hydro was "clean energy." Simeon greatly appreciated the support of the Patagonia Foundation and its founder, Yvon Chouinard, who she called "an amazing defender of rivers." As the campaign grew, so did the support, especially from Sierra Club members and donors.

"I feel that fighting for the Peace Valley was the most important thing that I've done, not just as part of my eleven years in the Sierra Club, but in my life," said Simeon. "It was truly love at first sight, a love that has grown as I spent time in the valley and got to know the fearless defenders of the Peace among the Treaty 8 First Nations and the farming community, and so many people from all corners of the province who became part of this movement."

After eleven years wearing various hats at the Sierra Club, Simeon left in November 2016 to work for RAVEN (Respecting Aboriginal Values and Environmental Needs). Galen Armstrong took over as Sierra Club BC's Site C campaigner. At the time of our interview, Simeon was much encouraged by the ongoing and growing grassroots movement to stop Site C. "The story of the Peace inspires great passion in people. People are not giving up, no matter what. First Nations have just filed a constitutional challenge and an injunction application. Groups are form-

Ana Simeon visits the grasslands at Churn Creek on the western bank of the Fraser River south of Williams Lake. *Photo by Tom Martin*

ing all over the province to fundraise for this legal work. One way or another the Peace will have the last word." She thought Sierra Club BC's fight against the dam was fitting given the history of its founder, John Muir. "Back in the 1800s, he fought so hard against the Hetch Hetchy dam and some people think that the grief [due to the dam going ahead] contributed to his early death. Fighting against dams is in our DNA. I'm so proud to be part of this organization." ▲

Northern Watersheds

THE KHUTZEYMATEEN INLET FORMS A SMALL ARM OF PORTLAND Inlet on the far north coast of BC near the Alaskan border. The Save the Khutzeymateen campaign began in earnest in the mid-1980s, when concerns about extensive helicopter logging on the slopes of the inlet suggested that logging would spread to the watershed, with its old-growth forest and significant and irreplaceable grizzly habitat. The area had originally been proposed as a candidate for an ecological reserve as early as 1974.[43]

In the 1980s, the Khutzeymateen watershed, from its estuary all the way to its headwaters, was still relatively untouched; a tree farm licence had been granted but a cutting permit had not yet been issued. The push was on to provide scientific evidence for the necessity to protect the habitat in order to protect the bears, including monitoring the use of the park by them. Sierra Club BC was the first to act on this need, although others stepped in along the way to take on leadership roles, notably the Friends of Ecological Reserves with Vicky Husband. When Husband came to work for Sierra Club BC in 1988, she continued the campaign.

In 1994, the province established the Khutzeymateen/K'tzim-a-deen Grizzly Sanctuary as a Class A provincial park and the first grizzly bear reserve—resulting in the first undisturbed estuary of its size to be protected along the north coast of the province. In 2008, a number of conservancies were added at the periphery, and the protected area was extended to include traditional use areas of the Coast Tsimshian (Metlakatla and Lax Kwa'alaams First Nations), including the Khutzeymateen Inlet Conservancy and the Khutzeymateen Inlet West Conservancy.[44]

Similarly, the watershed of the Babine River, a tributary of the Skeena River found in central BC, was subject to a plan to initiate logging around 1986—one that involved clearcutting and building three bridges to facilitate the removal of logs. The river is considered to be one of the best steelhead fishing areas in the world, and is a favourite destination for whitewater kayakers and rafters. Its sockeye run is integral to the commercial fishery at the mouth of the Skeena, not to mention a feeding ground for the large grizzly population. Sierra Club BC called on its membership and the public to send letters to the government stressing the importance of protecting the grizzly bear population of the area.

A number of individuals and businesses reliant on wilderness tourism formed the Wilderness Tourism Council in 1987, with Ric Careless as its first executive director, and the group, along with Sierra Club BC, lobbied the provincial government to protect the area—arguing that it made better economic sense to protect the resources than to destroy them. The area for the Babine River Corridor Park was set aside in 1990, and the park was eventually established in 1999.

The Skeena River, the second-longest river entirely within BC, originates at the southern end of the Spatsizi Plateau and flows southwest to the Pacific Ocean. *Photo by Sam Beebe/Ecotrust*

Sierra Club BC's Impact on Northern BC

NORTHERN BC'S VAST EXPANSE IS FILLED WITH LARGE POWERFUL rivers, towering mountains, splendid beauty, and a copious variety of plants and animals. Its population is spread thinly throughout in small towns, rural areas, and many First Nation territories. Sierra Club BC contributed significantly to preserving many of its special regions placed at risk, as well as the area's biodiversity. This is especially evident when the campaigns discussed in later chapters, dealing with mining and oil and gas issues, are also considered. The club often acted as a conduit to help people in the north explain to those in the southern, more urban areas what would be lost if steps were not taken. With the persistence that environmentalists are noted for, many of these campaigns achieved success.

We will never see these ancient forests again. We have to change our course before everything is gone.

—Vicky Husband

5

Old-Growth Forests— Conflict in the Woods

COASTAL TEMPERATE RAINFORESTS, ONE OF THE RAREST ECOSYS-tems in the world, make up less than 1 percent of the Earth's surface. These old-growth forests with their lush undergrowth support an abundance of plants and animals and play an important role in sta-bilizing global climate patterns and maintaining biodiversity, water regulation, and nutrient cycling. They also provide a secure habitat for many endangered species, including marbled murrelets, north-ern goshawks, and Roosevelt elk, some of which can only thrive in unlogged forests. Second-growth forests only regain the essential characteristics of old forests over hundreds of years. Long before that, they are cut again!

BC's forests have been logged since the arrival of the first pio-neers. However, the process became more industrialized in the 1930s and '40s and the pace of cutting exploded between 1950 and 1970. The landscape was soon dominated by vast clearcuts that looked like war zones. With them came significant erosion and stream-bed contamination, devastating both fisheries and wildlife. By the 1970s, not all forested land had been cut by any means, but virtually everything left had a date assigned for when it too would be on the chopping block.

The stage was set for a public backlash—*and it happened!* There were many actors but the SCBC was a leader in the movement and members were often in the thick of the action.

Foundational Forestry Campaigns

TO UNDERSTAND HOW THE REVOLUTION AGAINST INDUSTRIAL FOR-estry in BC began, one must begin with two epoch-making conflicts: South Moresby and Clayoquot Sound. They brought the situation in BC's forests to the public eye. They also trained and radicalized a generation of activists and showed them that they could win if they pushed hard enough. Crucially, they also brought First Nations' concerns and rights to the forefront of the debate.

South Moresby

IN 1974, THE HAIDA FIRST NATION INITIATED WHAT BECAME A VERY public, high-profile campaign to protect the old-growth forests of South Moresby—the southern wilderness archipelago of Haida Gwaii (historically known as the Queen Charlotte Islands). This area has been called the "Canadian Galapagos" due to the large number of species native to the region.

Sierra Club BC's involvement began at the Skidegate Museum Symposium, sponsored by the Islands Protection Society, on November 29, 1977, when the club presented a brief calling upon the provincial government and Rayonier Canada (B.C.) Ltd. to support the "completion of a comprehensive assessment of development alternatives for the Southern Moresby Wilderness." Suggested possibilities included an ecological reserve, provincial park, national park,

Many celebrated the South Moresby success including these en-vironmentalists. LEFT TO RIGHT: Vicky Husband, Sharon Chow, John Broadhead, Mr. Suzuki (father of David Suzuki), Kevin McNamee and Elizabeth May. *University of Victoria Archives*

biosphere reserve, or world heritage area. The club also requested that public hearings be launched to discuss the issue.

Sierra Club BC, along with 150 other organizations, lobbied the government to halt logging on South Moresby, and donated funds to support the Haida campaign. Opposition from the forestry and mining industries was intense. The situation on the islands became charged with hostility, which simmered for years afterwards. Elizabeth May, in her book about the South Moresby fight, *Paradise Won*, described loggers angrily waving placards at federal Environment Minister Tom McMillan when he landed at the Sandspit airport in the fall of 1985. In his first major speech in that role, he had commit-ted to protect South Moresby.[45]

Nevertheless, logging continued, and later in 1985, the Haida des-ignated the southern third of the archipelago as a Haida Heritage Site, setting up a blockade on Lyell Island that resulted in the arrest of sev-enty-two members of the Haida Nation. Their implacable opposition and the continued lobbying by multiple groups and individuals eventually led to the South Moresby Memorandum of Understanding in 1987, followed by the South Moresby Agreement in 1988. The latter set the terms for creating a National Park Reserve; this was followed by the Gwaii Haanas Agreement in 1993, which secured the protection of the area—about 50 percent of Haida Gwaii.

In 1988, Sierra Club BC, along with the Council of the Haida Nation and several other groups and individuals, received the Fred M. Packard International Parks Merit Award from the Commission on National Parks and Protected Areas for working "tirelessly" over a thirteen-year period to preserve the area.

Clayoquot Sound

THE SECOND SIGNIFICANT BATTLE INVOLVED CLAYOQUOT SOUND, which is situated on the west coast of Vancouver Island and is a network of inlets, bays, islands, and three watersheds. The latter contain one of the largest intact temperate rainforests in the world and some of the oldest and largest trees on the west coast. It is home to the Nuu-chah-nulth First Nation.

The roots of the Clayoquot conflict lie in a rapid increase in logging in the 1970s and '80s that many considered unrestricted. The Friends of Clayoquot Sound was established in 1979 to pursue better forest practices and a transition to an environmentally friendly economy.[46]

The opening salvo of what became known as the "War in the Woods" was at Meares Island. Plans to harvest timber there were made public in 1980 and were opposed by local First Nations for whom the island had spiritual significance. After an unsuccessful planning process to explore alternatives to large-scale logging, in 1983 the government granted MacMillan Bloedel the right to harvest 90 percent of the land.[47] Soon after, First Nations designated Meares Island a tribal park and set up a blockade to prevent MacMillan Bloedel from accessing the island. An injunction to stop the logging was also obtained on the grounds that Aboriginal title had not yet been settled.

The Tla-o-qui-aht and Ahousaht First Nations declare Meares Island as Canada's first tribal park on April 21, 1984. *University of Victoria Archives, photo by Andrew Dorst*

A blockade in 1988 tried to stop a logging road from being built in Sulphur Passage, and another in 1992 protested MacMillan Bloedel's logging on the edge of an intact Clayoquot River Valley.

In 1993, a new NDP government endeavoured to settle the issue by imposing the Clayoquot Sound Land Use Decision. While claiming to balance the environmental, economic, and social needs of the area, it earmarked 45 percent of the land for logging, 33 percent for parks, and 17 percent for "special management," with 5 percent awaiting determination of Aboriginal title. An SCBC mapping analysis concluded that, in fact, 74 percent of the ancient temperate rainforest was slated to be clearcut while much of the proposed protected area was actually bog and marginal forest. Environmentalists were outraged.

What followed was the largest peaceful civil disobedience protest in Canadian history. Over 12,000 people attended the Clayoquot Summer blockade, and 856 were arrested and charged.[48] More than 200 protestors also stormed the BC legislature. An international boycott of BC wood was set up by Greenpeace. In short, Clayoquot gained international attention.

The government eventually capitulated and established the Clayoquot Sound Scientific Panel, a blue-ribbon science panel tasked with developing "world-class logging standards." In 1995, the government accepted all 127 recommendations of the panel and the conflict was over. A third of Clayoquot was protected and a further 21 percent was put under special management. Small-scale logging continues, primarily by First Nations–owned Iisaak Forest Resources Ltd., established in 1998 as the first company under Indigenous management to hold a tree farm licence. Although MacMillan Bloedel closed its operation in 1998 and there have not been any more blockades, controversy continues to permeate the region to this day.

Sierra Club BC's involvement in the Clayoquot conflict was less overt given its practice of limiting its engagement to legally sanctioned advocacy. However, the club actively supported the protests through public education and lobbying.[49] Some members also participated in the week-long, coast-to-coast Clayoquot Express, organized by Elizabeth May of the Sierra Club of Canada. This was a rail caravan of protesters that made its way from the Maritimes to Vancouver. The Express was described as going from the east coast, "the sea without fish," to British Columbia, "the forest without trees."[50] As well, Sierra Club BC's mapping project played a key role in convincing the public and the decision makers that the area needed protection.

In 2002, Clayoquot Sound was designated a UNESCO World Biosphere Reserve.

Campaigns by the SCBC

WHILE SIERRA CLUB BC'S INVOLVEMENT IN THE HAIDA GWAII AND Clayoquot campaigns was mainly supportive, SCBC played a critical role in amplifying the growing public rage over forest practices, particularly on Vancouver Island, and projecting it onto much wider areas.

In 1972, the Victoria Sierra Club group found out that the government was providing logging companies with timber rights in areas of Strathcona Park—in exchange for lands that the Parks Branch wanted to acquire elsewhere. Brian Pinch reported in a 1974 paper he wrote about BC environmental groups, "One of these trades involved the exchange of 90 acres of property worth $300,000 at Cape Scott for the cutting rights to 5260 acres of Strathcona, worth $10,000,000."[51] SCBC was outraged by these questionable trades and called for an investigation. Bob Williams, the minister of lands, forest, and water resources, agreed and although results of the investigation were not made public, it seemed to put a halt on timber trades.

An early project was undertaken by Ric Careless and the Victoria Sierra Club during the Nitinat Triangle campaign to assess the remaining wilderness on Vancouver Island. As satellite imagery did not yet exist, Careless and two others took weeks to look through thousands of aerial photographs to determine where logging roads had been built by tracing every logging road that they showed. They then pieced these results together to form one map. With this they were able to identify a few unlogged areas of great interest, in particular the Tsitika-Schoen—the last significant unlogged watershed on the east coast of Vancouver Island.

Along with the BC Wildlife Federation, the Steelhead Society of BC, and the Federation of BC Naturalists, Ric Careless and the Victoria group became very active in opposing timber cutting in the area, including in the Adam, Eve, and Tsitika-Schoen watersheds. An early victory was the establishment of Schoen Lake Provincial Park in 1977. The Tsitika watershed, however, remained unprotected. When the BC government set up what they called an Integrated Resource Plan for the area in 1978, Sierra Club BC campaigners argued that it was a thinly disguised logging plan. In the 1980s, SCBC's Tsitika campaign passed from its lead campaigner, Bruce Hardy, to George and Kay Wood.

Robson Bight, located where the Tsitika River enters Johnstone Strait, received particular attention. This stretch of coastline contains the world-famous rubbing beaches of the orcas. Paul Spong, a long-time whale researcher, suggested that whales likely find rubbing to be a pleasant experience, much like a visit to the spa for a massage.[52] The whales added recreational and scenic value to the lower Tsitika watershed, making for an even stronger case for preservation.

In 1982, the Robson Bight Ecological Reserve was established, which banned boats and set strict guidelines around watching the whales. However, this did not protect the forests around the bay, which were deemed critical to its ecological integrity. Thus, the fight continued.

Sierra Club BC presented six briefs to the government on the Tsitika-Robson Bight issue, and the government produced a number of reports on the area with input in many of them from George and Kay Wood. Throughout the 1980s, the club corresponded and had meetings with various provincial government departments as well as Parks Canada. Campaigners issued news releases, created brochures, wrote letters to newspaper editors, made TV appearances, and did slide shows, all to keep up pressure and to publicize the area. Eventually, when logging was imminent in a nearby area below Catherine Creek, George Wood requested that the Wilderness Committee step in and they set up a protest camp. Thirty people established a blockade and were arrested. Although George Wood was not one of them, he was named along with the WCWC leaders in a BC Supreme Court lawsuit. Ultimately, the government placed a five-year logging moratorium on the Lower Tsitika Valley and the adjoining Schmidt Creek. Final protection did not come until after the CORE process in 1994 (described later in this chapter).

The SCBC also worked ceaselessly on forest policy. An early opportunity came when the government appointed the Royal Commission on Forest Resources, chaired by Dr. Peter Pearse, in June 1975. Sierra Club BC volunteers from both the Vancouver and Victoria groups submitted briefs.[53]

Brian Pinch of the Victoria group recalls working along with Eve Howden and others "for months and months." They had help from a forester who provided significant input about poor forest practices and how the logging companies misrepresented estimates of the volume of wood available for logging. For example, there was what was known as the "fall-down effect," which referred to the fact that the first harvest of a forest produces a much larger volume of wood than a subsequent harvest. "In fact, there is a lot more to it than that. We didn't understand that the second rotation would have a much poorer quality of wood as well, which is a big deal." Pinch was the Victoria group's witness before the commission and spent an afternoon being cross-examined.

Although Pearse was critical of many aspects of forest policy and indicated that other uses for forested lands needed to be considered, his recommendations did not endorse many of the issues about sustained yield raised by Sierra Club BC and other environmentalists.[54] His view on clearcuts was also opposite to that put forth by environmentalists, indicating that it was an appropriate method of harvesting and with proper safeguards any harmful consequences could be mitigated. Nevertheless, an important finding that emerged from these hearings was that there were only a few companies controlling most of the harvesting rights and manufacturing in the province and Pearse made a number of recommendations regarding the tenure system.[55]

In the mid-1980s, two people joined the SCBC and became possibly the most dynamic forest campaigners in the history of the province, namely Peter McAllister and Vicky Husband.

Peter McAllister returned to Victoria in 1988 after eighteen years in the Okanagan. A flight over Vancouver Island revealed devastating clearcuts covering the landscape and obliterating his favourite fly-fishing haunts. He was soon a committed member of the SCBC and its chair. While McAllister's campaigns were diverse, he was especially attached to the Carmanah, a mostly untouched valley on the west coast of Vancouver Island sitting behind the West Coast Trail. Randy Stoltmann had discovered "giant" Sitka spruce trees in the valley and word got to McAllister via Bristol Foster, head of the Ecological Reserves program.

McAllister related that he immediately called MacMillan Bloedel. The chief forester of the company had never seen the area so a helicopter trip was arranged to fly McAllister and Sharon Chow, along with the chief forester and other company officials, into the valley. Stoltmann and Clinton Webb, both acting for the Wilderness Committee, were standing there in the pouring rain to meet the helicopter. All were awestruck by the Carmanah's stunning trees.

SPEAK UP FOR CARMANAH

The fate of Carmanah Valley . . . lies with the public — ordinary British Columbians — (who) will decide how much of the valley is logged, how much is saved, by the way they react to MacMillan Bloedel's park proposal over the next few weeks.

A mighty hue and cry will tell the provincial government that it had better preserve much more than MacMillan Bloedel has in mind at the moment.

The new park reserve includes only a fringe of trees flanking the lower reaches of the creek . . . (a) snake-thin park proposal.

A sensible interim step for the government would be to put a logging moratorium on all of Carmanah until the year 2000.

TIMES-COLONIST EDITORIAL JAN 30/1989

WHO GAVE MacMILLAN BLOEDEL CONTROL OVER THE PUBLIC'S FORESTS?

HELP SAVE CANADA'S TALLEST TREES AND VANCOUVER ISLAND'S PRICELESS NATURAL HERITAGE FOR FUTURE GENERATIONS.

* **WRITE** Premier Vander Zalm and tell him how you feel about Carmanah. Parliament Buildings, Victoria V8W 1X4.

* **ATTEND** Ministry of Forests "Carmanah Open House" 11 a.m.-8 p.m. Feb. 20/21 at the Bedford Hotel, 1140 Government, across from Eaton's.

* **FILL OUT** Ministry of Forests Questionnaire.

FOR MORE INFORMATION CONTACT

SIERRA CLUB

#314-620 View St., Victoria, B.C. V8W 1J6   386-5255
Donations to help pay for this ad are appreciated.

Sierra Club BC used the media effectively to help mobilize the public.
University of Victoria Archives

Once they were back at MacMillan Bloedel headquarters, McAllister told them: "This is world-class heritage stuff. You've got to stop that logging road and I suggest you stop it for forty days while we get to the bottom of this." Remarkably, the company agreed, and with the help of Tony Gooch, Sierra Club BC raised enough money to initiate an immediate environmental assessment of the Carmanah. The results were released to the premier, cabinet ministers, MLAs, the press, and the public, emphasizing the importance of moving quickly to protect the area. McAllister also announced at the annual Sierra Club convention in San Francisco that Sierra Club BC had located the largest spruce trees in the world.

The Wilderness Committee remained active in the Carmanah, and Stoltmann himself was responsible for building many of the early trails that allowed the public to come and see the trees for themselves. The Carmanah Forestry Society, led by Sid Haskell, also played an important role in building trails and transporting people to the area. Sharon Chow recalls the SCBC designing and selling thousands of Carmanah T-shirts to boost the visibility of the issue.

In 1990, the lower part of the Carmanah was designated a provincial park. The upper part remained unprotected until 1994.

McAllister emphasized that he did not work alone on these campaigns. There was a growing cadre of Sierra Club BC volunteers armed with a host of valuable skills and talents. McAllister recalled "much socializing, boating and hikes, adventures in Clayoquot Sound and genuine camaraderie that kept us going up until about 1992. The stories many of those Sierra Club friends could tell would fill a very entertaining book."

McAllister was pivotal in bringing the logging practices of the time, often shocking, to the public's attention. In 1988, he became fast friends with Joseph (Jup) Weber. Weber was a key player in founding Luxembourg's Green Party and later became a member of the European Parliament. He was also at the forefront of the first boycotts of tropical rainforest timber products coming from the Amazon area of Brazil.

McAllister and Weber decided to bring prominent journalists, filmmakers, and forest ecologists together to draw attention to BC's clearcutting practices. Ultimately a documentary film was made by Channel 4, Britain's premier public service broadcaster. It was called *Battle for the Trees* and received wide circulation in Canada and abroad. In McAllister's words, "they shot scenes of destruction that shocked the outside world."

This publicity was effective. Dominic Gill, the owner of *Loot*, one of the largest daily buy and sell newspapers in Great Britain, saw *Battle for the Trees* just as he was about to renew his contract with Fletcher Challenge, a major west coast timber producer, for a large order of newsprint. He put the contract on hold, called McAllister, and arranged to come to BC to "see for himself." After a flight over Vancouver Island, Gill announced that he was cancelling his contract and would have nothing further to do with British Columbia lumber producers. It was the first highly publicized economic embarrassment suffered by the timber industry and a forerunner of the international consumer boycotts later on.

In 1989, McAllister received a tip that *National Geographic* magazine was doing a story on the clearcut destruction of forests in the western United States. He called Rowe Findley, an assistant editor, and convinced him that BC should also be included in the story; he told him that BC had clearcuts that would surpass any logging destruction documented in the US. Findley, along with photographer Jim Blair, accepted the invitation.

McAllister took them up the coast to Kyuquot where Blair photographed a massive clearcut of Mount Paxton that extended down to the ocean. It was later published as a triple-page foldout in *National Geographic*. This became an iconic photo that made an impression around the world.

Around this time, McAllister spoke as a Sierra Club representative to a national forestry convention in Toronto, a federal government and timber industry affair. He noted that a consumer boycott could be effective in changing logging practices. The audience was appalled and McAllister was denounced. Not since the seal hunt reprisals had boycotts threatened a Canadian industry. McAllister was flattered to be compared to that enemy of Canada, Brigitte Bardot, the French movie star who championed the seal hunt boycotts.

In 1990, McAllister began exploring the forests of the mainland coast, which would later become known as the Great Bear Rainforest. This was his focus for the next five years. Initial work was done under the auspices of the SCBC but McAllister soon formed the Raincoast Conservation Society and worked under that label

Michael Blades kayaks by the infamous clearcut slope on Mt. Paxton north of Kyuquot Sound. *Photo by Mike Sheehan*

thereafter. (McAllister's work on the Great Bear Rainforest is described in chapter 10.)

Vicky Husband came to the scbc in 1988 after playing a leading role in the Friends of Ecological Reserves campaign to protect the Khutzeymateen Valley, a grizzly sanctuary north of Prince Rupert. Over most of the next two decades, she was a high-profile spokesperson for the club, a formidable lobbyist and a key fundraiser. She and Ric Careless were leaders in bringing us foundation funding into Canada for forestry campaigns and a wide range of other issues, such as marine protection and the Flathead Valley. As noted in chapter 2, this paved the way to professionalizing the club with permanent staff.

SCBC Mapping Program

HUSBAND'S PROUDEST ACCOMPLISHMENT WAS THE SCBC MAPPING program. Tired of fighting one battle at a time, Husband had the idea of determining what the big picture was and starting with that. In particular, she wanted to know the status of remaining old-growth in the forests. Husband enjoys telling the story about her talk with the then chief forester, John Cuthbert, who, when asked how much old-growth forest was left on Vancouver Island, thought it would be easy to find out from the Inventory Branch. However, he was told that the government had no idea as so much of the inventory information was held by the tree farm licence holders—in other words, the logging companies.

Dave Leversee, scbc's mapping specialist. *University of Victoria Archives*

This led Husband to initiate the Sierra Club's highly successful mapping project. At a geographic information system (GIS) conference in Vancouver in the late 1980s, she met Dave Leversee, who introduced himself and said he had a dream of satellite mapping Vancouver Island. He had already been doing this type of innovative mapping for the Wilderness Society in Washington state. "That's when it all began," said Husband. "It took me a year to raise the money so that we could pay Dave and the Wilderness Society to do the maps."

The first map was released in 1991—a composite of forest cover maps from 1954 compared to the 1990 satellite imagery map of Vancouver Island. It displayed very graphically how much of Vancouver Island's old-growth, ancient forests had been logged in that period of time and how much was left. Logged areas were shown in a sand colour and were so extensive that the project was nicknamed the Desert Storm Map. It created a media firestorm.

The map showed that between 1954 and 1990, 770,000 hectares of forest had been cut, leaving approximately 828,000 hectares. Leversee estimated that if this rate of logging was maintained, all unprotected ancient temperate rainforest on Vancouver Island would be lost by 2022.[56]

Subsequently the club's mapping expertise was used to help with many campaigns, notably Clayoquot Sound and the Great Bear Rainforest.

At one time or another, Husband fought for pretty much every scrap of significant old-growth on Vancouver Island. When she was awarded the Order of British Columbia in 2000, she was acknowledged for almost single-handedly working to protect the Tahsish, Kwois, Silburn, Nasparti, Power, and Battle watersheds on the northwest coast of Vancouver Island.[57]

Husband's effectiveness was due to three factors. First, in the SCBC tradition, she worked very hard to always have her facts straight. She made sure that she was informed by experts like Ray Travers, Bob Nixon, and Herb Hammond. Second, she cultivated many contacts among the press, civil servants, and politicians. Last but not least, she worked very hard at being an effective public speaker. In particular, she stressed the importance of using effective sound bites in interviews.

Speaking to a class of students she told them, "if you don't have the passion, don't do this. You can't survive." Husband advised young environmentalists of the importance of public speaking: "You've got to learn to be able to express yourself, you've got to know how to communicate." She told them that a

Some memorable Husband quotes:

"I have to have my facts correct, and I have to be able to quote scientific arguments. It's what I do. But I can also see with my own eyes. There's something wrong out there. I've walked in thirty-to-sixty-year-old second-growth forests, and they're biological deserts. A deer would have to pack a lunch in there!"[58]

"In the last fourteen years we've cut as many trees as were cut in the previous eighty-six. We're overcutting by 40 to 50 percent and we're running out; we're running off the cliff."[59]

"Environmentalists have become scapegoats for the timber industry. Job loss is due to technology, mechanization, and company restructuring to reduce the payroll, not to protection."[60]

person has to speak in a way the public understands in order to have an impact.

Jeremy Wilson described the effectiveness of one of Husband's slide shows in his book *Talk and Log: Wilderness Politics in British Columbia*.[61] Dave Parker, the forests minister at the time, was losing the confidence of Premier Bill Vander Zalm and his fellow cabinet members. During one of the cabinet meetings, the premier had asked Husband to show them a slide show that she called Vicky's Clearcut Horror Show. Parker reportedly was embarrassed by a satirical slide that caused the room to burst into laughter—a photo of a family picnic in a clearcut area. The caption said, "multiple use, BC style."

Commission on Resources and Environment (CORE)

THE ELECTION OF AN NDP GOVERNMENT IN 1991, WITH MIKE HARcourt as premier, profoundly changed the landscape of the forest wars. On the negative side, as discussed above, the government's inept attempt to resolve things in Clayoquot Sound resulted in the largest peaceful civil disobedience protest in Canadian history. On a more positive note, it established the Commission on Resources and Environment (known as CORE) headed by former ombudsman Stephen Owen with Denis O'Gorman as its deputy commissioner in 1992.

Essentially, CORE was established with two objectives. First, Canada had recently signed the Convention on Biological Diversity at the 1992 Earth Summit in Rio de Janeiro, committing itself to establishing 12 percent of its land base as protected area. Harcourt charged the commission with fulfilling British Columbia's contribution and doubling its protected land base to 12 percent. Second, by doing this, Harcourt hoped that all sectors would come to an agreement on what lands should be protected and that the ongoing fight over land use in BC would be settled once and for all.

CORE was designed to be a collaborative process wherein agreements would be reached through consensus by "tables" of multiple stakeholders, including members from industry, community groups, environmental groups, local and provincial governments, and First Nations. Specifically, it was to come up with integrated land use plans for Vancouver Island (excluding Clayoquot Sound) and the East and West Kootenays. Thanks to input from Ric Careless,[62] the Cariboo-Chilcotin also became one of the designated areas.

Initially, there was considerable opposition within environmental groups about whether to participate. Colleen McCrory of the Valhalla Wilderness Society led the opposition, claiming that CORE was just another instance of "talk and log." Brian Pinch of SCBC circulated a memorandum that made the case for participating, noting that there was little to lose and potentially much to be gained. The SCBC board backed this position and many other environmental groups in BC were soon committed to being involved.

CORE published its final recommendations in 1994. Of the four tables, only the East Kootenay one came close to achieving consensus on its land use recommendations, agreeing on 90 percent of the proposals.[63] Because no table reached a conclusive agreement, the CORE staff made their own recommendations for final land use status based on the massive amount of material that had been submitted and the extensive discussions of the tables. The Vancouver Island section was especially contentious. Not only were the environmentalists unhappy with the outcome but so were the loggers. On March 21, 1994, a vast parade of logging trucks with thousands of loggers and their families and friends, known as the Yellow Ribbon Caravan, made its way down the island to protest at the legislature. They were dissatisfied with Owen's recommendations and the job losses they thought would result.

Harcourt's cabinet got the message loud and clear. It effectively rejected the CORE recommendations and designated Doug McArthur, the premier's deputy, to find compromises more acceptable to the forest industry and unions. This involved appointing regional negotiators Murray Rankin and Grant Scott in a process described by the negotiators as being very political.[64] The government also sought to soften industry and union opposition to regional agreements through programs to offset job losses, notably Forest Renewal and Skills Now.

By the end of 1996, cabinet had approved land use plans for all four areas that had been considered by CORE. While, on the face of it, the consultative processes of CORE were unsuccessful, Jeremy Wilson noted that the tables and Owen's reports were beneficial in preparing the ground for the final deals.[65]

The final cabinet-approved Vancouver Island Land Use Plan was released in April 1995. It resulted in only a slight increase in protected areas but some locations that had been on the SCBC wish list for a very long time were saved, notably the remainder of the Carmanah Valley, the Walbran Valley, the Tahsish-Kwois, Nitinat Lake/Hitchie Creek, and the lower Tsitika River adjoining Robson Bight.[66]

Forest Practices

THROUGHOUT THE 1990S, SIERRA CLUB BC CONTINUED TO WORK ON forest policy as well as protecting specific areas. It produced a report in 1993 that put forward recommendations for a new forest policy for British Columbia.[67] It emphasized that it was too simplistic to see change merely in terms of a trade-off between jobs and the environment; that, if the status quo was allowed to continue, it would accelerate the downward spiral and result in an untenable situation. The report provided a vision "of an ecologically sustainable forest and a sustainable forest economy" which could only "become a reality when the long-term needs of the forest become the preconditions for meeting the short-term needs of people."[68]

Another important SCBC initiative related to the Forest Stewardship Council (FSC). The council was established in Toronto in 1993 and introduced an "ecolabel" plan to identify sustainably sourced forest products. This label would help consumers make informed choices about wood or paper products: if it was present they could be sure that the products came from forests that adhered to principles that had been agreed upon internationally.[69]

Merran Smith, a new forest campaigner with SCBC, along with others, successfully convinced the Forest Stewardship Council that BC should be considered a separate region with its own standards. By the late 1990s, the time came for negotiations about what these BC standards would entail and Lisa Matthaus became what was termed an "environmental chamber" representative on the committee. It was a hugely complex process that went on for several years. Fortunately, they had helpful advice from knowledgeable technical people who worked with them. Matthaus was pleased with the end result, although she noted, "it is tough, as it should be."

Sierra Club BC and several other BC environmental groups went on to push logging companies to adopt the standard, and to encourage consumers of BC wood to ask for the FSC logo when making wood and paper purchases—creating awareness at the same time about the hidden costs of buying cheap products from unknown sources.

In 1998, Jill Thompson was hired as an SCBC forest campaigner. Thompson was a veteran of the Friends of Clayoquot Sound and had recently been the coordinator for the Vancouver Island section of Forest Watch. Forest Watch was a strategy to monitor the forest industry that had been developed by the BC Environmental Network and Sierra Legal Defence Fund. Through a series of training workshops on forestry law and investigative techniques, it taught volunteers how to hold logging companies accountable to the law. Participants learned how to investigate the causes of landslides and beetle epidemics, monitor forestry practices, get involved in operational planning processes, and generate investigations through the Forestry Practices Board and other legal avenues.[70] In the late 1990s, Sierra Legal Defence lost its funding for the program.

Thompson, however, was able to keep Forest Watch alive under SCBC. It helped that many members of the Sierra Club's local groups were also members of Forest Watch. Thompson continued to provide training and coordination for groups of volunteers in Quadra Island, Powell River, Victoria, Clayoquot, Port Alberni, Cortes, Nootka Sound, Courtenay, and other communities.

Thompson spent a fair bit of time in Ministry of Forests offices reading plans that the Forest Practices Code required forestry workers to write. Every forestry plan had a sixty-day public-input period. She and the volunteers went out to the forests to evaluate the situation. After examining the plans, they determined whether, for example, a planned cutblock was far enough from a fish-bearing river and whether there were fish in the river. "The forestry plan might classify a stream as 'no fish' and if we found fish, then we reported that to the Ministry of Forests and demanded the larger stream buffers that fish-bearing streams get." Thompson gave special accolades to the Quadra Island group as they were very dedicated in doing this kind of work. "I think they walked every cutblock that was proposed, measuring and taking careful notes and meeting with the logging companies to demand better attention to detail. They were just dogged."

Thompson described a novel way of communicating with the provincial Ministry of Forests. In 2001, SCBC staff members realized that their second-floor office windows on the 500 block of Johnson Street looked across a parking lot to those of the ministry on Pandora Avenue. They began hanging banners outside the window to promote ideas such as the importance of obtaining value from the wood that was cut by augmenting it with manufacturing (i.e., not simply shipping raw logs). Their banner read "Value, not volume."

Thompson indicated that the message was directed at Larry Pedersen, the chief forester, and his deputy, Ken Baker. SCBC staff knew that their messages were being received. Not only did they sometimes receive phone calls in response, they also heard about the banners during an impromptu snowball fight between the ministry staff and SCBC.

Despite being quite different in their views about forestry issues, Matthaus and Thompson had cordial relationships with Pedersen and Baker and sometimes they even teased each other. As snow in Victoria is a rare event, a January snowfall prompted Matthaus and Thompson to send a fax to the ministry office, "Snowball fight. 12:00. Be there." A return fax indicated that their challenge was accepted. At noon, all the SCBC staff headed outside, taking with them an office partition with a large marmot poster to use as a shield. The ministry staff were there with a comparable number of people and snowballs were pelted good-naturedly back and forth. "What's wrong with volume?" one ministry staffer bantered.

As they seemed to be an effective means of communication, the banners continued with various messages over the next several months.

Eventually an article appeared in the local newspaper to explain to the general public the meaning of some of these cryptic messages.[71]

Thompson was involved in another challenging campaign regarding logging on private land. Sierra Club BC tried to expose the fact that most of BC's laws are written to protect Crown (i.e. public) land, however, on the east coast of the Island, from Victoria to Campbell River, there is almost no Crown land; it is mostly private land. As a result, there was no overall planning to deal with maintaining endangered species or forest ecology; private landowners were allowed to do their own management. Sierra Club BC wrote a report about private-land logging called *Private Rights and Public Wrongs*, advocating that the Forest Practices Code should also apply to private land. "But unfortunately, it went the other way and the Code got gutted," Thompson said.

In 2004, the detailed standards of the Forest Practices Code were eliminated and replaced by the "results-based" Forest and Range Practices Act (FRPA) and what is known as the professional reliance model. Essentially, the forest industry was given control of supervising itself with the companies' "forest professionals" ensuring that sustainable practices were followed. The public was assured that there would be stiff penalties if standards were not followed. But with limited staffing to provide the inspections, this seemed optimistic.

A 2004 report by Ben Parfitt and Kerri Garner, *Axing the Forest Service*,[72] written for Sierra Club BC, discussed the effects of the loss of funding and the many positions within the Forest Branch that were cut as a result. Because of the decrease in staff, the number of inspections by Forest Service field officers between 2001 and 2005 decreased by 46 percent. This allowed a range of abuses to occur, including illegal logging, log theft, unmarked logs (which meant stumpage fees were not paid), and environmentally destructive logging practices.

Not only environmentalists were troubled about the changes. An investigation by the BC Forest Practices Board revealed that logging companies were high-grading cedar and spruce on the central coast with thousands of usable hemlock logs being left behind. As well, there was limited reforestation of valuable tree species.[73] A 2008 report written by union workers concerned about the loss of jobs in the

Ken Meadows stands among the old-growth Sitka spruce trees (approximately 78–79 metres tall) known as the Three Sisters in Carmanah Valley. *Photo by Bo Martin*

industry cited the report and the author, Briony Penn, wrote, "The citizens opposed [to the professional reliance model] come from every corner of British Columbia, whether rural or urban, white or First Nation communities, resource or tourist towns, Mackenzie or Metchosin."[74]

Soon after the provincial election in 2017, BC Environment Minister George Heyman appointed Mark Haddock to do an independent review of professional reliance within the natural resource sector, not just forestry. Sierra Club BC made a submission in January describing some of the problems with the present system and offering ten recommendations for improvement.[75] Haddock's final report was published in June 2018[76] and it provided 121 recommendations, a major one being the creation of an Office of Professional Regulation and Oversight to monitor and direct resource professionals. The government promises to follow through on this recommendation and will also need to pass legislation to make it work.

A 2016 publication produced by both Sierra Club BC and the Wilderness Committee[77] pointed out other problems in the forestry industry that also contribute to job losses. The handout discussed the controversial practice of exporting raw logs and advocated that it was time for a ban. Instead, these raw logs should be processed in mills in

BC to provide jobs for BC workers and, as well, allow forests to have more time to rejuvenate. The report also advocated for longer harvesting cycles, selective logging, and the elimination of slash burning and wood waste to reduce both greenhouse gas emissions and the loss of carbon storage capability. Not only is it important to protect endangered old-growth but second-growth forests need to be planted to ensure adequate species habitat, clean water and air, and appropriate settings for tourism to help promote a diverse economy.

Our Majestic Ancient Forests are a Living Treasure

THE FOLLOWING IS AN EXCERPT FROM VICKY HUSBAND'S 1990 address to the National Round Table on the Environment and the Economy.[78]

> While I do not claim to be an expert on the state of Canada's forests, I do know something about the forests of British Columbia. BC has been blessed with some of the world's biggest and oldest tress, and they grow in some of the most productive forests on the entire planet. I am referring, of course, to our coastal forests, the rare and remarkable ancient temperate rainforests.
>
> These majestic forests are every bit as old as the classical ruins of Greece and Rome, and every bit as inspiring. But, unlike the aging relics from those very great and very dead civilizations, this historical treasure is very much alive.
>
> This ancient forest is not a renewable resource. It is a gift to humanity that comes once in the lifetime of a planet. But in the next two decades, the best of what remains of this priceless heritage will be clearcut.
>
> In these ancient forest ecosystems, veterans have accumulated more individual growth rings than there are years on the Christian calendar. The biggest trees in the rainforest power their way to the sky for more than 300 feet—an

accomplishment few skyscrapers in downtown Vancouver can equal.

This ancient temperate rainforest is a complex, largely unstudied, and poorly understood ecosystem that has been seeking structural perfection for 10,000 years.

Many of us living in BC have been fortunate to have the opportunity to walk among these spectacular old-growth trees. Husband's words eloquently describe why these trees need to be preserved—so that we can continue to do this, and so that others can also experience this wonder. One can only have a feeling of awe when standing among these giants, contemplating how many centuries they have stood there. They are definitely a treasure worth much more than any price based on their volume of wood.

Peter McAllister: Forestry Warrior

Peter McAllister is descended from Captain James McAllister, who founded McAllister Towing, one of the oldest and largest family-owned towing and transportation companies in the US, in 1860. He grew up on Long Island, New York, in a wealthy family that spent summers in the Hamptons. In 1963, McAllister headed to California to attend graduate school in marine biology. While en route, his father suggested he get a job and offered him one at a McAllister subsidiary, Island Tug and Barge in Victoria. The idea appealed to McAllister and he headed north. He never forgot the tugboats and log barges coming into the Victoria Harbour with massive logs, often up to two metres in diameter, some of them from the central coast around Rivers Inlet. He would recall these memories when he was later working to protect the Great Bear Rainforest.

After working for Island Tug and Barge, McAllister led an eclectic life, running a farm in the Fraser Valley, working as a stockbroker, and entering politics to preserve the rural character of Langley, where he lived. He was instrumental in protecting the Fort Langley flood plain with an injunction against a corporation affiliated with his family. Prior to returning to Victoria he turned to ranching in the North Okanagan near Vernon. In 1986, he joined the campaign to save South Moresby.

Through this initiative, McAllister became acquainted with Colleen McCrory (founder of the Valhalla Wilderness Society in 1975 in the New Denver area of the Kootenays), which enabled him to join a delegation to Haida Gwaii with Environment Minister Tom MacMillan, his assistant Elizabeth May, and other environmentalists. Their plane landed at Sandspit, where they were met by a contingent of RCMP officers who escorted them to the hall. McAllister remembers being happy to have them as bodyguards: "The atmosphere was just a tinderbox with these angry loggers. They were ready to kill."

Elizabeth May later described the all-night potlatch that ensued in her book *Paradise Won*.[79] It was here that McAllister met an old friend, Moira Johnston,[80] who had written a story about the Haida's fight to save their land for *National Geographic* and finished it months before. Realizing the international implications, he urged Johnston to get it published immediately. It was soon available on newsstands all over the world. McAllister remembers that "it was a blockbuster and changed a lot of politics and embarrassed the government."

McAllister had also met Brock Evans, one of the leading environmentalists in the US, through the Audubon Society. Evans, at that time, was active with the Sierra Club in Washington, DC. When McAllister asked for help with the South Moresby fight, Evans told him he would take a delegation of environmental lobbyists to the Canadian consulate in Washington, where Allan Gotlieb was the ambassador to the US. McAllister remembers that the delegation told the ambassador that if the federal government in Ottawa did not hurry up and protect South Moresby and make it into a national park, the Americans would boycott Expo 86. "I think that probably had some influence on Ottawa."

McAllister is an inveterate storyteller. He likes to recall the time he took Jim Blair, a photographer for *National Geographic*, into the Carmanah. It was October and despite driving McAllister's tough Toyota Land Cruiser, they had difficulty navigating the logging road

In 1989, Peter McAllister (on right) hired Jerry Lang (now deceased), the founder of West Coast Expeditions, to guide his group around Kyuquot Sound and partway up the Tahsish River. *Photo by Stephen Ruttan*

into the valley. McAllister will never forget: "The winds were howling; it was gale-force winds. The rain was torrential and the two of us watched as the earth completely drained down the hillside through these fresh clearcuts. The earth moved. It was just mud pouring down and we could look down into the Nitinat Lake and it was turning red." The winds were so strong that the Land Cruiser was rocking back and forth as they sat inside. Blair was unable to take any photos in those conditions, but they managed to park close enough to the Carmanah Valley to hike down to a grove of trees.

McAllister described their descent into the valley of the giants as a miraculous transformation: up above there had been howling winds, torrential rains, and mudslides, while below the wind was merely a breeze, with a little mist coming down through the canopy. Here, Blair was able to spend most of the day taking photographs. When they arrived back at their vehicle, the road out was blocked by mudslides. Fortunately, a night watchman was on duty in a nearby

Members of Peter McAllister's group find a fallen pole on Acous
Peninsula, evidence that Indigenous people had a long history in
this area. *Photo by Stephen Ruttan*

shed and was able to radio MacMillan Bloedel. McAllister laughed
as he remembered hearing the watchman say, "Hey, you're going
to have to come in and get these guys, and you will not believe who
they are."

On a more serious note, McAllister recalled, "Thanks to the Sierra
Club, I got to appreciate the crucial importance of forming alliances
and joining forces with First Nations. Searching for culturally modified trees in Clayoquot Sound to establish lawsuits against inroads
by the timber industry, discovering ancient burial sites in Kyuquot,
coming across long abandoned village sites . . . with signs of cultural
heritage, thousands of years old, everywhere I went on Vancouver
Island in the course of confronting the timber industry and documenting their destruction on the traditional territories of the First
Nations."

McAllister attended the fourth conservation forum of the International Wilderness Congress held in Estes Park, Colorado, in 1987.
It was there that McAllister heard Steven Schneider, the leading climate scientist, introduce to conservation leaders from all over the

world the stark, irrefutable evidence of global warming. McAllister became an active member of the Sierra Club International Committee, and served as a delegate to the Congress of the International Union of Conservation and Nature (the conservation arm of the United Nations), held in San José, Costa Rica, in 1988. He attended the congress along with Vicky Husband.

McAllister was not popular in some spheres: "Because of the film work I was doing and my public persona at the time, I can remember Jack Munro [the president of the largest forest workers' union] accusing me of treason." He recalls, with some humour, that there were "wanted" posters of him (along with Vicky Husband and Paul George of Greenpeace) in the MacMillan Bloedel head office in Vancouver. His image was also on the cover of *BC Business* magazine in December 1989 with the headline, "Is this man the Enemy?"

After establishing the Raincoast Conservation Society and campaigning for the Great Bear Rainforest for the next five years, McAllister gradually became less active in the campaign and his son, Ian, took over, first as executive director of the Raincoast Conservation Society, and more recently as co-founder and executive director of Pacific Wild.

Nevertheless, McAllister remains a committed environmentalist and, now that he lives on Salt Spring Island, he has become involved with local issues. He founded a new organization, the Salt Spring Ocean Stewards, focused on marine conservation, shoreline inventories of forage fish, and surveys of nearby kelp and eelgrass beds. Birdwatching continues to be a favourite pastime and, when we spoke, he had recently spent a month in Argentina birdwatching with his wife, Bernadette. ▲

Vicky Husband: Mama Grizzly

Vicky Husband inspires strong opinions, both pro and con. She has had her photo on loggers' dartboards and has been affectionately called "Mama Grizzly" for her tenacious campaign to protect the Khutzeymateen grizzly sanctuary. She has accomplished much since she first became involved in the environmental movement in the 1970s, and she has been recognized with several prestigious awards, including the Order of BC in 2000 and the Order of Canada in 2002. She joined Sierra Club BC in 1988 and was a full-time volunteer, major campaigner, and spokesperson for the chapter for eighteen years.

Husband was born and raised in Victoria. She graduated with a bachelor's degree in fine arts and history from the University of British Columbia. In 1964, she financed a trip around the world by selling drawings to a local Victoria newspaper, and the next year, she put on a one-woman show at the Art Gallery of Victoria.

Husband grew to love the wild west coast of Vancouver Island, including Long Beach and Clayoquot Sound, and spent a lot of time there from the early 1970s on. In the early 1980s, she became involved in the fight to preserve Meares Island. She started lobbying and doing slide shows with George Watts, a Nuu-chah-nulth leader, and Simon Lucas of the Hesquiaht First Nation. She recalled Moses Martin, the chief of the Tla-o-qui-aht at the time, standing up at the Easter Festival in 1984 to declare Meares Island a tribal park.

In 1983, she and Karl Spreitz produced a film about what was then known as Ninstints, the UNESCO World Heritage Site and Haida totem pole village at the south end of Haida Gwaii, now known as SGang Gwaay. It was through that project that she met Miles Richardson, Guujaaw, John Broadhead, Thom Henley, and Bill Reid and was drawn into the South Moresby fight.

Bristol Foster, director of the government's Ecological Reserves program, was instrumental in her joining the Friends of Ecological Reserves. This led Husband to the fight to protect Windy Bay on Lyell Island in Haida Gwaii as an ecological reserve, within Gwaii Haanas, and later to the Khutzeymateen Grizzly Bear Sanctuary on the north coast.

Husband emphasized the need for passion, dedication, and perseverance when talking to funders. She learned to be adept at raising money and was successful in finding significant funds for the Sierra Club: "I actually was a leader in bringing, for better or for worse, US foundation funding into Canada."

Husband has fought for a long time and it has not been easy. There were times when she felt threatened: "When I went out into those forestry communities and they wanted my head . . . and you had to stand up and speak out. They threatened me. It was much worse for women." She thought back to those times in the 1990s: "Fighting, fighting, fighting. I was either told that 'you've sold out' or that I was a government collaborator, a tree hugger or I was spiking trees. It was a fine line to keep your focus on the goal and vision that you were trying to achieve."

Vicky Husband stands in front of the poster of the 1954 and 1990 contrasting maps of Vancouver Island's Ancient Temperate Rain-forests. *University of Victoria Archives, photo by Karl Spreitz*

Husband summed up her role in Sierra Club: "I always saw Sierra Club as an organization that could be strengthened and be a vehicle so that we could achieve bigger goals. You set a goal, whether it's protection of ancient forests, changing forest practices, or a focus on sustainable fisheries and ocean protection. You had to have some kind of strategic vision, a bigger vision."

In 2006, due to differences between Husband and the executive director, the SCBC board relieved her of her authority to act or speak for the club. Despite many years passing, Husband expressed resentment about her forced departure from the SCBC.

Now in her 70s, Husband continues to work independently, remaining a formidable champion for the environment, raising her voice over ancient forest protection, forestry issues, fisheries, climate change, Site C, wildlife, and many other conservation concerns. ▲

*Dream no small dreams for they have the power
to move the hearts of men.*
—Johann Wolfgang von Goethe

6

Campaigns in the Southern Interior

SIERRA CLUB BC STARTED IN VANCOUVER AND ON VANCOUVER ISLAND, so it is not surprising that many high-profile campaigns occurred on the coast. Nevertheless, as the club's reputation grew and its effectiveness in lobbying politicians and spreading the word about particular issues became known, many groups and individuals in other parts of the province decided it would be worthwhile to join the club or to ally with it to fight for the issues that they thought needed to be dealt with.

Okanagan Valley

IN THE EARLY 1970S, KATY MADSEN, ACTIVE IN THE OKANAGAN AND A founding member of both the Okanagan Similkameen Parks Society (OSPS) and Sierra Club BC, directed the club's attention to an OSPS campaign to protect Brent Mountain—a beautiful alpine area just west of Penticton that developers wanted to develop into a ski resort. Working with OSPS on this issue created another of the club's early alliances.

Brent Mountain was the only Okanagan mountain without a road to the top at the time, despite logging operations all around it. Although clearcutting was a common practice in many of the Okanagan watersheds, campaigners were hopeful that they could achieve protected status for the peak and the surrounding area. A long battle was fought and eventually the Brent Mountain Protected Area was established in 2001, becoming the only alpine area protected in the Southern Thompson Upland Ecosection.

Southeastern BC

IN ANOTHER PART OF BC, THERE WAS CONTROVERSY OVER CONSTRUC-tion of the Revelstoke Dam, situated on the Columbia River just north of Revelstoke. Sierra Club BC member Terry Simmons intervened in the BC Utilities hearing process in 1976. He said that the outcome of hearings sometimes seems predetermined: "you are . . . waving this flag, being a helpful nuisance, making your point sometimes redundantly." Nevertheless, he still thought it was a valuable undertaking. At this hearing, he raised concerns about two issues. The first was about the potential risk of a large rock slide behind Revelstoke Dam giving way and causing extensive damage from flooding. The other was about load forecast, that is, "whether you actually needed this power." Indeed, in 1984, when "it came on-line, it generated electricity that was completely surplus. That's because load forecast correlates very closely with economic growth and activity and [there] was a real dip in the economy in the early '80s."

Sierra Club BC also lent support to the campaign to protect the Valhalla Range, which sits above the western shore of Slocan Lake in the Slocan Valley. The campaign was launched by the Valhalla Wilderness Society. The campaign began by blocking the construction of a logging road into an area slated for logging by Slocan Forest Products, and what followed has been described as one of the most intensive park advocacy campaigns in BC history. Sierra Club BC's contribution, as in so many campaigns, was to spread the word throughout the Lower Mainland, Vancouver Island, and other urban centres about why this area was special and needed to be protected. As well, SCBC's proximity to the legislature allowed it to lobby the relevant decision makers about the issue. After a highly ambitious resource planning program[81]—which laid the groundwork for the first provincial park protecting an entire mountain ecosystem from lake shoreline to high alpine—Valhalla Provincial Park was established in 1983. It was also considered significant for protecting low-elevation interior cedar-hemlock forests, a forest type with trees commonly up to five hundred years old, that had not often been targeted for protection.[82]

Also in the southeastern part of the province, Ric Careless, who at this time was working independently, was active with a campaign in the mid-1980s with the Palliser Wilderness Society. He became the society's executive director and decided that the area needed a more compelling name, changing it from the Palliser Wilderness to the Height of the Rockies, as it is now known. The area straddles the Great Divide in the Kootenays south of Banff National Park, and contains the Palliser River Valley and Mount Joffre. With its seven mountain passes, numerous small lakes, and two major river valleys, it is home to a large concentration of elk, mule deer, bighorn sheep, moose, cougar, black bears, grizzly bears, and mountain goats. This area had been proposed as a provincial park in the early 1900s, and by 1986 logging roads and swaths of clearcut forests had claimed vast areas of forest nearby in the southern Canadian Rockies. It was seen as one of the last refuges for the region's wildlife.

Careless had built a large support base around the Kootenays but realized the campaign needed wider-spread support. He returned to Sierra Club BC to achieve it and took a seat on the board. At this time, attention was so focused on protests about coastal forests and the War in the Woods in Clayoquot Sound that it was difficult to shift consideration to concerns about the interior of the province. Nevertheless, having the chapter headquarters in Victoria made it easier for Careless and SCBC to lobby politicians.

Finally, in 1987, after two years of hard campaigning and negotiation with the government and logging companies, the coalition of environmental organizations, with Sierra Club BC's help, succeeded in having the area designated a Forest Service Wilderness Area. This was a new designation in BC that provided protection under the auspices of the BC Forest Service rather than the Parks Branch. By 1995, legislation had created the Height of the Rockies Provincial Park. Hikers can now follow in the ancestral footsteps of Ktunaxa (Kutenai) First Nations, whose people traversed trade routes through the passes of North Kananaskis and Palliser to the plains beyond for thousands of years.[83]

Cariboo–Chilcotin Region

IN THE LATE 1990S, THE SIERRA CLUB JOINED THE MOVEMENT TO protect an area in the southern portion of the Chilcotin ranges in the southwest region of the province, about ninety-five kilometres west of Lillooet. This area, with its gently sloping valleys, rolling hills, alpine ridges, lakes, and grasslands, provides significant grazing land for cattle and horses, as well as horseback riding opportunities offered by a number of guide outfitters. It is located in the rain shadow of the Coast Mountains and is considered ecologically important, with a grizzly bear habitat that links those found in the northern and southern regions of the province.[84] An initiative to protect this area from mining and logging was proposed as early as 1937 by wildlife filmmaker Charlie Cunningham and was supported by the guide outfitters in the area.

The Cariboo-Chilcotin was one of the areas designated by the government for the Commission on Resources and Environment (CORE) to develop a land use plan. The commission met in 1993, but there was no consensus on the land use recommendations tabled in 1994.[85] Further negotiations were needed so the government embarked on another process under the Land Use Coordination Office.

Bill Wareham, Sierra Club BC executive director, and campaigners Tom Nichols and Doug Radies, played strategic roles in the ensuing land use planning process. Under their leadership, Sierra Club BC contributed its satellite mapping expertise and conservation analysis while attempting to mediate discussions with the forestry industry in order to develop a conservation, recreation, tourism, and community-based proposal for the government to consider prior to the election in 2001.

The rolling hills of the Cariboo-Chilcotin area provide ecologically important grizzly bear habitat linking areas in the south to those in the north. *Photo by Jens Wieting*

SCBC developed briefing materials to identify priority conservation areas, proposed a grizzly bear recovery program, challenged logging plans, and undertook a risk assessment of the biological values in the Lillooet region.[86] Following extensive negotiation at the land use planning table, the area now known as the South Chilcotin Mountains Provincial Park was designated as a protected area in 2001. Its boundaries were eventually revised to remove three "mining and tourism" areas[87] from the original protected area, after which the remaining land was designated as a Class A provincial park in 2010.

Flathead River Valley

OVER ON THE OTHER SIDE OF THE PROVINCE, BEGINNING IN 2007, Sierra Club BC became involved in an ongoing campaign to preserve the Flathead River Valley in the territory of the Ktunaxa people in the southern BC Rockies. Described as "the heart" of the Rockies, the valley has been identified as a highly biodiverse ecosystem. It includes

The mountains within the Flathead River area provide habitat for mountain goats such as this juvenile. *Photo by Joe Riis*

one of the last wild gravel-bed river basins in Canada, renowned for the quality of its water. It is an important grizzly bear habitat, and a critical link for migratory wildlife and genetic diversity along the Yellowstone-to-Yukon connectivity corridor.[88]

The Flathead Valley has also been characterized as the "missing piece"[89] in the Waterton–Glacier International Peace Park—established in 1932 as a partnership joining the Canadian Waterton Lakes Park with the American Glacier Park. The parks straddle the Alberta–Montana border, and the partnership highlighted the similar conservation objectives that both countries have for this region. UNESCO also designated both Waterton Lakes Park and Glacier National Park as Biosphere Reserves in 1979, and proclaimed the entire Waterton–Glacier Park a World Heritage Site in 1995, emphasizing the importance of the region.

As early as 1911, John George "Kootenai" Brown, the first superintendent of Waterton Lakes National Park, suggested that the borders of the park be extended to protect fish breeding grounds in the Flathead but his lobbying efforts over the years proved unsuccessful. Parks Canada had proposed to have this area protected; it was the BC government that resisted due to the area's potential for lucrative coal mining and coalbed methane extraction. The North Fork Flathead River, from the Canadian border downstream to its confluence with the Middle Fork in Montana, had been designated a "National Wild and Scenic River"[90] in 1976, and the ongoing lack of protection of the river on the other side of the border in Canada was long a point of contention between the two countries. In 1988, in light of an open pit mining proposal for the Flathead, the International Joint Commission, established under the Boundary Waters Treaty of 1909, ruled that such a mine would violate the terms of the 1909 treaty.

In 2006, there was a proposal for an open-pit coal mine in the Flathead quite close to the US border and Glacier Park. This suddenly gave the campaign a sense of urgency. Campaigners realized they had to increase its profile in the populated areas of BC, like the Lower Mainland and Greater Victoria. The groups asked Sierra Club BC to become involved in the campaign and author and journalist Sarah Cox, who worked for the Sierra Club from 2006 to 2013, remembered when Sierra Club BC jumped into the campaign. "[The Flathead Wild Team] wanted a strategic communications element, not just putting out press releases and calling media but leveraging moments in the campaign and strategic opportunities to get that media coverage."

SCBC joined the Flathead Wild initiative: the message was "protect it, connect it." Cox described it as very much an international campaign with six organizations involved, four from Canada and two from the US: Sierra Club BC, Wildsight, CPAWS BC, the Yellowstone to Yukon Conservation Initiative, Headwaters Montana, and the National Parks Conservation Association (US). "It was a very tight campaign in the sense we were always in communication with each other. We used an internet hub base camp to communicate. We were in daily touch with each other on the campaign and had many, many conference calls. It was just a very highly functioning campaign team."

Sierra Club BC encouraged high-profile British Columbians to become "Friends of the Flathead" to boost the profile of the campaign—including, among others, former federal environment minister David Anderson, Vancouver mayor Gregor Robertson, Victoria mayor Dean Fortin, and adventure photographer Pat Morrow.

Cox cultivated media coverage at the right time to move the campaign forward and she was involved with government relations as well. She gave public presentations and helped organize opportunities for publicity. One of these occurred in 2009 when the International League of Conservation Photographers arranged a Rapid Assessment Visual Expedition, or RAVE. The event involved a group of professional photographers trekking around the Flathead Valley to take photographs of the wildlife, plants, and other stunning features. Sierra Club BC spread the word about this endeavour and helped to arrange showings of the photos at places such as Vancouver's Science World.

The Flathead Wild team also petitioned the UNESCO World Heritage Committee to declare Waterton-Glacier International Peace Park a World Heritage Site in Danger because of the mining threats. The team strategically released media coverage about the petition and managed to be always one step ahead of the provincial government, making various announcements to raise the profile of the Flathead. The World Heritage Committee agreed to send a mission to the valley, exploring the area and talking to various stakeholders. They concluded that if the government allowed the coal mine to go ahead, then, yes, they would recommend that Waterton-Glacier be considered a World Heritage Site in Danger. Meanwhile, the Montana government expressed its concerns to BC premier Gordon Campbell about the impacts a coal mine would have on downstream water. On the eve of the 2010 Winter Olympics, held in Vancouver, the BC government announced it would permanently ban mining and energy development in the Flathead River Valley and passed the legislation in November 2011. While this was welcome news for biodiversity and wildlife connectivity, the valley is still threatened by plans for industrial logging, new road access, rock quarrying, and off-road vehicle use. The fight to protect the Flathead was far from over.

Dedicated individuals have kept the pressure on the government to protect the area from these destructive activities. Scientists, including from the Royal BC Museum, participated in bioblitzes during which they surveyed the Flathead Valley, recording as many species as possible in a short period of time. The first bioblitz, in 2012, focused on insects and molluscs. The scientists, surprisingly, found no introduced species and even discovered a new species of spider that they named *Apostenus ducati* after the Italian motorcycle; Cox said the scientists told her "they had never seen a spider move so quickly." [91] The next was a bird bioblitz in 2013. Again, the ornithologists found an incredible array of species with no introduced ones. The 2014 bioblitz focused on bats and a fourth bioblitz examined the land that Teck Resources Limited had purchased for conservation in 2015, compiling a catalogue of species within the area. Opportunities such as this help keep the valley in the public eye. Sierra Club BC continues to advocate for protection of "this unspoiled wilderness pathway for migratory birds, grizzlies, wolverines and other species in alignment with the wishes of the Ktunaxa First Nations."[92]

Over the years, successes were achieved in the Okanagan, Valhallas, Chilcotin–Cariboo, and the southern Rockies. Sierra Club BC proved to be a useful ally for other groups that needed help to push forward their campaigns. The club had the resources and talent to provide the scientific backing or media strategy needed to convince the public and politicians. As well, its proximity to the legislature and large urban areas was valuable to those who were coming up against stumbling blocks in spreading the word about their issues.

Sarah Cox: Communications Specialist

Sarah Cox, with her extensive experience in journalism and interest in conservation, was an excellent choice for the job of communications director at Sierra Club BC in 2006. Because there was not enough funding for a full-time position, she took on the second role of running the Flathead River Valley campaign, becoming the club's representative on the international Flathead Wild team.

When Premier Campbell was about to make a surprise announcement about the Flathead in his Throne Speech in 2010, Cox received a tip about it on her way to work. She recalled, "I just turned around and went home to change out of jeans and at the same time phoned a contact to get me a ticket for the Throne Speech so I could be there. So, I was in the legislature when it was announced, which was very exciting." Camp-bell announced a ban on energy and mining development in the entire Flathead.

Sarah Cox. *Courtesy of Sarah Cox*

Cox left Sierra Club BC at the beginning of September 2013 to work for the Yellowstone to Yukon Conservation Initiative for two years. In 2016, she returned to inde-pendent journalism and began writing about the controversial Site C hydro dam on BC's northern Peace River, which a Statement of Concern signed by more than two hundred of Canada's leading scholars said would cause more signif-icant adverse environmental effects than any project ever examined in the history of Canada's Environmental Assessment Act.[93]

Cox had been working at Sierra Club at the time of the BC gov-ernment's announcement, in April 2010, that it would seek regulatory approval for the dam, and she had visited the Peace River Valley for both Sierra Club BC and while working at Y2Y. She recalled going to the area for the annual Paddle for the Peace: she "fell in love with the valley. It's just a remarkable area." After learning more about the Peace and the impact of the Site C dam on the environment and Treaty 8 First Nations, she felt compelled to write about an issue that had received scant provincial and national attention, and wrote a book on the topic.

"It's just a very important issue and it's out of sight, out of mind for most British Columbians. Essentially, we will be paying for a com-pletely unnecessary and hugely destructive project that violates inter-national human rights standards and will destroy a farming valley that is historic and scenic and forms the heart of the traditional ter-ritory of the Treaty 8 First Nations. Site C is by far the most expensive, most destructive and riskiest way to generate new energy in BC. This is crazy." The book, published in 2018, is entitled *Breaching the Peace: The Site C Dam and a Valley's Stand Against Big Hydro.* ♠

*The goal is not to shut down the mining industry
... it is to make sure that the projects that would
have really negative impacts to water or species
or habitat aren't viable projects.*

—Susan Howatt

7

Mining
Campaigns

BRITISH COLUMBIA'S GEOLOGY HAS PROVIDED IT WITH A WEALTH OF
mineral resources; however, the processes that led to their formation also made their extraction risky. Due to potential seismic activity, hazards may occur when mines are situated in unstable valleys or
on mountain ridges susceptible to high precipitation and erosion. Up
until the 1960s, most mining in BC took place underground, but then
the feasibility of open-pit production increased, resulting in the opening of several large copper mines, including the largest open-pit operation in Canada—Highland Valley copper mine near Logan Lake.[94]

Open-pit mines tend to be large, with low-grade deposits that
produce vast amounts of mining waste (tailings). These wastes frequently contain toxic substances that can leach into nearby watersheds and, as a result, require proper storage for decades or longer.
According to MiningWatch Canada's website there are ninety-eight
tailings dams at sixty operating and closed mining sites within
BC, some the size of small lakes. Many of these tailings dams are
becoming much higher and holding back even greater amounts of
waste mixed with water, thereby increasing the possibility of them
breaching. Reportedly half of the serious tailings dam failures in the

past seventy years occurred between 1990 and 2009.[95] The costs are enormous when this happens, and as mining companies often have difficulty obtaining insurance, taxpayers may be left with the bill, especially when a mining site has been abandoned and the company no longer exists.

Even after mines shut down, they can continue to pollute nearby watersheds. For example, the Britannia Mine that closed forty years ago continues to affect sea life in Howe Sound because of the millions of tons of tailings and litres of metal-laden waters that were discharged into the sound. Remediation efforts have been ongoing since 2001 and although beneficial effects have been noted, with the return of pink salmon and mussels to the region, metals still contaminate the water.[96] So far, the twenty-year contract that the government signed with a private remediation company for $27.2 million dollars is being covered by funds collected from the former owners of the mine. However, when this contract ends, taxpayers will have to cover any future costs of treating the acid run-off.[97]

Strathcona Park

STRATHCONA PROVINCIAL PARK ON VANCOUVER ISLAND WAS founded in 1911 and is the oldest provincial park in British Columbia. Mineral claims had already been staked in the park and amendments to the Strathcona Park Act in 1918 opened it up to numerous additional claims. Although the park was eventually elevated to the status of a Class A provincial park in 1957, the government granted Western Mines (a precursor of Boliden Westmin) permission to build an open-pit mine in 1961 and dump its tailings in Buttle Lake, and in 1965 the park was reclassified to Class B. Additional mining interests were encouraged in 1967 when Cream Silver Mines was allowed to stake out claims at Cream Lake.

In the mid-1970s, Sierra Club BC member Brian Pinch, who had hiked extensively in Strathcona Park, learned that Cream Silver Mines was proposing an access road and mine in what he considered the heart of the park. He alerted the Victoria daily newspaper and was stunned to see the issue as the front-page headline the next day. It quickly became a major concern. Pinch, with the help of Gordon Price, developed promotional materials, "a pretty slick brochure," to garner publicity. At that time, Price was working for Hansard (the legislature's transcription service) and had access to one of the few good word-processing computers in Victoria, which was able to produce high-quality brochures. He also advised Pinch about how to deal with the media. Pinch was interviewed by the local television channel in his small apartment, which was furnished in the typical student way with second-hand, makeshift furniture. Nevertheless, they were able to place Pinch in front of his bookshelves of texts, making him look distinguished and trustworthy.

Pinch arranged a meeting with several government ministers and their deputies. Deputy Minister of Mines Jim Fyles spoke first and seemed somewhat supportive of the SCBC position, as he did not think that there were high mineral values in the Cream Lake area. However, Bob Ahrens, the director of parks, who spoke next caused jaws to drop when he said, "Let's face it, there is going to be mining there someday." In the end the mining company did not get its permit and further industrial expansion was halted. Pinch recalled, "It just died and the whole thing disappeared. I have been to Cream Lake many times since and it's absolutely gorgeous. Mining there would have gutted the park."

Unbeknownst to Pinch at the time, the issue would re-emerge in 1985[98] when the parks minister gave Westmin Resources a permit allowing the company sole and exclusive mining rights for twenty-five years to over six thousand acres in the park. In 1987, significant changes were made to the composition of the park, which opened large tracts of land to mining and logging by "deleting" them from the original park, while adding new tracts from the periphery. Sierra Club's Cowichan group was involved in lobbying against these developments—as were the Friends of Strathcona Park and the Vancouver Island section of the Alpine Club. The Friends of Strathcona Park set up a blockade across the road to Cream Lake in 1988, resulting in the arrest of sixty-four people. This was the first time in Canada that people were arrested for actively protecting a park in this way.

In response, the government formed the Strathcona Advisory Committee to review the park boundaries and consider the ongoing industrial activity within it. The Cowichan group submitted a brief, *A Plan for the Future of Strathcona Park*, that not only addressed the need for a sustainability plan but also promoted strategies that would protect jobs. This position won the Cowichan group widespread support among those who saw job loss as a natural outcome of the move to protect areas from industrial development and resource extraction. On the basis of the committee's recommendations, the government decided to revert the park to Class A status, stop all new mining exploration, and return the Cream Silver claim area to the park. Most of the people arrested went free due to a technicality—a particular provincial order-in-council, on which part of the case was based, had not been proved to exist.[99]

Okanagan Valley

IN 1975, KATY MADSEN, SIERRA CLUB BC'S OKANAGAN MEMBER, SET off a landslide of public debate. She had been examining maps at the courthouse in preparation of a brief about Brent Mountain when she found that, in addition to the small gold mining claims she had noted dotting the maps previously, there were now multiple other claims from north of Vernon down to the US border. The official told her that they were uranium claims. She had been aware of people objecting to uranium claims in the Kelowna watershed area because of concerns about radioactive material leaching into the water system, so she was surprised to see so many claims.

Madsen tried to publicize her discovery but was unable to get the newspaper to print anything about it and suspected political reasons, due to the ongoing provincial election. After the NDP lost, the mining company responsible admitted that they had been making uranium claims for two and a half years. This information was supposed to be available to the public and technically it was, if people knew where to look. Madsen thought the NDP would have won the election if the public had known about the claims sooner.

Then, during an appointment, Madsen's hairdresser said that she had noticed stakes and pipes in the ground near where she lived west of Penticton. Madsen went with her the next day to take photos of the stakes laid out in a grid, forming the boundaries of a claim. With this information, she was able to refute the mining company spokesperson at a public meeting who said there were no claims on the west side of the lake. Madsen produced her concrete evidence, along with the story that she had learned about it, not from the spokesperson, but from her hairdresser, which caused the audience to "howl with laughter." She noted that "people pay attention when you make them laugh."

Madsen became concerned that other communities may also have such claims and travelled throughout the Okanagan to the various government offices where the claims are registered, going as far as Princeton, Merritt, and Kamloops. While driving along the back roads to the various communities, she recalled the account of Karen Silkwood, who had worked for a uranium mining company and was pushed off the road and killed while on her way to tell people what she knew. Madsen identified with her, driving alone with a No Uranium Mining bumper sticker on her car. However, nothing sinister happened.

Upon her return, she wrote a press release with the help of a friend. Once people knew the situation, there was vehement opposition and Bill Bennett, the premier at that time, who relied heavily on Okanagan support, was instrumental in having a seven-year moratorium placed on uranium mining in 1980. This ban on both mining and exploration was not renewed. In 2008, the government established a "no registration reserve" under the Mineral Tenure Act, which meant that uranium and thorium would be excluded from any mineral licences in the province, thereby ensuring that all uranium deposits remain undeveloped.[100]

Windy Craggy Mountain

IN 1988, IN A MUCH LESS POPULATED AREA IN THE FAR NORTHWEST corner of British Columbia, near both the Alaska and Yukon borders, concerns were raised about Windy Craggy Mountain becoming the site of a large-scale copper mine. In the centre of this wilderness area, making up what is now Tatshenshini-Alsek Provincial Park, Geddes Resources proposed to first construct an open-pit mine and about a decade later dig an underground mine. The ore would be transported by a 242-kilometre pipeline to Haines, Alaska, and then shipped to Japan for processing while a second pipeline would send fuel to the mine site. These two pipelines would be buried a metre underground and would parallel the access road.

An estimated 151 million tons of acid-consuming waste rock would be deposited on the nearby North Cirque and Marie glaciers with the expectation that the glaciers would break it down and disperse it via the moraines. As well, 100 million tons of acid-generating waste rock and 124 million tons of tailings expected from the mining would be kept in an impoundment under 1.25 metres of water. This would necessitate building two dams in the Upper Tatshenshini Valley.

Opposition to the Windy Craggy copper mining project grew, becoming intense around 1992. There was controversy about both the construction of the road and the pipelines, which would affect fish and wildlife—particularly the grizzly habitat and the Chilkat Eagle preserve, where 3,500 eagles gather for the fall salmon run. As well, the disposal and storage of the tailings and acid-consuming and acid-generating waste rock[101] had the potential to contaminate the watershed. The area is considered to be the most seismically active in North America: the largest recorded earthquake on the continent had occurred only 120 kilometres away. Landslides and avalanches were also prevalent due to heavy precipitation in the area. All this placed the dams and the storage of the tailings at high risk.

Ric Careless became involved and established Tatshenshini Wild, an alliance of environmental groups opposed to the project, and by 1991 Tatshenshini International was established, linking together a network of the top fifty conservation organizations in North America and representing a combined membership of about ten million people. In addition to Sierra Club BC, the alliance included the Canadian Parks and Wilderness Society, Wilderness Committee, and the

World Wildlife Fund as well as powerful US conservation organizations such as the US Sierra Club, National Audubon, Wilderness Society, American Rivers, and American Wildlands.

Campaign members lobbied politicians not only in Victoria and Ottawa, but also the US Congress and eventually the White House, where they achieved the active involvement of then Vice President Al Gore. Eventually there was outcry across North American and the US Congress began to act on the need to protect the river.

The hard-fought campaign eventually convinced the BC government that something had to be done. It was at this time that the Commission on Resources and Environment (CORE) was involved in land use planning in other parts of the province. Premier Mike Harcourt decided that the CORE process should also become involved in this area and through it, he enabled the planning process for the Tatshenshini-Alsek region.[102] The CORE report provided three options, one being that the area be protected as wilderness. Premier Harcourt chose this option and announced in 1993 that the area would be a Class A provincial park—effectively terminating the Windy Craggy project.

The Tatshenshini-Alsek Park was to be co-managed by the Champagne and Aishihik First Nation and the BC government. In combination with the adjoining national parks, the creation of this new BC park completed the world's largest international park complex (approximately 8.5 million hectares).[103] The following year, with acceptance from the Champagne and Aishihik First Nation, the park became part of the International World Heritage Site with the Yukon's Kluane National Park and Alaska's Wrangell-St. Elias National Park and Glacier Bay, making it one of the largest trans-boundary protected ecosystems in the world.

The aftermath of Windy Craggy also led Careless to form the Environmental Mining Council of BC (EMCBC), a network of environmental groups in BC and the Yukon, in 1993. Its mission was to allow activists to coordinate more effectively in countering the environmental threats that irresponsible mining posed to wilderness, fisheries, and water quality. It also helped provide advice and support to groups

confronted with having to make sense of mining proposals.[104] Tatshenshini Wild, the non-profit organization established by Ric Careless,
was renamed BC Spaces for Nature and provided funding for the network. Careless recruited board members and Alan Young, a key Yukon
campaigner for the Tatshenshini, became the first executive director.

The EMCBC reviewed mine proposals, monitored the post-cer-
tificate permitting and operations of mine developments, lobbied
for improved mining practices and regulation, and networked with
other groups involved in mining. Sierra Club BC was a founding member, with Rosemary Fox as the club's representative. She was involved
with the EMCBC review of several mine proposals in the northwest
section of the province in the 1990s, including Kemess, Red Chris,
Bronson Slope, Tulsequah Chief, Telkwa Coal, and Silvertip. EMCBC
folded in the early-to-mid-2000s due to a loss of funding. However,
it had been a member of the pan-Canadian initiative MiningWatch
Canada, formed in 1999, and after its demise, MiningWatch took
over its watchdog role in BC.

BC's Mineral Tenure Act and Other Contentious Mining Proposals

SUSAN HOWATT, SIERRA CLUB BC'S CAMPAIGNS DIRECTOR FROM 2008
to 2013, described BC's mining laws as extremely outdated. Compared to other areas nearby (Washington, Montana, Alberta), "we
were the only jurisdiction that hadn't touched our mining laws since
Confederation." The Mineral Tenure Act had been derived from the
Goldfields Act of 1859, which was intended to promote settlement
in BC, and had changed little since then. Howatt argued that it was
much too easy to obtain an exploration licence, especially given that
the act allows "online staking claims to be made within city limits,
on private land and on land of ecological and First Nations importance."[105] Once a tenure is obtained and an exploration site is staked,
it trumps all other land uses—for example, a town would not be able
to establish a park in that area or decide to prioritize forestry, tourism, or some other industry for the site.

Howatt recalled that rather than continuing to try to fight these highly controversial fights site by site, the SCBC campaigns team decided a better strategy was to focus on fixing the system. "And to do that we kind of stepped outside of our toolbox and built some unusual alliances with local governments and other members of industry." The club partnered with West Coast Environmental Law, MiningWatch Canada, and First Nations Women Advocating for Responsible Mining (FNWARM). Howatt said that MiningWatch Canada "really carry the banner in terms of responsible mining and advocacy." FNWARM is also an important ally, as often proposals for mines are on First Nations' territory.

There were several other contentious mine proposals in recent years. KGHM Ajax proposed an open-pit copper and gold mine to be located in Kamloops just two kilometres from a residential area. As early as 2006, residents were worried about the potential hazards of a tailings pond, and dust that could affect the air quality. As well, the Stk'emlupsemc Te Secwepemc First Nation claimed the territory, which holds spiritual and cultural value for them. Sierra Club BC was asked to get involved and in 2016 they commissioned the report *Ajax Project Review—Review of Predicted Water Contamination* by Dr. Kevin Morin, which found that the risks of water contamination from the mine were significantly underestimated by the mining company. However, it was not until 2017 that the newly elected NDP government denied the proposal, after the BC Environmental Assessment Office found that the "adverse effects of the Ajax project outweighed the potential benefits."

Another controversial mine proposal concerned Fish Lake (also known as Teztan Biny), 125 kilometres southwest of Williams Lake in the headwaters of the Chilcotin River watershed on the territory of the Tsilhqot'in First Nation. It is one of the top ten fishing lakes in BC for rainbow trout. Taseko Mines acquired the Prosperity property in 1991 and a feasibility report was completed in 2007. The proposal was for a massive open-pit gold and copper mine right next to the lake, and the company planned to drain the lake and use its bed to contain the mine tailings. The BC Environmental Assessment Office concluded that, while the project would have significant adverse effects, the undertaking was nonetheless justified. However, although the federal minister of the environment took into account BC's assessment review, she noted that the 2010 federal review panel rejected the mine proposal for a number of reasons, a main one being Taseko's plan to drain the lake for the tailings.[106]

Taseko responded by changing its proposal. After a heated campaign by Sierra Club BC, other organizations, and First Nations, Taseko's New Prosperity Mine proposal was again rejected by the Canadian Environmental Assessment Agency in 2014 after concluding that the mine would have significant harmful effects on water quality, fish, and fish habitat in a lake considered sacred by the Tsilhqot'in First Nation. Nonetheless, Taseko continued to push the project forward, proposing to build roads and perform seismic line tests in preparation for mine construction. The Tsilhqot'in First Nation continued to advocate for protection of the area.

In 2014, in a court case that went all the way to the Supreme Court of Canada, the Tsilhqot'in won the right of aboriginal title over 1,700 square kilometres of land. This meant that the government had a greater burden to justify economic development on their land. In October 2014, the Tsilhqot'in Nation announced that Dasiqox Tribal Park would be designated and that a land use planning process would be undertaken for several hundred thousand hectares surrounding Fish Lake with mining and other industrial activity no longer being allowed. After further lobbying by environmental groups and First Nations, finally in 2017, a Federal Court judge ruled against Taseko, upholding the federal government's decision to reject the proposal for environmental reasons. Nevertheless, a drilling permit was issued by the provincial government in July 2017—four days before the NDP were sworn in as the new government—requiring the Tsilhqot'in to return to court to contest the permit. The legal challenge to protect Fish Lake continues as of the printing of this book.

On another front, Sierra Club BC became concerned about an open-pit copper mine that Imperial Mines proposed for Catface Mountain after the company conducted test drilling in 2010. The mountain overlooks Tofino and the nearby Pacific Rim National Park Reserve on the west coast of Vancouver Island, which attracts almost a million tourists each year. The proposal to remove the mountain top in order to dig out the minerals would result in noise and reduced air quality, detrimentally impacting the tourist business. Sierra Club BC soon had the town's mayor onside as a very passionate advocate. As well, the local Ahousaht First Nation claimed the area as part of its unceded traditional territory and was not supportive of a mine. To date the opposition has succeeded in staving off further development.

In 2014, British Columbia experienced the largest mine-waste disaster in Canadian history at Imperial Metal's Mount Polley gold and silver mine near Williams Lake. A tailings pond breach released millions of cubic metres of toxic water into the environment. An award-winning short film, *Chasing Wild: Journey into the Sacred Headwaters,* produced by three intrepid cyclists in partnership with Salmon Beyond Borders depicts the devastation caused by this disaster as well as the stunning beauty of the Sacred Headwaters area that they bikepacked and rafted through in 2017.[107]

Sierra Club BC responded to the Mount Polley tragedy quickly by making recommendations for an independent review. Those recommendations were adopted by the provincial government. Two years later, MiningWatch Canada initiated private legal action against the corporation, taking the position that the province was negligent and, after two and a half years, had failed to lay charges and enforce the Fisheries Act, despite clear and ample evidence.[108] The Federal Crown ultimately stayed the charges on the grounds of insufficient evidence, among other reasons.

Sierra Club BC continues to advocate for a reformed BC Mineral Tenure Act that will define areas that are off limits to new mineral claims and leases, and end compensation for claims that have been staked in areas that have been designated as ecologically important and earmarked for protection. These off-limit areas would include private and residential lands, dedicated community amenities, such as recreational areas, watersheds, fish-bearing waterways, ecologically sensitive areas, private conservation lands, and other areas incompatible with mining for environmental, First Nations, or health reasons.[109]

Katy Madsen: Okanagan Hero

Katy Madsen was involved with the Sierra Club since she was eleven years old, first in the San Francisco area and later in the Okanagan, where she lived from 1968 to 1993, and finally in Victoria. She attended the first meeting arranged by Terry Simmons in 1969. During our interview, Madsen, a spry, fit woman in her nineties, was excited to talk about her Sierra Club experiences and wore a T-shirt featuring a drawing she had designed many years ago—Ogopogo inside a heart with the slogan "Don't tread on me with 2,4-D"—for a campaign against using the chemical in the Okanagan Lake system to kill milfoil.

She recalled the Sierra Club–sponsored hikes she did with her dad and brother in the area south of San Francisco. If they were leading one of the weekly hikes, they did a trial run the day before to ensure that everything was in order. She enthusiastically continued even when her father was unavailable, getting a ride with others at the pick-up spot, and maintained her Sierra Club membership throughout her life.

Madsen graduated from San Jose State University with a degree in biological sciences and, while there, she met and married her husband. It was wartime and he had joined the navy, stationed first in San Diego and then in Hawaii. Madsen was offered a fellowship to study at Stanford, but she declined as she had a child and thought she should be with her husband.

Harold Madsen survived the war and went on to get a PhD in entomology. He held a teaching and research position at Berkeley and one year he had a sabbatical position at the Summerland Research Station in the Okanagan. Katy Madsen was impressed by the contrast of the relaxed atmosphere in Canada with that of the McCarthy-era us, with its communist fears and loyalty oaths. When her husband was offered a position to return as head of the entomology section at the Summerland Research Station in 1964, she encouraged him to jump at the chance.

Madsen became involved with her new community right away. She was surprised to find out that California bighorn sheep were found in the Okanagan. It upset her to realize they had no protection and that some were being shipped to the US for repopulation purposes. She contacted the local MLA to express her concern but found no support from the Social Credit government.

She met Steve Cannings, a photographer at the research station, who also had concerns about environmental issues in areas around Summerland. Madsen and Cannings, with his extensive contacts throughout the Okanagan Valley, were founding members of the Okanagan Similkameen Parks Society (OSPS) in 1966. This group was successful in purchasing eight hundred acres of winter rangeland for the endangered bighorn sheep.

Madsen, with the backing of OSPS, was also involved in protecting Cathedral Lakes, a high-elevation area of lakes and trails at about 2,100 metres, which became a park in 1968. She recalled going to Kamloops for a meeting with the head forester with her maps showing the area in question. The forester's first comment to her was that BC was a "timber-oriented province" and when she asked what was going to be logged in that area, he told her Douglas fir—a tree that Madsen knew only grew at much lower elevations. After looking at the relevant maps, it became clear that Madsen was right about the lack of trees in this area: "It was like he was a big balloon that got a puncture in it." Finally, he conceded, asking her, "What are we going to name the park, Katy?" By 1975, she and Ric Careless, who at that point was working with the BC government Environmental Land Use Committee Secretariat, were able to convince the government to enlarge the park to 33,454 hectares.

Despite living in the Okanagan, Madsen was keen to help with Sierra Club BC's formation and became its delegate to the Pacific Northwest Chapter meetings in Oregon, fitting them in with her frequent travels to California to visit her mother. She became knowledgeable and supportive about the campaigns focused on the coast (e.g., Cypress Bowl, Skagit Valley) while also bringing Okanagan concerns to the group.

As soon as she was able, Madsen became a Canadian citizen. During the ceremony, the judge, aware of her environmental work, commented that he was glad that she was now a Canadian.

Madsen laughed about how she had lived up to the stereotype of being a loud, sometimes pushy American. She thought it was important to let politicians and others know about her concerns. Madsen acknowledged that obtaining the uranium moratorium was her biggest win.

Art was important to Madsen as well. She often used it in the campaigns in which she was involved and in 1982, she returned to painting portraits and landscapes as well as teaching art. Her award-winning paintings have hung in galleries across North America. Madsen moved to Victoria in 1993. In 2012, she was awarded the Queen's Diamond Jubilee Medal for her role in conservation efforts with the Sierra Club and the Okanagan Similkameen Parks Society. She lived comfortably in her own home until she died in July 2017 at the age of ninety-six. ▲

Katy Madsen. *Photo by Nori Sinclair*

Susan Howatt: Natural Resource Protector

Susan Howatt left her birthplace on Prince Edward Island to attend Acadia University in Wolfville, Nova Scotia, where she became an energetic student activist on social justice issues and was inspired by the solidarity movements in South Africa and Latin America. She completed an undergraduate degree in political science and, after graduation, moved to BC.

In the 1990s she volunteered for CUSO International (a non-profit organization involved with international development with a posting in Indonesia. "I went for one year and stayed for three." She worked with the Indonesian Mining Advocacy Network, which is part of Friends of the Earth, Indonesia. "I did human rights investigation work with communities that were impacted by the Canadian mining industry . . . I saw first-hand the impacts of poor corporate social responsibility on the rights of human beings and the environment. I saw really polluted rivers and just widespread poverty and at the same time, record-breaking profits for Canadian mining companies. It didn't square with the kind of world that I wanted to live in."

Howatt was in Indonesia just after the country had overthrown its military dictator and was able to witness its very first free democratic election. "It was quite inspiring and [it meant that] my colleagues and life-long friends were legitimate for the first time. NGOS were not allowed under the military dictatorship and were very tightly controlled. Indonesia had no free press and lots of human rights issues happening." Despite these disturbing observations, she was impressed with the vibrancy and joyfulness of the people she visited in various communities.

Howatt returned to Canada where she landed a job as the national waters campaigner for the Council of Canadians and was able to learn from Maude Barlow, "one of the world's best storytellers." She travelled throughout Canada learning and talking about water issues and came to understand that there is a "myth of abundance" and that a lack of government oversight can result in dire problems for Canada's water resources.

One day in 2008, she had a conference call with Sierra Club BC's Sarah Cox and Kathryn Molloy about a water issue in Kamloops. A group of concerned citizens had sought the club's help about a water licence application for a bottling operation. With Howatt's advice about wording for a letter sent to both the municipality and the local newspaper editor, the application was withdrawn within twenty-four hours. "I think that was the fastest campaign," she recalled. When Molloy questioned Howatt about whether she ever thought of returning to BC, she replied "every day." Molloy quickly made a job offer and within a week Howatt had a one-year contract as Sierra Club BC's campaigns director.

She and the other Sierra Club BC campaign staff had discussions about possible "game-changing environmental laws" and out of those discussions, Howatt decided to advocate for three issues. In addition to tackling BC's outdated mining laws, she would focus on an endangered species law and better water protection.

A highlight was working on the run-of-the-river issue. Bute Hydro Inc. proposed a dam on the Bute Inlet that would have a significant impact on endangered species habitat. Sierra Club BC campaign staff took donors and supporters on a boat trip up the Bute River to see what would be affected by the proposed dam. "It was a glacial-fed river. We saw bears and we saw otters and dol-

Susan Howatt. *Photo by Nori Sinclair*

phins and it was a really magical place." They returned determined to fight for its preservation. The project had been referred to a panel for an environmental assessment and thanks to the lobbying efforts of Sierra Club BC and others, Bute Hydro Inc. decided in 2011 not to proceed with the project.

After Kathryn Molloy left the executive director position, Howatt replaced her as acting executive director until George Heyman came on board. In 2013, Howatt left Sierra Club BC. She had recently obtained a master's degree from Royal Roads University in the field of human security and peace building. The Site C Dam issue had inspired her major research paper on how the public is consulted and involved in decision-making regarding large dam projects. She had interviewed someone from International Rivers for the paper and a few months later the organization called her to interview for a campaign position in Berkeley, California. She became their lead campaigner for the Mekong River in Southeast Asia. She has since returned to Vancouver where she does a variety of consulting work.

🌲

Progress is impossible without change, and those who cannot change their minds cannot change anything.

—George Bernard Shaw

8

Oil and Gas Issues— Pipelines, Tankers, and Fracking

IN 1969, INADEQUATE SAFETY PRECAUTIONS CAUSED A BLOWOUT TO occur at an offshore oil well off the coast of Santa Barbara, California. The explosion was so powerful the ocean floor cracked in five places, allowing crude oil to spew out at four thousand litres per hour.[110] This went on for a month before it could be stopped, resulting in eleven million litres spreading along the coast for fifty-five kilometres, killing thousands of birds, fish, and sea mammals. The Santa Barbara spill sent shock waves through the US as the media showed photos of oil-covered birds. New environmental legislation was passed and people wanted change. In the two years after the spill there was a doubling of Sierra Club memberships in the US.

It was the worst oil spill in North American history—until twenty years later, when an Exxon Valdez oil tanker hit a reef and spilled forty million litres off the coast of Alaska. That spill killed a quarter million seabirds, hundreds of sea otters and harbour seals, 250 bald eagles and more than twenty killer whales. About two thousand kilometres of shoreline was affected and oil continues to wash up every year.[111] Exxon eventually paid $125 million in criminal fines and $900 million for civil penalties.[112]

Canada also had its own major oil disaster on the east coast in 1970 when the aging Arrow oil tanker ran aground during a storm. It spilled about 9.5 million litres of oil that ended up on the beaches of Cape Breton, Nova Scotia, affecting three hundred kilometres of shoreline and costing millions of dollars to clean up over a period of months.

In 1968, oil was discovered in Prudhoe Bay, Alaska, resulting in a proposal to build a 1,300-kilometre pipeline south across Alaska to the port of Valdez, where the oil would then be transported by tankers along the coast of BC to markets in the US. There was much opposition to the Alaska pipeline. A nine-volume environmental impact statement was put forward in 1972, followed by a number of court actions, resulting in a rise in public awareness about the risks involved in pipeline construction. David Anderson, Member of Parliament for Esquimalt–Saanich from 1968 to 1972, in his capacity as a member of the BC Wildlife Federation, was one of the litigants in the (failed) effort to stop this pipeline in the early 1970s. With memories of the Santa Barbara and Arrow oil spills fresh in their minds, Canadians were overwhelmingly against this proposal. In 1971, the BC legislature passed a resolution opposing tanker traffic on the west coast. The federal government established the Department of the Environment, and in 1972, the House of Commons unanimously supported the motion that tanker traffic along BC's coastline from Alaska to Puget Sound would be detrimental to Canadian interests.[113] In 1973, after a sharp rise in oil prices in the US, the US Senate passed an act authorizing the building of the Trans-Alaska Pipeline.

The federal government imposed a moratorium on crude oil tanker traffic along the Inside Passage (Dixon Entrance, Hecate Strait, and Queen Charlotte Sound)—a decision based on the recommendations of the Commons Special Committee on Environmental

Control, chaired by David Anderson, the environment minister and MP from Victoria. Not long after the moratorium on tanker traffic was announced, the Canadian government extended it to all offshore oil and gas activities on the west coast.[114] The Trans-Alaska Pipeline, one of the world's largest systems, was completed in 1977. It was not until the disastrous Exxon Valdez spill in 1989 that BC announced a similar moratorium for waters not under federal control.

Alberta had meanwhile been extracting oil on a large scale since the 1940s and moving it through various provinces via pipelines. These pipelines were designed to deliver oil being sold by American companies to (largely) American companies. In 1976, a consortium of six companies announced their intention to support a Trans Mountain Oil Pipeline Company proposal to construct a pipeline that would run from Kitimat to Edmonton. The idea was to connect the new Alaskan supply of oil to an existing pipeline system running from Edmonton to the US Midwest, where the projected demand was located.

Rosemary Fox, in her capacity as chair of Sierra Club BC's Lower Mainland group at the time, characterized the proposal to build a terminal at Kitimat as "one of the most serious single threats to the environment faced by British Columbia, without assuring any significant benefit to either BC or Canada."[115] The club sent telegrams to the federal and provincial cabinets demanding that plans for dealing with hazards and construction be made public, that impact studies on the oil transport, port and pipeline facilities be developed, and that a ninety-day interval between impact assessment and public hearings be instituted.[116] It also presented submissions to the National Energy Board hearings.

In 1977, the federal government appointed Andrew Thompson as commissioner of the West Coast Oil Ports Inquiry and asked him to consider the environmental, social, and navigational aspects of oil port proposals (Kitimat and other possibilities, including Vancouver, had been suggested). He noted that there were "general public concerns," which he saw as nonetheless real fears not to be dismissed: "Despite my familiarity with this history of determined opposition to tanker traffic, I have been surprised to find it so universal. In my preliminary meetings throughout the province and in the formal and community hearings of the Inquiry held to date, the oil port proposals have inspired few advocates other than the proponent companies themselves."[117] Following the filing of the results of this inquiry, the federal departments of environment, fisheries, and transportation rejected the Kitimat oil port proposal in 1978.

Tom Hackney. *University of Victoria Archives*

In addition to concern about tankers, oil ports, and pipelines on the central coast, Sierra Club BC became concerned about another pipeline. Tom Hackney was a dedicated volunteer whose main reason for joining the organization was to address the issue of climate change. In 2000, he helped launch a campaign to oppose a proposal for a natural gas pipeline known as the Georgia Strait Crossing (GSX), which would run from the mainland to Vancouver Island. Hackney was convinced that increasing the use of fossil fuels on the Island was misguided.

The provincial government, interested in development, and noting the low price of gas, had decided that over the next several decades, BC Hydro's generation should switch to gas-fired power plants on Vancouver Island. The underwater power lines that brought power to Vancouver Island from the mainland's northern hydroelectric dams were becoming old and needing expensive replacement. The government decided to put in a gas pipeline instead.

BC Hydro had made a deal with Williams Gas Pipeline Company and was trying to figure out a route through Cobble Hill. Several hundred people attended information sessions in Cobble Hill to express strong objections to the proposal. On behalf of Sierra Club BC, Hackney attended the meetings and objected as well. The local people started to organize and one of them, Arthur Caldicott, created an email listserv and a website. Those concerned about the issue formed an organization known as the Georgia Strait Crossing Concerned Citizens Coalition (GSXCCC). Sierra Club BC became a leading member with Hackney as president of the coalition. The campaign used a multi-prong approach to achieve its objective.

Because the pipeline was going through international waters, there was a need for a federal review. The coalition decided to intervene in the process and one of its first acts in the National Energy Board process was to successfully call for a Joint Panel review of the project rather than a lower level review.

Sierra Club BC was able to get funding from the Environmental Dispute Resolution Fund administered by West Coast Environmental Law. They hired Bill Andrews, a lawyer in independent practice, who has continued to work in this capacity with Hackney ever since. Hackney found his involvement a vital learning experience in figuring out how the process worked: "We tried to read our way through these enormous long applications running for thousands of pages. We were still enormously under-resourced. The proponents had professional lawyers and staff that were very familiar with these kinds of materials. We had no budget to speak of, except for a very small amount of legal advice."

With Andrews's help, Hackney tried to argue that greenhouse gas emissions associated with the pipeline should be a factor considered by the National Energy Board (NEB). That argument was rejected and the NEB ruled that only the pipeline and the environmental concerns associated with building it would be considered, and not what was flowing through it.

Each side had presented its evidence and, in the end, the National Energy Board approved the pipeline project. By Hackney's calculation, the more advanced Joint Panel review process caused a delay of at least a couple of years. During that time, the price of gas went up, making gas-fired power much less cost effective than it had seemed in the year 2000. As well, Centra Gas (now Fortis Gas) became aware of the pipeline proposal and indicated that they could transport gas to the Island with less expense than the GSX project. "Who knows why but for whatever reason BC Hydro had not secured Centra Gas's agreement and support to connect to their gas system." In the end, although the pipeline had been approved, BC Hydro decided not to proceed with it after all, due to a combination of public pressure and the price of gas.

At the same time these hearings were occurring, the government was planning the power plants that the gas from the pipeline was meant to fuel. The coalition had more success there. The first project that came forward was the Port Alberni Generation Project, utilizing a combined cycle gas turbine to produce electricity. Representatives from the coalition (including Hackney) talked to people in Port Alberni and gave a presentation to the city council. There was a strong public reaction against the project; a major concern was the health hazard of breathing in the fine particulate matter formed when the gas is burned. The municipality decided not to support it and denied zoning.

The government next tried to build a power plant in Nanaimo and after several iterations, eventually attempted to secure a site at Duke Point. A new provincial government with the Liberals in power had just been elected. The energy minister was persuaded to put the proposed power plant before the Utilities Commission for a review to determine whether it was in the public interest. Sierra Club BC (through the GSXCCC) decided to intervene in that proceeding as well. This process was initiated at about the time the National Energy Board review of the pipeline was winding down, around 2004.

Sierra Club BC was able to mount what Hackney called "a half-decent fight" during the Utilities Commission review process as the commission allowed arguments about climate change. "We argued that [there was an] unacknowledged liability to BC Hydro, in that if they kept on emitting greenhouse gas emissions, somewhere down the road there would be a liability because they would have to do something to curtail their emissions or they might get sued." Sierra Club BC also argued that BC Hydro had exaggerated their load forecast on Vancouver Island and, as such, there was no great urgency to build the power plant. Sierra Club BC won the first round when the commission concluded that BC Hydro had not proved that the power plant was necessary.

This was a triumph for Sierra Club BC, but an environmental activist's job is never done and this was another case demonstrating the need for passion and persistence. BC Hydro tried another tactic to get the project approved. This time they put out a call for independent power producers to produce power on Vancouver Island. A project very similar to the one that had just been defeated was put forth, except that it was now being proposed by a private company rather than by BC Hydro. Sierra Club BC intervened again to fight it. It was much harder this time to argue about greenhouse gas liability because BC Hydro simply said that it was not their problem—BC Hydro would have to assume that the private power producer had somehow or other made allowance for the liability cost. The project was approved; however, Sierra Club BC appealed the approval to the BC Court of Appeal. Although that appeal was ultimately not successful, again they had delayed the project long enough and created enough negative political energy around it that enthusiasm for building the power plant had waned. As well, the price of gas by that time was fairly high. As a result, BC Hydro discarded the plan in 2004—a result that can be considered, at least in part, due to Sierra Club BC's persistent campaign.

Hackney continues to work with Bill Andrews before the BC Utilities Commission to advocate for renewable energy and environmental conservation issues. They become involved in reviews, not only of BC Hydro's energy plans, but also those of Fortis, Pacific Northern Gas, and other utilities. To this day, they regularly bring up issues about climate change and greenhouse gas emissions. The most common theme they address is the need for BC's utilities to invest in energy conservation and to get their customers to conserve more energy. They have intervened in seventy to eighty proceedings over the past ten years, some very small and others needing multiple experts to provide evidence. Hackney was proud to report that BC Hydro has improved over the years so that it produces fewer gas emissions. "I think we can claim that as a victory, that that is now acknowledged in law and policy and we've had some influence in that happening."

In 2004, Sierra Club BC submitted a brief to the federal panel on offshore oil and gas (also known as the Priddle Panel, for its chair, Roland Priddle), which was examining whether the moratorium that had been in effect since 1972 should be lifted. Interestingly, the Council of the Haida Nation asked the Haida people not to participate to avoid having the hearing mistaken for fulfilling the duty to consult.[118] The report tabled in October that year showed that the public was intensely divided, and that, in fact, 75 percent wanted the moratorium to be maintained.[119] The risk of an oil spill was thought to be too great, and with it the potential to harm marine species too high; the negative effect of a spill on the economically important recreation and tourism industry was also highlighted.

It seemed that the collective memory of previous oil spills, with their widespread environmental impacts—particularly the 1989 Exxon Valdez spill in the Gulf of Alaska—continued to haunt the public. According to the report, there was "near consensus" that there were still significant knowledge gaps about the effects of oil on lifeforms in the ocean and the possible environmental and socio-economic impacts of a spill. The report also pointed out that participants in favour of the moratorium wanted these gaps filled before lifting the moratorium, while those in favour of lifting the moratorium thought the only way to fill in the gaps was to lift the moratorium.[120] First Nations also participated in the federal First Nations Engagement Process, again with the caveat that this was not to be considered as consultation.[121] The report indicated that the vast majority of First Nations participants thought that lifting the moratorium was not in their best interests, while others were not prepared to draw any conclusions at that time.

Kitimat remained of interest to the oil and gas industry as a strategic gateway; in 2010, a pipeline going the opposite way (moving Alberta oil from the growing oilsands production to the coast) was proposed. Enbridge Northern Gateway Pipelines filed an application to build a twin (eastbound/westbound) pipeline between Kitimat and Bruderheim, Alberta, again proposing terminal facilities for loading and unloading and marine transportation. Opposition centred around the risk of leaks and spills and the prospect of increased tanker traffic through Douglas Channel.

Sierra Club BC campaigner Caitlyn Vernon became active in opposing Enbridge's Northern Gateway pipeline and tankers proposal, as a result of hearing significant concern from members of coastal Indigenous communities. After working for years to protect the Great Bear Rainforest, she knew that an oil spill would jeopardize not only Indigenous cultures, coastal communities, and the marine ecosystem but, because of the well-known connections between marine flora and fauna and those based on the land, it would be devastating for the land ecology too.

Other environmental groups also opposed the Enbridge proposal and, although there was not a formal coalition, the groups coordinated their involvement with conference calls, an electronic mailing list, and occasional in-person meetings. While each group had its own tactics, the campaigners strove to have an overall coherent strategy. The connections and relationships with coastal Indigenous communities was a key contribution of Sierra Club BC to the loose coalition. As well, SCBC organized rallies and educational events, and encouraged people to speak at the Joint Review Panel.

In addition, Vernon focused her efforts on supporting community-based activities along the Enbridge route, whether that be events, film screenings, rallies, or other creative means to engage and educate northern residents. For example, Sierra Club BC partnered with various northern groups to organize photo exhibits from Haida Gwaii to Prince George and to raise awareness of the cultural and ecological values at stake along the proposed oil tanker route.

The National Energy Board once again held hearings in 2012 and 2013, and in December 2013, despite tremendous opposition, recommended in favour of the pipeline (contingent on 209 conditions being met).

After the federal government approved the Enbridge Northern Gateway pipeline and tankers project, seven First Nations went to court to defend their territories. Legal fees are expensive, and it seemed unfair for the First Nations to have to shoulder all the costs, when success would provide benefits not only to them but to everyone concerned with a livable climate, salmon rivers, and an oil-free coast. A community group in Terrace held a spaghetti dinner to raise funds for the First Nations in court, then reached out to Vernon to mobilize the rest of the province to do the same. Vernon contacted

Denman Island Chocolate produced chocolate bars with labels critical of the building of Enbridge's Northern Gateway pipeline, and portions of the sales were contributed to the Pull Together campaign. *SCBC Photo Files*

the legal defence fund RAVEN Trust,[122] and together the two organizations partnered to launch Pull Together, a campaign to raise moral support and funds for the First Nations in court through a variety of community events and business initiatives. By the end of the campaign, over $600,000 had been raised for the seven nations: the Gitxaala, Gitga'at, Haida, Hciltsuk, Nadleh Whut'en, Nak'azdli, and Kitasoo/Xai'xais, who were all involved in legal actions.

All of the Pull Together donations went directly to the nations' legal fees, minus an administrative fee to RAVEN Trust. There was some concern that this campaign was a financial risk for Sierra Club BC. Some feared that donors would become confused, donating to Pull Together and overlooking the club's other needs. Nevertheless, Vernon felt it was the right thing to do, emphasizing that solidarity with First Nations does not just mean standing beside them when they are speaking up but also letting them take the lead and being willing to give up something as an individual or an organization.

The First Nations won their court challenges and the court overturned the federal approval of Enbridge's Northern Gateway project. After the election of the new federal Liberal government headed by Justin Trudeau in 2015, the proposal was quashed altogether, with a promise of an oil tanker moratorium. Vernon travelled to Ottawa to be a witness for a parliamentary committee, in an attempt to strengthen the oil tanker ban. While imperfect, the federal Oil Tanker Moratorium Act was introduced (Bill C-48) in 2017. When passed, it will prohibit tankers carrying more than 12,500 metric tons of crude oil from stopping or unloading the oil at ports located along British Columbia's north coast from the northern tip of Vancouver Island to the Alaska border.

After the defeat of the Enbridge pipeline proposal, concern shifted to Kinder Morgan's 2016 proposal to twin its Trans Mountain pipeline to carry heavy oil (diluted bitumen) from the oilsands in Alberta—from Edmonton to the Westridge Marine Terminal in Burnaby. The 1,150-kilometre pipeline has been in operation since 1953, but the proposed expansion would almost triple the amount of oil being transported and result in a high proportion of it being exported. Although estimates vary slightly depending on the source, an article by *Global News* reported that currently, five tankers per month leave the Westridge Terminal through Burrard Inlet and that the expansion would see as many as thirty-four tankers a month making their way through the waters around Vancouver and into the Salish Sea.[123]

This pipeline would not only increase the risk of contamination on land; escalated tanker traffic would add to underwater noise levels for whales and other marine fauna, and a bitumen spill is a risk that most people do not want to contemplate. Bitumen is different from refined or crude oil, which floats and can be removed to some extent with skimmers and dispersants. Diluted bitumen sinks—with no known way to attempt a cleanup.

As well, environmentalists are concerned that continuing to build pipelines will enable the expansion of the oilsands, and make it impossible for Canada to meet its commitment to reduce carbon emissions under the Paris Climate Accord. Moreover, research strongly suggests that as the supply of oil is increased, over the long term more will be consumed globally,[124] thus increasing overall global emissions.

Sierra Club BC has lobbied government, circulated pamphlets, staged rallies, participated in hearings, and advocated intensively against the pipeline. Another Pull Together campaign was launched to support the Coldwater Indian Band, and Tsleil-Waututh, Squamish, and Stk'emlupsemc Te Secwepemc First Nations with their legal challenges, with over $650,000 raised by September 2018. In addition, the club continues to engage the public with events publicizing energy alternatives and demonstrating how to transition to a fossil fuel-free economy. In 2018, Vernon co-hosted a new Sierra Club BC podcast series entitled *Mission Transition: Powering BC's Clean Energy Economy.*

The NDP campaign prior to the 2017 provincial election promised the party would use "every tool in the toolbox" to ensure that the pipeline is not built. Following the election, the NDP government finds itself pitted against Alberta and the federal government, both insisting that the pipeline must be built. Sierra Club BC, along with numerous environmental groups, First Nations, and politicians continue to lobby heavily against the prospect of such a pipeline. Federal Green Party leader and MP Elizabeth May and NDP MP Kennedy Stewart, as well as over two hundred other citizens, were arrested and criminally charged for violating a court injunction to stay at least five metres away from the Burnaby terminal.

On August 30, 2018, the Federal Court of Appeal released its ruling that overturned the federal government's approval of the pipeline and provided two reasons for doing this. First, the panel of judges indicated that the National Energy Board had not adequately considered the marine shipping component with its increase in tanker traffic and impact on marine species such as orca whales. Secondly, the federal government had not consulted meaningfully with the First Nations that would be affected by the pipeline.

Despite this ruling, shortly afterwards the federal government completed the contract it had signed with Kinder Morgan to purchase the existing Trans Mountain pipeline and its assets for $4.5 billion, and promised it would provide funding for the expansion project.

Sierra Club BC condemned this action in a press release. Three weeks later, the federal government announced that the NEB would reconsider the parts of the Trans Mountain application that related to marine shipping. There would also be new consultations with Indigenous communities, with Supreme Court justice Frank Iacobucci appointed to oversee the proceedings.[125]

The NEB had twenty-two weeks to produce its report by February 22, 2019. It decided to limit its consideration to the shipping area between the Westridge Marine Terminal and the twelve-nautical-mile territorial sea limit rather than Canada's two-hundred-nautical-mile exclusive economic zone. In January 2019, the government of BC filed its submission[126] against the project, indicating its concerns about the impacts of an oil spill and the potential effects of increased tanker traffic on resident orca whales. It also maintained that the case for twinning the pipeline has not been proven to be necessary. Rather than intervene in the process, SCBC, along with other environmental groups, used its resources to mobilize the public to send over 66,000 faxes to the NEB to share their concerns about expanding the pipeline.

On February 22, the NEB released its recommendations endorsing the expansion of the pipeline, despite acknowledging that there would be "significant adverse" effects on endangered orca whales, increased greenhouse gas (GHG) emissions, and, although "not likely," the environmental effects of a spill would be significant.[127] The report indicated that the economic benefits outweighed these impacts and provided 156 conditions with which the company must comply and sixteen recommendations that would help reduce the impact of increased shipping in the Salish Sea. The not-yet-completed consultations with Indigenous communities would continue in order to determine how to accommodate their concerns. Sierra Club BC continued to speak out against the pipeline expansion. Caitlyn Vernon's statement on the website said, "As the climate crisis worsens and the costs to taxpayers of this project increase, it's time for the prime minister to step away from this climate-polluting pipeline and invest in a clean energy economy instead."[128]

Liquefied Natural Gas

ANOTHER FOSSIL FUEL THAT PLAYS A ROLE ON THE CLIMATE CHANGE stage is liquefied natural gas (LNG). Sierra Club BC's Rosemary Fox voiced her concern as early as 1996 when a proposal to build an LNG plant at either Kitimat or Prince Rupert was being considered. At that time, the primary concern was that exploration and drilling in northeastern BC would have a negative effect on the east slope of the Rockies, with its boreal forest habitat. Sierra Club BC's current concern is environmental damage caused by the method of producing the gas and its effect on increasing greenhouse gas emissions.

Extraction of LNG employs hydraulic fracturing, or fracking, which involves drilling deep into the earth and injecting a high-pressure stream of water mixed with sand and chemicals to stimulate the release of the gas. Not only is this method heavily reliant on surface water (potentially needed for drinking and irrigation), it may also contaminate underground water and water-dependent habitats, and possibly cause earthquakes.

In 2013, Ecojustice brought forward a lawsuit on behalf of Sierra Club BC and the Wilderness Committee, seeking a Supreme Court order to declare that the BC Oil and Gas Commission's practice of repeatedly granting short-term water withdrawal approvals to oil and gas companies for fracking and drilling operations was unlawful. Encana Corporation, one of BC's major natural gas players, was also named in the suit. The groups were concerned about the impact on lakes, rivers, and streams in northeastern BC and the communities and wildlife that depend on the water. However, the court ruled that the oil and gas industry and other major industrial users do not require a water licence for long-term access to the province's freshwater resources. In what appeared to be a backdoor way of dealing with the court case, the BC government had passed a Water Sustainability Act days before the case was heard, legalizing the practice being challenged in court. This outcome did not negate Sierra Club BC's concern about the issue and the need for continued advocacy.

The LNG process can also result in the fugitive emission of methane, a greenhouse gas that is even more damaging than carbon dioxide for its ability to trap heat within the earth's atmosphere. As well, a substantial amount of energy is required to liquefy the gas at the marine terminal in order to transport it. Researchers at the Pembina Institute concluded that "even if LNG Canada and Woodfibre LNG [two of the proposals being considered at the time of their report] and their associated upstream operations were developed using only clean energy and best practices, the greenhouse gas emissions from natural gas extraction, processing, transportation, and liquefaction would use up almost half of the total allowed emissions for all of BC. This would make it extremely challenging for BC to meet its climate target without almost completely eliminating emissions from the rest of the economy."[129]

In the summer of 2018, the BC government announced sales tax concessions, among other measures (including a carbon tax break), in order to attract LNG investment in the province, while offering assurances that the facilities would have to meet the "cleanest" operating standards.[130] On September 20, 2018, Sierra Club BC's executive director, Hannah Askew, wrote a letter to Premier John Horgan, Minister of Environment and Climate Change Strategy George Heyman, and Minister of Energy and Mines Michelle Mungall, calling on the BC government to demonstrate strong and meaningful climate leadership by strengthening targets and ending its support for LNG.

In a SCBC press release,[131] Jens Wieting said, "To willfully ignore the science and promote fossil fuel expansion is a new form of climate denial . . . [Recently] California set a goal of achieving zero emissions by 2045. We are calling on the BC government to follow this example and commit to climate action based on the latest science, including more aggressive carbon pollution targets and a robust climate test for new energy projects." Nevertheless, on October 2, 2018, LNG Canada, with five investors from five different countries, agreed to move forward on building a LNG pipeline from Dawson Creek to a terminal at Kitimat. Both Prime Minister Justin Trudeau and BC Premier John Horgan were present to make the official announcement. This was done despite warnings from SCBC and other environmental groups that it would be difficult to meet provincial climate targets, since it would require far too drastic GHG cuts in other sectors of the economy.

A special report from the UN's Intergovernmental Panel on Climate Change[132] was released October 8, 2018. It indicated that "rapid and far-reaching" transitions to the world economy and net-zero carbon pollution are required by mid-century if we are to limit global warming to 1.5 degrees Celsius. Moreover, Canada has to cut its emissions in half within twelve years if it is to reach targets that many of these experts believe are necessary to avoid significant repercussions. It is because of scientific evidence such as that cited in this report that Sierra Club BC continues to advocate strongly for the transition to a fossil fuel-free economy.

Caitlyn Vernon: Coastal Defender

Caitlyn Vernon grew up in East Vancouver, often spending family vacations on Salt Spring Island and along the west coast of Vancouver Island, camping at Long Beach and hiking in the coast mountains. Her family was often involved in social justice issues related to labour concerns, women's rights, and international solidarity. They went to rallies, walked on picket lines, and participated in marches—a great education for Vernon's career in environmental activism.

Vernon completed an undergraduate degree in biology at Simon Fraser University in 1997, with the idea of becoming a biologist. While at university, she became interested in environmental issues; she and two friends were the driving force of SFU's environmental group at the time. After graduation, she did fisheries and wildlife fieldwork in northern BC, and became disillusioned with the limited role of a biologist in protecting ecosystems. Instead, she became interested in resource management decision-making, and joined the Department of Fisheries and Oceans' marine use planning process in the Great Bear Rainforest area. After that, she travelled to Mexico, where she worked with the Forest Stewardship Council on making forest certification accessible to community forest workers and Indigenous communities, before coordinating a CIDA-funded project working with Indigenous communities on organic and fair-trade certification and community forests. Throughout this time, she also worked at the Falls Brook Centre in New Brunswick, coordinating projects on non-timber forest products, forest certification, and community-based resource stewardship.

Subsequently, Vernon returned to university to complete a master's degree in environmental studies at York University in Toronto. Her research paper examined shared decision-making between the province of BC and First Nations, and questioned what form of decision-making could lead to outcomes that are both ecologically sustainable and socially just. She had become interested in this topic after witnessing resource management decision-making that excluded and disrespected Indigenous voices, and often resulted in decisions harmful to the environment. She wanted to explore how the dynamic could be changed to assure better, more ecological and just outcomes. Her paper was included as a chapter in a book called *Alliances: Re-envisioning Indigenous/Non-indigenous Relationships.*[133]

Vernon happily returned to BC and, after a brief stint with the Greater Victoria Compost Education Centre, was hired by Sierra Club BC in 2007 to assist Claire Hutton in providing outreach and support to the First Nations in the Great Bear Rainforest (GBR). Early on, Vernon was active in encouraging staff to recognize the ways in which environmental organizations have served to erase Indigenous peoples from the landscape through the use of particular language and approaches. For example, she encouraged staff to stop using words like "untouched" or "pristine" when referring to landscapes that had in fact been used and managed by Indigenous peoples for thousands of years.

After Hutton left, Vernon took on the leading role as outreach worker in the GBR campaign. At that time, SCBC recognized that the people working on the ground in communities needed to have more information about what was being negotiated by their political leaders, and the First Nations people needed improved capacity to implement and monitor the new agreements as part of governing their territories. Hutton and Vernon helped Sierra Club BC provide a

Caitlyn Vernon (second from left) joins others involved with the Pull Together campaign. LEFT TO RIGHT: Susan Smitten (executive director, RAVEN), Marilyn Slett (Chief Councillor, Heiltsuk Tribal Council), Harvey Humchitt (Hemas—i.e., hereditary chief—of Heiltsuk First Nation), Kelly Brown (director, Heiltsuk Integrated Resource Department).
Photo by Andy Cotton

series of ecosystem-based management learning forums in partnership with the Coastal First Nations Great Bear Initiative.

Vernon also helped establish the Regional Monitoring Strategy with the Coastal Guardian Watchmen Network. The network standardized the work that was being done to monitor the coast with consistent methodology and a data-capturing system. Vernon was also involved in ecosystem-based management and conservancy planning for the Great Bear Rainforest with Jens Wieting. Later, she initiated a Sierra Club BC campaign against the Enbridge pipeline and tankers while continuing to do the GBR community support work.

With time, Coastal First Nations took on full coordination of the Guardian Watchmen program. Funders were keen to support the nations directly and Sierra Club BC stepped back. Vernon was then able to devote more time to the Enbridge campaign and gradually her work became more concerned with pipelines, oil tankers, climate change, and energy issues.

In 2013, Vernon became Sierra Club BC's campaigns director upon the departure of Susan Howatt. She supported the team of campaigners working on pipelines, energy/climate, old-growth forests, the Flathead River Valley, and Site C, while also becoming deeply involved in organizational management and leadership. Following the departure of executive director Bob Peart in 2017, Vernon acted as part of a three-person executive team until the next executive director was hired. She is often a media spokesperson for the club and has participated in a variety of events including rallies, speaking at a convention about green jobs, and joining a panel to discuss women's contributions to environmental leadership.

Outside of her Sierra Club BC work, Vernon also fit in publishing an award-winning non-fiction book for young readers, called *Nowhere Else on Earth: Standing Tall for the Great Bear Rainforest*, in 2011.[134] The book encourages young readers to pay attention to what is happening in the world around them and inspires them to take action, speaking out for the future they want to live in. Vernon's passion is an inspiration not only for young people but for all of us concerned about the future of our province and the need to address environmental issues in a socially just and sustainable manner. ▲

Eelgrass beds and salt marshes effectively bury carbon for thousands of years—probably the most efficient carbon removal mechanism on Earth—and we should make good use of it while we still have a chance to avoid the worst climate scenarios.

—Colin Campbell

9

Marine Campaigns— Protecting Oceans and Sea Life

THE NEARLY THOUSAND-KILOMETRE COASTLINE OF BRITISH COLUMbia—much longer if the coastlines of each of the innumerable fiords and islands are taken into account—provides a rich and irreplaceable habitat for a great variety of invertebrates, fish, birds, whales, and other ocean mammals. This coast is nourished by countless rivers, creeks, and estuaries, each vital to ensuring a healthy network of ecosystems.

It has long been clear that certain logging practices have a significant and often toxic impact on fish spawning grounds in the creeks and streams that drain into the ocean along the coast of BC. Vicky

Orca whales may be one of three distinct forms—resident, transient or offshore—and differ in diet, social structure, habitat, and genetics depending on their type. *Photo by Sherry Kirkvol*

Husband of Sierra Club BC emphasized that "clearcuts kill salmon by destroying stream bank integrity, by silting up spawning beds and by raising stream temperatures when shade trees are removed. If we are to avoid the collapse of our fishery, as we have seen on the east coast, the important issue of habitat destruction must be on the table."[135] As early as 1972, SCBC lobbied against the destruction of salmon-bearing streams. Local fishers in Ucluelet on the west coast of Vancouver Island had formed an organization called Save Our Salmon (SOS). SCBC coordinated a campaign with this group as well as the Amalgamated Conservation Society (ACS), the Society Promoting Environmental Conservation, the Federation of BC Naturalists, and the United Fishermen and Allied Workers Union. The coalition sent a telegram to the federal minister of fisheries and forty Ucluelet fishers demonstrated in front of the BC legislature. It resulted in the federal government promising to provide additional funds to clean up the salmon streams.[136]

Sharon Chow, on behalf of Sierra Club BC, made a submission in 1994 to the Fraser River Sockeye Public Review Board, which was asked to investigate what appeared to be a significant decline in spawning sockeye salmon throughout the Fraser River watershed—more than a million less than usual.[137] The review board made a number of recommendations and recognized the importance of conservation to all those involved in the fishery. The report emphasized the need for a timely and reliable system for recording catch data that provided a readily apparent and up-to-date status to everyone in order to reduce the risk of overfishing.

In the late 1990s and early 2000s, Terry Glavin, Scott Wallace, and David Levy, separately and together, authored several scientific reports for Sierra Club BC that addressed a number of aspects of the BC fisheries. These reports gave weight to Sierra Club BC when it subsequently sounded the alarm about the state of groundfish and the critical decline in Strait of Georgia lingcod and inshore rockfish. Sierra Club BC publicized various harmful fishing practices, including overfishing and bycatch—unwanted fish species inadvertently caught by fishers in their nets. It also called for a moratorium on the expansion of salmon farming and lobbied that all salmon farming permits should be subject to environmental impact assessments.

Sierra Club BC also proposed that the provincial and federal governments implement a wild salmon conservation policy involving habitat protection, more stringent commercial and recreational fishing restrictions, better enforcement of regulations, establishment of a Pacific Fisheries Resource Conservation Council, better scientific data, and the phasing out of open net-cage salmon farms. Sierra Club BC emphasized that salmon are important not just as a food source but also as "the lifeblood of BC's temperate rainforest," pointing out that "wildlife such as grizzly bears, wolves, and bald eagles eat their fill of returning salmon; the spent fish carcasses provide essential nutrients to the stream environment and literally fertilize the valley forests. In return the new eggs thrive in the clean, cold water that only intact forest watersheds provide."[138] In 2005, the federal government enacted a wild salmon policy.[139]

To help promote sustainable fisheries in the early 2000s, Sierra Club BC developed a consumer guide identifying fish harvested with sustainable fishing practices. In an article printed in the *Sierra Report*,

Canada's
Seafood
Guide

SeaChoice
healthy choices, healthy oceans

Sierra Club BC produced the seafood wallet card to aid consumers in making more sustainable choices. *SCBC Photo Files*

Bruce Hill, lead marine campaigner in 2000, identified three categories: "guilt-free," "OK for now," and "don't you dare"[140]—a precursor to Sierra Club BC's popular *Citizen's Guide to Seafood*, produced in 2003 as a wallet-size insert with traffic-light red, yellow, and green indicators.

Although alternative seafood guides were circulating at the time, Sierra Club BC wanted one to include species often listed on local restaurant menus in order to provide information that was relevant to BC consumers. For example lingcod, which was suffering from a decline in stock in BC at that time, received a "questionable" rating. As well, differences in Canadian and American regulations could affect the degree to which fish harvests were questionable. For example, American environmentalists rated wild pacific salmon as one of the better seafood choices, whereas Sierra Club BC called this choice "questionable," based on the fact that American fishermen continued to harvest salmon runs that spawned in Canadian rivers and were known to be at risk.[141]

In 2006, Sierra Club BC, together with the David Suzuki Foundation, the Ecology Action Centre, and the Living Oceans Society, launched SeaChoice,[142] a partnership designed to help seafood consumers, chefs, and retailers make informed choices in favour of sustainable harvesting practices. Seven years later, Sierra Club BC stepped back and is no longer contributing actively to this successful program.

Another of the club's marine programs involved the Pacific North Coast Integrated Management Area (PNCIMA), identified by the federal government's Department of Fisheries and Oceans (DFO) in 2007. This was one of seven large ocean management areas the federal government had targeted for development of an ecosystem-based management plan.[143] PNCIMA encompasses 88,000 square kilometres, approximately half of which is considered ecologically and biologically significant by Fisheries and Oceans. It includes the waters around Haida Gwaii, extending to the mainland and down around the northern part of Vancouver Island—in other words, about two-thirds of BC's coast.

According to an article in the *Sierra Report*, "thirty-two species in the PNCIMA area are listed as endangered, threatened or of special concern. Twenty-five coastal communities and 35,500 residents rely variously on commercial fishing, aquaculture, shipping, forestry and tourism. Kelp forests, 9,000-year-old [glass] sponge reefs and cold-water corals provide crucial breeding habitat for rockfish and other organisms. Shipping, trawling and fish farms are threats to these assets that need to be fully understood and controlled. It is time to include the oceans in the landscape of our minds as we plan a sustainable future."[144]

The above-mentioned 9,000-year-old glass sponge reefs (which were thought to have died off about 40 million years ago) were identified near Haida Gwaii in Hecate Strait in 1987 as part of a scientific program to map the ocean floor. The Canadian Parks and Wilderness Society—along with others, including Sierra Club BC—worked for quite a number of years to have the reefs protected from fishing gear (trawl nets, prawn traps, anchors, and cables)—especially in light of the slow-growing nature of reefs and their importance in providing a home for a host of marine species. In May 2008, the BC government announced fishing closures for all bottom-contact fisheries within 150 metres of these fragile reefs (about twenty-two have so far been identified on the coast).[145]

Several environmental groups, along with Sierra Club BC, were key in the development of PNCIMA's management scheme, including the Living Oceans Society, the World Wildlife Fund, the David

Suzuki Foundation, and the Canadian Parks and Wilderness Society. The planning process officially launched in 2009 and the framework was developed over a three-year period. It was finally endorsed by the DFO in 2017 as a joint (federal, provincial, and First Nations) plan.[146] As well, the DFO designated four reefs as a Marine Protected Area— now known as Hecate Strait/Queen Charlotte Sound Glass Sponge Reefs MPA[147]—despite concerns raised in the fishing industry.

In addition to the oceans, the estuaries along BC's coast are also in great need of protection. Estuaries are formed at the point where rivers enter the ocean and fresh water mixes with the salt water, forming highly productive ecosystem zones that serve as breeding and feeding habitats for invertebrates, fish, marine birds, and mammals. Colin Campbell, science advisor for Sierra Club BC's marine program, wrote a plea for protecting them, indicating that they should be the "highest possible priority for conservation, restoration, and enhancement" because of their ability to store carbon, and because estuarine habitats are among the most rapidly disappearing ecosystems on earth, "disappearing in aggregate at rates from 2 to 15 times faster than forests."[148] Campbell emphasized that, like terrestrial forests, these "marine gardens" are capable of capturing and storing "immense amounts of carbon but much more efficiently." He points out that "blue carbon" is stored and stabilized in sediments: the salt marshes and seagrass meadows "stash away as much carbon as BC's portion of the boreal forests."

Campbell recommended the following: a comprehensive mapping survey of sub-tidal eelgrass in the coastal waters of BC; protection of intact estuarine vegetation under the Federal Fisheries Act; control of upstream erosion and monitoring of recreational use (including fishing and harvesting) by the province; and, at the local level, protection of eelgrass beds from chemical runoffs and construction with the establishment of vegetation buffer zones.

The club has also been active in raising public awareness of increasing ocean acidification with the advance of climate change. In 2009, Sierra Club BC launched a multimedia show entitled *Code Blue: Ocean Rescue and Resuscitation*, which was made widely available.[149] The acidification of oceans has come about as levels of carbon dioxide in the atmosphere have increased through human activity—an estimated 30-40 percent of this carbon dioxide is dissolved into oceans, rivers, and lakes. The potential harmful effects on marine life, particularly shellfish and corals that are sensitive to changes in the pH balance, have yet to be fully understood, but when these factors are combined with other environmental changes now well underway, it is clear that marine ecosystems are increasingly at risk. Sierra Club BC advocates intensively to encourage a reduction in carbon emissions, and continues to lobby for the establishment of marine protected areas to encourage resilience of these ecosystems in the face of climate change.

Colin Campbell: Science Advisor Emeritus

Colin Campbell grew up in Melbourne, Australia, and after high school he enrolled in a new university called Monash where there were young, bright professors from all over the world. Working with an American supervisor, he did a faunal analysis of aboriginal middens found on Tower Hill Beach, 250 kilometres west of Melbourne, and, as a consequence, he became interested in palaeontology.

He received a Fulbright scholarship to Berkeley, which at that time had a collection of the oldest Australian mammalian fossils. He commented, "It was a marvelous education. In the space of four years, in museums and at that university, I probably saw some piece or part of animal, plant, or invertebrate, from every living and extinct family. It was a huge exposure to the living world and that became my fully developed passion."[150] Noteworthy is the fact that Campbell has a species named after him—*Bulungu campbelli*, a species of bandicoot that lived in southern Australia 24–26 million years ago.

In the late 1990s, Campbell realized, after having worked at the Australian National University for a number of years doing research, that, although doing research is both important and interesting, it can be slow to achieve change in the world, and it was not really his strength. He had become concerned about human impact on the environment and, with this in mind, he decided to shift directions. As he was employed by the university, he was entitled to have his fees paid while he went to law school for two years, acquiring a master's degree in environmental law. "I am not a lawyer; it is a degree in legal studies. My classmates were all federal bureaucrats in Canberra who were responsible for existing legislation. They were there to learn the end runs around all the legislation. I was there to learn how this thing could be used more like a hammer. I was surprised I was the only environmentalist studying environmental law."

Campbell was married to a Canadian who, after being in Australia for ten years, was missing her large family and convinced Campbell to move to Canada. Although his environmental law degree would have been even more effective for an environmentalist living in Australia, Campbell still found it useful in Canada, where there are similar legislative principles and structures.

At first he worked for the BC Environmental Network in the Forest Caucus, which exposed him to the negotiation process between environmental groups and the government, as well as issues like the Forest Practices Code. He applied for a job at Sierra Club BC but was not initially hired. Instead, he was asked to run for a position on the board of directors, winning a seat in December 2003. At his first board meeting in January he was elected chair. Campbell explained, "I did it on the condition that I was still eligible to apply for jobs as they came up."

Six months later, in July 2004, Campbell was hired to start working for the Marine Program, which was funded by the Gordon and Betty Moore Foundation. "For the first few years I worked at the Sierra Club, the Marine Program was the most affluent and was led by Vicky Husband. To the extent that I was trained on the ins and outs of how this game is played, it was thanks to Vicky. She is a highly effective activist. She could be a bit stern and demanding, but always with the goal of peak performance. She often made me smile—I had never had anybody correcting my commas before."

Campbell was one of the environmentalists providing input to the PNCIMA Committee and resultant reports. He attended many meetings requiring quite a bit of travel. A highlight for Campbell was attending an Oceans Economic Summit in Singapore where Sylvia Earle, a highly respected oceanographer, spoke. As an activist, she had a huge influence on promoting marine protected areas. Campbell said, "Protected areas are the key and where they are firmly established, like in New Zealand, the fishermen do better. They all object to their establishment in the beginning; scarcely one of them ever supports it. But their financial and catch records in subsequent years show they have always done better. There

Colin Campbell explores a beach along the Juan de Fuca trail. *Photo by Nori Sinclair*

are bigger fish and more of them." Campbell brought these sorts of ideas to planning committee meetings, although he acknowledged that not everyone was willing to listen. "The conservation benefits are indisputable and it is then one of those things where the challenge is no longer scientific, it is sociological. It is necessary that people shift their value judgements."

As a palaeontologist and someone who has studied evolutionary history, Campbell has always been aware of the effect of climate. In the 1990s, his research involved a project on sea level change. "Palaeontologists and biologists use climate to explain everything—change in species adaptations, speciation itself, species extinction, and major changes in floral and faunal assemblages."

While working at Sierra Club BC and studying oceans, Campbell became increasingly concerned about other effects of climate change. "And by then I had become obsessed with the carbon dioxide question, especially what can be done with this carbon when clearly we are going to keep making it. Where is it going to go? There are not many choices. The ocean sequesters some of it; eel grass, salt marsh and mangrove ecosystems store a hell of a lot of carbon." This led to the publishing of Campbell's favourite paper,

"Blue Carbon–British Columbia: The Case for the Conservation and Enhancement of Estuarine Processes and Sediments in BC."[151]

Campbell always tried to ensure that in any recommendations he wrote for a PNCIMA report, there was a paragraph giving high priority to conservation of these high carbon-storing ecosystems. "Before you do any damage make sure there is no eel grass there. That is a bit naïve but I think in the beginning it is good to just have a blunt statement like that. I stopped following PNCIMA recently but the repetition worked." Campbell noted that PNCIMA continues to emphasize the need to conserve eel-grass areas.

Campbell's final project before retirement, after working just shy of ten years with Sierra Club BC, put his extensive scientific knowledge and experience to a task, and resulted in a draft of the visionary document *The Future Is Here*. Campbell reviewed the literature and "put together a position paper on how the future looks, where conservation science is leading us, what the modern thinking is and how our campaigns need to realign." The draft was the basis for the document being used by Sierra Club BC to guide the organization's future work. ▲

*British Columbians are showing that it is possible
to protect the environment and provide the economic foundation for healthy communities. This
innovative rainforest agreement provides a real-
world example of how people and wilderness can
prosper together.*
    —Lisa Matthaus

10

The Great Bear Rainforest

PETER MCALLISTER, WHO WAS CENTRAL TO A NUMBER OF IMPORT-
ant rainforest conservation campaigns on Vancouver Island in the
1980s (as discussed in chapter 5), turned his focus in the 1990s to
the forested watersheds in First Nations territories along the north
and central mainland coast of British Columbia. He was concerned
that timber companies operating far from the public eye were taking advantage of the growing controversy in Clayoquot Sound and
remembered all too well the flotillas of giant logs from his days at
Island Tug and Barge. An unpublished report by Keith Moore, *An
Inventory of Watersheds in the Coastal Temperate Forests of British Columbia*, had caught his attention and provided motivation. The data indicated that Vancouver Island had only four unlogged watersheds over
five thousand hectares, whereas the central coast still had close to a
hundred rainforest watersheds that size. These precious areas were at
risk but few among the general public knew about them.

McAllister paid to get the report published and took it with him
when he and his crew sailed north to the central coast in 1990. He
had decided that the best approach to making the region known to

the public was to explore and survey the coast to document the state of the forests—undertaking what would become known as the Raincoast Expeditions. With a small conservation team, McAllister sailed along the central coast, stopping to trek through the forests to film and document as many forest valleys as possible. He also conducted aerial surveys in a Cessna 172 outfitted with a wing-mounted camera. Spread over a number of years, these Raincoast Expeditions explored thousands of kilometres of rugged coastline north to the Alaskan border and documented hundreds of rainforest valleys under threat from logging. In 1994, McAllister named the large wild areas of BC's central coast, the "Great Bear Wilderness." Later his son, Ian, morphed this designation into the "Great Bear Rainforest" (GBR) and extended its reference to the entire central and northern coast.

The first voyage was aboard the famous three-masted, 17-metre sailing ship *North Star of Herschel Island*, captained by Sven Johansson, an Arctic navigator. Later the 15.5-metre *Pyacket I*, the sister ship of one owned by Walt Disney, was used to explore the area. McAllister gathered journalists, prominent conservation biologists, film crews, and wildlife photographers from Europe, the US, and Canada. Through their lenses and the outpouring of articles and documentaries, the outside world learned of the region's extensive ecological richness and cultural heritage. Also on board were a number of Sierra Club members, as well as McAllister's young son, Ian, working as a deckhand and learning first-hand the challenge of conservation campaigns and how to be a photographer.

The Koeye in the territory of the Heiltsuk First Nation was one of the first river valleys they investigated. McAllister was amazed by its abundance, noting, "You could almost walk across the salmon during the migration. And the grizzly bears all over the place!" He described trails along the river where it appeared the bears would "literally put their paws in the same print as the bear before them so over thousands of years you have these [deep paw prints]"—gesturing that they were about twenty centimetres deep.

This 18,625-hectare watershed, virtually unknown to the outside world, was on Macmillan Bloedel's shortlist for clearcutting. Upon his return to Victoria, McAllister presented to the Social Credit

Members of the newly formed Sierra Club BC campaigned for fourteen years before achieving success in protecting the beautiful Skagit River Valley from flooding. *Source: www.ihikebc.com*

Tsusiat Falls is a favourite view for photographers along the West Coast Trail. Lobbying for the inclusion of the trail within Pacific Rim National Park was one of SCBC's first major campaigns. *Photo by Jens Wieting*

Scenic sandstone cliffs and a rock shelf are on display at low tide on the West Coast trail. SCBC published a popular guide to the trail in 1972 that sold over 30,000 copies, with all royalties going to the club. *Photo by Jens Wieting*

Sharon Chow canoes across Hobiton Lake, one of the three lakes in the Nitinat Triangle that the Victoria group was able to save from logging. *Photo by Bo Martin*

A decade after the successful Nitinat Triangle campaign, Ken Gibbard (on the left) and a companion help to clear the trail to Hobiton, one of the three Nitinat lakes. *Photo by Bo Martin*

Sea lions bask on the rocks near Sombrio Beach along the Juan de Fuca Trail. After more than twenty years of campaigning by the Victoria group, the trail became a part of Juan de Fuca Provincial Park in 1996. *Photo by Bo Martin*

Botanical Beach at the north end of the Juan de Fuca Trail is renowned for its tide pools. In 1982 the Victoria group and others successfully negotiated the beach's purchase and management by BC Parks. *Photo by Caspar Davis, www.flickr.com/photos/heronsong/sets*

A vibrant ecosystem, the Botanical Beach tide pools teem with a variety of sea life. *Photo by Caspar Davis, www.flickr.com/photos/heronsong/sets*

Brian Pinch hikes along one of the many beaches of the Juan de Fuca Trail. An active SCBC member for over forty years, Pinch dedicated himself to the "far from glorious" but vital work of developing the group's board and management teams. *Photo by Diane Pinch*

The SCBC denounced a contentious plan to build a mine at Cream Lake in Strathcona Park, BC's first provincial park. Nine Peaks is visible in the background. *Photo by Brian Pinch*

Sharon Chow hikes up a peak on Haida Gwaii. SCBC was among the organizations recognized by the Commission on National Parks and Protected Areas for working "tirelessly" over a thirteen-year period to preserve the area. *Photo by Bo Martin*

An aerial view of Clayoquot Sound reveals large tracts of intact coastal rainforest. *Photo by W. C. Barnes/Tofino Photography*

Elders of the Haida Nation gather for a potlatch held in celebration of the South Moresby agreement. LEFT TO RIGHT: Dempsey Collison (Skidegate), Allan Wilson (Tiian), George Wesley (Cumshewa), Ernie Wilson (Skedans) *University of Victoria Archives*

scbc campaigner George Wood, pictured here in the Tsitika Valley in 1981, worked diligently for many years to protect its forests. *Photo by Bo Martin*

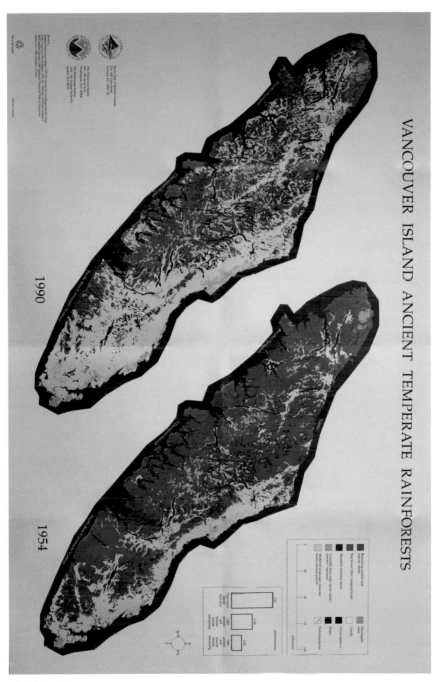

Dave Leversee produced contrasting maps showing the decrease in old-growth forests on Vancouver Island from 1954 to 1990. These maps were published in 1993 in poster format. *Photo by Brian Pinch*

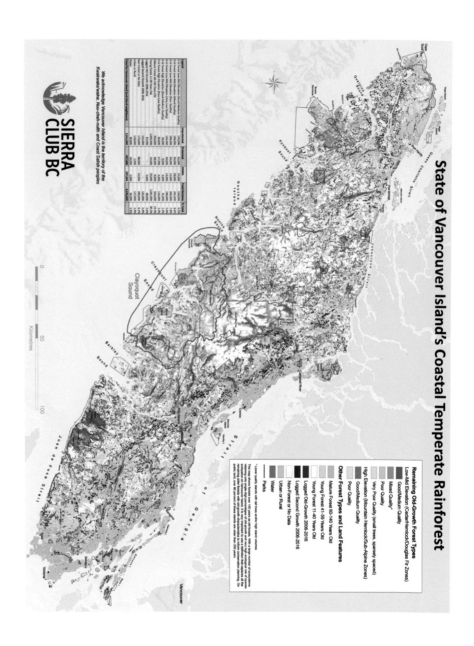

In 2018, Sierra Club BC published this map to show the state of Vancouver Island's ancient temperate rainforest and called it the "White Rhino Map." *SCBC Photo Files*

An orca whale swims offshore of a clearcut slope on the coast of Vancouver Island in the 1980s. scbc has been instrumental in raising public opposition to clearcut practices and campaigning for better forest management. *University of Victoria Archives*

Jens Wieting takes an aerial shot of logging clearcuts on Vancouver Island in 2018. *Photo by Jens Wieting*

This photo of the Klanawa Valley on Vancouver Island was taken in 2013 after it was logged. *Photo by TJ Watt*

SCBC campaigner Mark Worthing stands beside the cedar tree known as the "Leaning Tower," found in the Walbran Valley. *Photo by Torrance Coste*

Limestone Lakes is a majestic hike in Height of the Rockies Provincial Park. After two years of hard campaigning by SCBC and others, the area was designated a Forest Service Wilderness Area in 1987 before becoming a provincial park in 1995. *Photo by Brian Pinch*

In 1977, SCBC members Sharon Chow (on left) and Laura Porcher take advantage of one of the club's outings to explore the South Chilcotin mountains. SCBC helped negotiotiate for the protection of the area before it became a provincial park in 2010. *Photo by Bo Martin*

The mountains of the Chilcotin region feature some splendid panoramas. *Photo by Jens Wieting*

The Flathead River, one of the last wild gravel-bed rivers in Canada, is considered by many to be the heart of the Rockies. SCBC continues to advocate for the protection of this biodiverse ecosystem. *Photo by Garth Lenz, ILCP*

The Spatsizi River runs through the Spatsizi Plateau Wilderness Provincial Park. It has been described by some as the "Serengeti of Canada" due to its diversity of wildlife. *Photo by Gail Ross*

Sierra Club BC continues to advocate for the protection of the Peace River Valley from further damming at Site C. *Photo by Louis Bockner, www.louisbockner.com*

The 2017 Paddle for the Peace featured a blow-up "white ele-phant"—symbolizing the club's view that building the Site C dam involves excessive monetary and environmental costs. *Photo by Louis Bockner, www.louisbockner.com*

Sierra Club BC campaigner Galen Armstrong, participating in the 2017 Paddle for the Peace, displays a sign regarding the govern-ment's promise of reconciliation with the First Nations. *Photo by Louis Bockner, www.louisbockner.com*

The Kitlope watershed contains one of the largest continuous tracts of coastal temperate rainforest in the world *Photo by John Kelson*

An aerial shot provides an impressive view of the Great Bear Rainforest, one of the largest intact temperate rainforests remaining in the world (an area of roughly 12,000 square miles). *Photo by Andrew S Wright, www.cold-coast.com*

The "spirit" or Kermode bear—a rare subspecies of black bear born with white or cream fur due to a recessive gene—is found only on the central and north coast of BC, highlighting the importance of preserving this habitat. *Photo by Sherry Kirkvold*

Humpback whales have been making a comeback along the western coast, which was one of the factors impelling Sierra Club BC to launch a suit in 2014 to try to ensure their habitat remains intact. *Photo by Daryl Spencer*

SCBC's suit on behalf of the humpback whale was successful. The judge called the government's failure to implement the Species at Risk Act along the proposed Enbridge pipeline part of an "enormous systemic problem." *Photo by Sherry Kirkvold*

The various players involved in the negotiations celebrate the Great Bear Rainforest Agreements in 2006. *Photo by Jeremiah Armstrong. © Moresby Consulting Ltd.*

Douglas Channel, one of the principal inlets on the central coast, holds Kitimat (at the head of Kitimat Arm), the site of the proposed terminus for the Northern Gateway oil pipeline—officially rejected in 2016. *Photo by Caspar Davis, www.flickr.com/photos/heronsong/sets*

First Nations people and others rally to protest against Enbridge's proposed Northern Gateway pipeline in 2015. *Image by Wayne Wordan*

Orca whales are social animals and travel in pods. These particular ones were seen off the coast of the Great Bear Rainforest region. *Photo by Sherry Kirkvold*

The Cowichan group was inspired to campaign to protect the endangered Vancouver Island marmot and was eventually successful in establishing an ecological reserve in 1987. Here a juvenile marmot bonds with its mother. *©Jared Hobbs, Hobbs Photo Images Co.*

Wolves roam the central coast of BC where their diet, consisting primarily of seafood, is quite different from their inland cousins. SCBC pushed for an ecosystem-management scheme when it participated in the Wolf Working Group in the 1980s. *Photo by Sherry Kirkvold*

The Haida Gwaii group worked hard to protect the habitat of the northern goshawk. *Photo by Steven Garvie*

The Conservation of Marine Biological Diversity and Species Abundance on Canada's West Coast: Institutional Impediments

Groundfish: A Case Study

A Report by Terry Glavin
for the Sierra Club of British Columbia

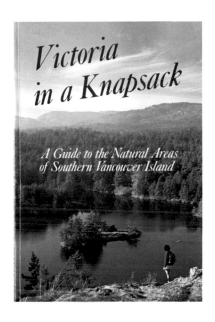

Victoria in a Knapsack

A Guide to the Natural Areas of Southern Vancouver Island

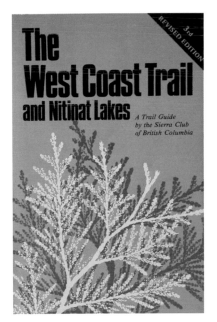

REVISED 3rd EDITION

The West Coast Trail and Nitinat Lakes

A Trail Guide by the Sierra Club of British Columbia

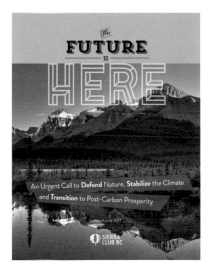

The FUTURE IS HERE

An Urgent Call to **Defend** Nature, **Stabilize** the Climate and **Transition** to Post-Carbon Prosperity

Updated June 2017

SIERRA CLUB BC

Sierra Club BC produced a variety of books and reports. *Top left and bottom right from SCBC photo files, others by Diane Pinch*

Is the Lower Mainland Going Under?

Global warming has already triggered a rise in sea levels that could reach 6 metres.[1]
We have 20 years to reduce carbon emissions or climate change will become irreversible.[2]

全球变暖可能令温哥华海平面升高

For SCBC's 2006 climate change campaign, Dave Leversee generated a map of the Lower Mainland indicating what would be under water if the average temperature increased two degrees. *SCBC Photo Files*

A rally against grizzly bear hunting was held at the BC legislature in 2009. *Photo by Moira Chaudhry*

A grizzly bear successfully captures a salmon on a beach in Bute Inlet, the site of a SCBC campaign to prevent a run-of-the-river hydroelectric project thought to be too large and devastating to the area. *Photo by Caspar Davis, www.flickr.com/photos/heronsong/sets*

Environmentalists, including many Sierra Club BC members, attend the Stand Up For What You Love rally on Valentine's Day, 2017. *Photo by Kat Zimmer*

Partners with the Rainforest Solutions Project assemble at the Koeye River in the Great Bear Rainforest in October 2011. LEFT TO RIGHT: Jens Wieting (SCBC), Jason Phillips (RSP), Eduardo Sousa (Greenpeace), Audrey Roburn (RSP), Suzanne Hawkes (facilitator), Valerie Langer (Stand.earth), Jenny Brown (TNC), Rachel Holt (RSP), Chris Allnutt (RSP), Caitlyn Vernon (SCBC), Chuck Rumsey (RSP). *Courtesy of Jens Wieting*

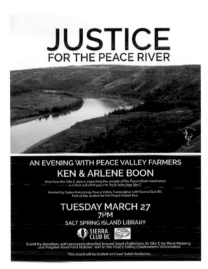

Sierra Club BC created posters to advertise many of its events. *All photos from SCBC Photo Files. Top left ©Wendy Shattill, iLCP*

Supporters for an oil-free coast rally at the BC legislature in 2014.
Photo by Michael Beach

A variety of sea life including colourful sea stars, sea anemones and mussels is found along the shores of Clayoquot Sound. SCBC campaigned for protection of the area, which was designated a UNESCO biosphere in 2002. *Photo by Jens Wieting*

While living in the ocean, sockeye salmon are blue with a tinge of silver, becoming a brilliant red and green when they return to their spawning grounds. Protecting salmon has been a perennial concern for SCBC. *Photo by Andrew S. Wright, www.cold-coast.com*

Sierra Club BC staff of 2018 enjoy being out in nature. BACK ROW, LEFT TO RIGHT: Jens Wieting, Amira Maddison, Summer Goulden, Tim Pearson, Lynn Bakken, Caitlyn Vernon, Galen Armstrong, Liz Reed. FRONT ROW, LEFT TO RIGHT: Maureen Yao, Britton Jacob-Shram, Mark Worthing, Kat Zimmer, Hannah Askew, James Davis, Roxanne Le-Goff, Kirsten Dallimore, Elisabeth Hazell. *SCBC Photo Files*

The 2011 education team used a variety of methods to stimulate children's interest in nature. LEFT TO RIGHT: Galen Armstrong, Meg Banavage, Kieran Dowling, Nadine Lefort. *Photo by Nori Sinclair*

The Sierra Club BC board of directors meet in 2012. BACK ROW, LEFT TO RIGHT: Caspar Davis (Victoria Group), Mike Bell (Comox Group), Doug McArthur, Rob Mitchell, Shirley Frank (treasurer). MIDDLE ROW, LEFT TO RIGHT: Elaina Konoby Sinclair, Gail Riddell, George Heyman (executive director), Stan Tomandl, Judy Leicester (Quadra Island), Patricia Molchan. FRONT ROW, LEFT TO RIGHT: Karen Palmer, Patricia Lane, Tim Thielmann. *Photo by Nori Sinclair*

SCBC volunteer canvassers provide information about the benefits of saving old-growth forests. LEFT TO RIGHT: Sarah Royston, Thea Melliza, Inder Dhaliwal. *Photo by Brynne Morrice*

SCBC Education staff person Kirsten Dallimore encourages students from South Park Family School in Victoria to hug an old-growth tree, demonstrating to them in a tangible way how big these trees really are. *Photo by Brynne Morrice*

With the 2017 ban of grizzly bear hunting in BC thanks to efforts by Sierra Club BC and many other organizations, this juvenile grizzly bear can rest easily in the Great Bear Rainforest. *Photo by Ian McAllister/Pacific Wild*

SCBC members gather at the legislature to present a petition to the government demonstrating the amount of support there is for protecting old-growth forests. *Photo by TJ Watt*

Grizzly bears drag salmon into the forest before eating them, which helps transfer vital nutrients such as nitrogen, promoting healthier soils and broader plant diversity. *Photo by Sherry Kirkvold*

government a fisheries officer's environmental assessment, endorsed by Sierra Club BC and the Wilderness Committee, proposing that the Koeye be protected from development. In 1991, the government agreed to make the Koeye a study area, deferring any logging activity. It later became a Protected Area Strategy study area—a designation developed when BC committed, in 1993, to doubling the protected land base by 2000—and remains one of the classic wild rivers of the GBR, the very first to be protected in the long campaign to follow.

While McAllister was doing this, the club became aware of another important area, the extensive Kitlope watershed, which terminates in the Kitlope River estuary at the head of the Gardiner Canal, north of Bella Coola. It was considered to be the largest continuous tract of coastal temperate rainforest in the world—with no history of logging or other industrial development.[152] Logging leases were granted to West Fraser Timber in the early 1990s, which prompted environmental agencies, including Sierra Club BC and the Haisla First Nation, to start lobbying for its protection. The company relinquished its lease in 1994 and the province established a protected area around the Kitlope in 1996 and a conservancy, co-managed with the Haisla Nation, in 2008.

Meanwhile, McAllister continued to explore the coastal valleys. He acknowledged that they had a lot of fun along the way: "Oh, boy, we ate well. I know that an army marches on its stomach." He recalled having a couple of journalists from the editorial board of the *Chicago Tribune* join him one summer on a sailing excursion. It turned out that they were also the food editors, and not only did they enjoy the food, according to McAllister, "they did several fantastic stories."

He also found it helpful to explore the area by air. In this endeavour he was aided by Mike Humphries, who was in his seventies at the time and had been a World War II fighter pilot. With the help of filmmaker Doug Cowell, cameras were attached to the wing of Humphries's Cessna, allowing the photographers in the plane to film both the clearcuts and the beauty of the central coast. McAllister incorporated much of this rare footage into documentaries that were broadcast internationally.

McAllister believes that making films was his best lobbying tool. They "put together some fantastic documentaries" of the Great Bear Rainforest, he said. At that time, there were no computers and no internet, but McAllister found other ways to distribute the films to a wider audience. Some won awards at film festivals and were shown on public television.

One documentary, *Legacy*, was especially well received, in part because of its juxtaposition of devastating clearcut images with the sound of David Darling's haunting cello score. The film, edited by Bill Weaver, also included captions that presented industry and government statements that ran counter to the images shown, such as logging companies insisting they no longer practised clearcutting despite obvious evidence that revealed the clearcutting was ongoing. McAllister also presented slide shows throughout North America and in Europe. He remembers sometimes introducing his slide shows with a ten-minute clip that had people crying before he even started to talk.

McAllister also remembers that, in the 1990s, the central coast First Nations groups varied considerably when it came to deciding whether or not to trust him and his environmentalist companions.

Nevertheless, he realized early on that it was important to seek their cooperation to achieve environmental goals. In 1993, McAllister organized a "sort of economic summit" with one of the First Nations, the Heiltsuk, and what he described as a "delegation of mostly old Sierra Club friends representing business, conservation, and forest management led by Ray Travers [a registered forester]. Filling the high school auditorium with almost the entire community of Bella Bella, an historic dialogue carried on for two days, covering ecologically sensitive economic development and ecotourism, all aimed at helping the Heiltsuk help themselves in taking back their ancestral lands from the timber industry." McAllister commended Larry Jorgenson, a respected community member, for playing a significant role in improving Sierra Club BC's relations with the Heiltsuk.

Although a lifelong member of Sierra Club BC, McAllister decided to found a separate organization in 1993, the Raincoast Conservation Society, to act as a flagship for the Great Bear Rainforest campaign. Establishing an organization separate from Sierra Club enabled him to strategize the campaign the way he thought fit and to endorse methodologies such as boycotts, which were not an accepted Sierra Club tactic. He continued to contribute articles to the *Sierra Report* and presented slide shows to the Sierra Club BC membership. McAllister also travelled throughout North America and Europe to gain international support for the cause. Here at home, it became obvious that Sierra Club BC had an important role to take on and the club became a key player in protecting this vast area.

After the Clayoquot campaign began to wind down in 1995, other environmental groups became involved with the GBR campaign, such as Greenpeace International, the David Suzuki Foundation, the Rainforest Action Network (RAN), the Natural Resources Defense Council, the Audubon Society, and the Wilderness Committee. Sierra Club retained a key role as well, lobbying and negotiating with various levels of the government and other parties as well as educating the public. Greenpeace and RAN helped spearhead the boycott campaigns, euphemistically called the international markets campaigns.

The GBR campaign was innovative and complex. It involved a number of stages with several coalitions and threads that meshed together to produce the end result. Rather than focusing on trying to preserve a well-defined region by advocating for the establishment of a park, environmentalists also took into account those dependent on the forest industry and the First Nations whose traditional lands represented a significant portion of the land base.

Just as it had in other regions in the province, the government set up a land use planning process (Land and Resource Management Plan, LRMP) on the central coast. Merran Smith, who had been hired by Sierra Club BC in 1996, recalled that although the club had participated in many of the other LRMP processes, it had recently made the decision not to participate in these particular planning talks until they were structured differently. The provincial government was working under the premise that a total of 12 percent of the land base in the region would be protected, as per the Convention on Biological Diversity accord signed by Canada at the 1992 Earth Summit (discussed in chapter 5).[153] As a result, the government expected that given that there were already some big chunks of protected land in the region, such as the Koeye and the Kitlope, only another 6 percent needed to be protected.

Sierra Club BC, on the other hand, thought the negotiations should start afresh without those kinds of expectations. Smith explained that the club teamed up with Greenpeace and ForestEthics and "we really stood our ground in a way I think hadn't been done . . . it had been done on Haida Gwaii when the First Nations first stood up for protection. It had been done in different ways and this was just the next step forward."

At first, the forest sector ignored their non-participation, however Greenpeace had launched a market campaign—Don't Buy BC Wood—that was growing in Europe and would expand later to the US. When companies such as Home Depot came on board, agreeing not to buy wood products from endangered forests, there was a change. The tipping point happened when a group of European publishers travelled to BC to see for themselves what was happening. They told the forest industry that they were not being told the truth about the logging practices, and advised the environmentalists that they should participate in the negotiations and work things out.

This started a whole new era of negotiation. Several of the forest companies and pulp and paper businesses allied to form the Coast Forest Conservation Initiative in 1999. As well, with the support of Tides Canada, three of the environmental groups—Sierra Club BC, Greenpeace, and ForestEthics—formed a coalition known as the Rainforest Solutions Project. These two collaborations joined in negotiations to form the Joint Solutions Project, an attempt to develop a fresh perspective on how to deal with the long-simmering conflicts over coast temperate rainforests.[154] News of this collaboration made it onto *Time* magazine's "Best of 1999" list. In a CBC radio interview, Charles Alexander from *Time* described the forestry companies' agreement to step back from logging a number of critical areas, and to negotiate with the environmentalists, as a very encouraging story. He went on to say that it was because of the innovative approach being used that they picked it as the best environment story of 1999.

Merran Smith was voted to be the one to go in and talk at the table—as she explained, "because I was the only one who owned a suit at the time." Smith recalled a lot of yelling back and forth, resulting in the mediator walking out of the room for half an hour. "Years later I said to him, 'Why did you do that? We were just yelling at each other. It was going nowhere.' And he said, 'Yeah, you guys had to do that. You had to get through that. You had to spew.' Smith recalled that the meetings reminded her of being in Central America when the "Guatemalan military police would have these shields that they would put up, these plastic shields, and I would feel like we would put up our shields and they would spew words. It would be like bullets across the table and they would just fall. They wouldn't touch us. And then we would put ours down and we would *stch-stch-stch*, fire back at them."

The meetings had an interesting gender and power dynamic, as the environmentalists were mostly women in their thirties and the other side consisted of senior, corporate men in their fifties and sixties. "You really had to mentally go in there and prepare yourself with your shield. But it really helped me understand the power of language and, you know, it was fun. We could trigger them. I could watch myself. I could trigger them, set the whole meeting on fire just by using certain language. Or I could actually try to talk the language that they could understand. And I'd say what we really learned, what I really learned, was listening to them."

Rather than just countering the other side with a negative statement, Smith learned to ask the question, "Why can't you?" When given an answer that made sense, she was left with problem solving another way of handling the situation. Her team shifted from making demands to trying to solve the problem. Of course, the environmentalists were more motivated to change the dynamic. But they also realized that they had power as the wood and pulp and paper buyers were backing them. However, they were not backing them to just sit at the table making demands; they wanted the problem solved. This required creativity. Smith said, "More importantly, you have got to keep making the pie bigger. If this is what we're stuck on, we have got to make the pie bigger; make it bigger; make it bigger. So, where can we find a solution for you that is not the thing that we are gridlocked on? The solution is going to lie somewhere else. It was very interesting, very creative, and we came up with solutions and it wasn't just the logging companies that we had to listen to."

The Great Bear Rainforest is home to over twenty First Nations groups and by 2003 several of these groups had allied to form a common front to negotiate with the government—the Turning Point Initiative, later known as Coastal First Nations. Other First Nations groups coalesced into the Nanwakolas Council. In 2004, the province and the amalgamated First Nations groups began their first-ever government-to-government deliberations.

The First Nations convinced those at the Joint Solutions table that it was important to have meetings in the communities, where they could actually see for themselves what they were talking about. In this way, they could go to the sites they were discussing and address the feasibility of the suggestions. For example, the loggers could see that a particular slope was actually too steep to build a road on, so that area could be protected. On the other hand, the environmentalists could agree that heli-logging in another area would not impact the fish-bearing streams, so even though they did not want to have an area logged, they could agree that logging it would not impact the values they were concerned about.

The First Nations were also at the bargaining table. She found that the communities made her think about and discuss issues in a way foreign to her way of thinking. She described their conversational style as being very inclusive and noticed that they took the time to think things through, both the particular decision under discussion and the consequences over generations. When told by the government that a problem had to be solved within a month, their reaction was, "If we do not solve this in a month, we have time. No one can pressure us to . . . make an ill-informed decision because somebody has put a timeline on it."

Smith found that the answers and the approach that they were looking for was much more holistic. This led to people feeling frustrated. "They weren't sitting and participating in the way that they had been structured to do. That whole structure didn't work for them for different reasons than it didn't work for us in the environmental community." Smith concluded that "everybody was going through a real learning process." Eventually the participants got past the anger, past the yelling at each other, past the demands on all sides, and were able to sit down and listen.

It became apparent that in order to have the First Nations onside, it was important to deal with their economic concerns. There were few well-paying jobs for them outside of the resource-extraction sectors. After some research to understand the scope and scale of conservation funding needed to support communities, environmentalists came up with the creative solution of raising $120 million to kick-start First Nations businesses and allow them to do conservation management. Smith recalled, "You know, at the time people said we were nuts. They just laughed at us. That's just crazy. But we did it. You know why? Because there was such a vision. And the thing that was so powerful about the Great Bear Rainforest was that you could paint that picture of conservation, protection of rainforest, protection of wildlife, of salmon, and the spirit bears, and the grizzly bears, and the whales, with communities living with economic development and those communities becoming healthier. You could paint that picture. You could take people up there. They could see it."

Because of this tangible and optimistic vision, philanthropists

Salmon is a major source of food for bears—in this case, a spirit bear. *Photo by Andrew S. Wright, www.cold-coast.com*

wanted to invest their money in the region and be part of making something both exciting and sustainable. Smith said, "People were part of this picture and it was going to be done in a way that was healthy and environmentally sound. People got excited. It was a black time in the US with George Bush and stuff. So, that was part of the success and the people in the Great Bear Rainforest, they were powerful speakers. It was not just a vision of the environmentalists; it was a vision owned by the First Nations and even the logging companies eventually came to see that it was worth doing something differently there."

The framework was agreed to in 2001. It involved the deferral of logging in the hundred intact valleys and other key ecological areas; a team of independent scientists to guide the process; a commitment to the "new" approach of ecosystem-based management; a $35 million financial package to assist workers and contractors impacted by logging deferrals, while agreeing to diversify resource use and attract new capital to support the protection of biodiversity; and the signing of a government-to-government protocol agreement between the province and the First Nations groups with traditional territory in the GBR areas.[155] A moratorium on further logging was put in place while talks proceeded.

For several years, Sierra Club BC paid an outreach worker to work directly with some of the First Nations communities. Claire Hutton replaced Robin Hood in 2003. While others were trying to negotiate a framework integrating social, economic, and ecological factors that would satisfy all parties, Hutton did a lot of the background work to help ensure the success of these proposed solutions. At the time that Hutton started, Guardian Watchmen programs were beginning to be established. The communities told her that they needed more people on the water and on the land to monitor what was happening. She had forged a connection with Larry Jorgenson, an important person in the Heiltsuk Nation's territory in Bella Bella and a close Sierra Club BC connection since his early meeting with Peter McAllister. Jorgenson runs an organization called Qqs (the Heiltsuk word for "eyes," pronounced "kucks") Project Society, so named because the program is designed to open the eyes of young people to their responsibility as stewards of their environment and culture. Sierra Club BC provided some support to Qqs for their summer science and culture camp for youth.

Jorgenson and Hutton decided to look for funding to bring together people from the various coastal First Nations communities who worked in some monitoring capacity as Guardian Watchmen—the eyes and ears on their lands and waters. They were successful and organized an initial Guardian Watchmen meeting. Out of this initial meeting came a clear need and desire to build a network of people working on the ground as guardians. The participants also identified more organized training and certification as essential, which resulted in a Guardian Watchmen training program being developed by coastal communities and delivered by Northwest Community College in later years. The initial meeting also led to the development of the Coastal Guardian Watchmen Network, which brought together on-the-ground staff from First Nations throughout the GBR. The network grew and evolved over time and still exists today, providing support, training, and coordination for First Nations' Guardian Watchmen programs.

Ecosystem-based management (EBM) was a term used in the GBR agreements, but when Hutton asked the people in the communities who worked at a technical level in resource management about EBM, they were unclear about the term and what it actually meant. "It became apparent that a lot of people who were working on issues to do with land use and resource management for their own nations didn't always have a clear idea about the implications of the agreements or the specifics of how they would roll out and be implemented. The agreements had been negotiated by the political people but the actual people who were responsible for the on-the-ground work were not always in the loop."

She recognized that, "it doesn't matter how great your agreement is if people in the communities are not on board and don't fully understand the agreements, or don't have the technical capacity to implement the agreements that have been negotiated at a political level . . . what's it going to be in five years, ten years? It's going to be an agreement on paper, not change on the ground." It became clear to Hutton that it would be beneficial to have some sort of forum for resource people in the field to get together for learning sessions about what ecosystem-based management involved.

Hutton was instrumental in starting a series of forums, which were later continued by Caitlyn Vernon when she replaced Hutton. Hutton discussed a presentation at one of the first forums, later coined the EBM Learning Forum. The complex GBR agreements had involved a long process, with many steps to achieve the final results. In order to help clarify them, Hutton thought it might be useful to present it visually as a puzzle. "We made all the components of the deals, what had been signed with the province, and when. There was a plethora of documents and agreements and deals and processes and bodies that were overseeing things. So, we put each one on a square piece of paper and painted the entire wall with it. We played a Vanna White–type game show. And for years, people would say 'Where's the EBM puzzle? We want to see the EBM puzzle again. Can we play that game show?'"

After Merran Smith left Sierra Club BC in 2001 to work for Forest-Ethics, Lisa Matthaus took over her role with the Rainforest Solutions Project (RSP) at the negotiation table. Smith continued to participate but was now affiliated with ForestEthics instead of Sierra Club BC. All of the participants involved in the negotiations had recently reached an agreement to hire a group of independent scientists, known as the Coast Information Team (CIT), in order to get past the issue of whose science should be used. The three groups—industry, government, and the environmental agencies—each contributed a million dollars to hire the science team, to be co-chaired by the provincial government and First Nations, making this one of the first government-to-government pieces in the negotiations. If negotiators had science questions that needed to be answered in order to make well-informed land use decisions, the CIT responses would be accepted by all sides as the relevant science—a leap of faith on everyone's part. The team also developed the *Ecosystem-Based Management Planning Handbook*.

The environmentalists had a long list of valleys that they thought should be protected, while industry and government continued to be convinced that 12 percent was the right amount of protection and thought the scientists would agree. Matthaus said, "They must have believed that. They put their money in; we all basically put our money in the pot to see what would come out."

Surprisingly, the conclusions of the team of scientists were that not only were the environmentalists right, they were more right than they had thought. The scientists concluded that more valleys had to be put on the list to be protected, because there were not enough to maintain the ecological integrity and sustainability of the region. "The government and companies were pretty stunned," Matthaus recalled. "It was that kind of external validation that helped keep a lot of us going through some really tough times."

A consensus land use decision for the central coast was achieved on February 7, 2006, protecting one-third of the region—2.1 million hectares—from logging and shifting forest management to the new ecosystem-based management approach across the other two-thirds of the region. Merran Smith described it as the "most comprehensive conservation achievement in North American history."[156] Sierra Club BC—along with Greenpeace, ForestEthics, the BC government, the First Nations and the forestry companies—received the World Wildlife Fund's Gift to the Earth award in June 2007 in recognition of the innovative conservation achievements.

Jens Wieting replaced Matthaus in January 2007, for the implementation phase, which was expected to be completed in three years, by 2009. Little did he know when he began that it would actually take nine years to finish the job of fully realizing the vision announced in 2006. He was able to get up to speed relatively quickly thanks to the other experienced team members—Jody Holmes, previously with Sierra Club BC and now employed by the RSP, and Valerie Langer, with ForestEthics, who had been involved with the negotiations from the beginning. Eduardo Sousa, with Greenpeace, joined a little later, in 2008. Caitlyn Vernon joined Sierra Club BC shortly after Wieting and took over Hutton's work with the First Nations, building capacity for implementation and monitoring of ecosystem-based management in the region. Wieting's job involved a lot of travel between Vancouver and Victoria because Sierra Club BC had its office in Victoria and the offices of the other organizations, including the RSP, were in Vancouver.

The RSP team decided that in order to successfully reach full implementation by 2009, they needed a work plan with a clear set of milestones to provide both accountability and transparency, and to ensure everyone understood the timeline that was involved. As well, the need for some kind of watchdog mechanism led the team to create a website called Great Bear Watch. They negotiated a series of sixteen milestones with the logging companies in order to meet the agreements' goals of ecological integrity, community well-being, and sustainable forestry. Once these agreements with industry had been reached, they were shared as recommendations in talks with the BC and First Nations governments, which had asked industry and environmental groups for joint input as stakeholders, knowing that a negotiated proposal would be much more helpful than receiving conflicting perspectives.

Although the agreements were announced in 2006, it was not until 2009 that all of the 2.1 million hectares of new protected areas were formally protected through legislation. Among these were more than one hundred new conservancies, a new protected-area designation that honoured First Nations traditional uses while still protecting the landscape. Commercial logging and mining are prohibited in these areas and the generation of hydro power is limited to local run-of-the-river projects. As well, harvesting of fish and wildlife requires a valid permit.[157] Another seven hundred thousand hectares of rainforest were set aside from logging under the "lighter-touch" ecosystem-based management approach,[158] and by March 31, 2009, the legislation for their protection was enacted. This step, combined with stricter logging regulations, meant that half of the region's rainforest was off-limits to logging. These finalized agreements between the provincial and First Nations governments were made with the proviso that further planning and negotiations were required to ensure support for the communities' economic and social well-being in the region. It took another seven years to fulfill this proviso, and to meet the goal of setting aside 70 percent of the region's rainforest.

Even then, there was still further work required. The three environmental groups and the industry representatives struggled to agree on details such as the additional conservation steps that were required for wildlife habitats in the area, among other interim precaution management requirements. These steps were supposed to be in place during the five-year period between 2009 and 2014 (the year all had agreed to move to 70 percent of the land being under low ecological risk management). After extensive unproductive talks, the two groups changed course and decided to focus their energy on increasing protection to 70 percent sooner, thereby avoiding expending energy on interim solutions. This resulted in a huge amount of technical work, reviewing a myriad of different scenarios. Wieting described this process as "trying to square the circle, i.e. figuring out how to move from about 50 percent of land that was off-limits to logging to 70 percent" while still allowing logging to take place in parts of the region. In early 2014, the environmentalists and industry were able to share a proposal with the province and First Nations. It took another two years of review and modifications to finally reach the 2016 Great Bear Rainforest agreements.

The insistence of the environmental organizations that the science-based conservation recommendations needed to be fully implemented turned out to be critical for keeping pressure on the BC government. This was particularly important when Premier Gordon Campbell—who had been fully behind the implementation of the agreements in 2006—was replaced by Premier Christy Clark, and pressure was required from the environmental groups and the public to regain the government's commitment.

Wieting pointed out that the Great Bear Rainforest agreements are important not only in themselves but also for providing a science-based conservation model tied to a regional framework, including socio-economic benefits for communities, Indigenous and non-Indigenous, agreed to by provincial and First Nations governments, and supported by environmental organizations and the logging industry. The model can be used by communities in other parts of the province to reach similar agreements incorporating ecosystem-based management plans that take into account human well-being while respecting nature's limits. Using this approach allows communities to combine conservation targets with their intimate knowledge about a particular area in order to propose which forests need to be protected—such as ones holding significant cultural or ecological value—rather than leaving it to industry and government to make decisions based primarily on economic factors.

In 2016, the intensive campaign to protect this rainforest culminated with the signing of the historic Great Bear Rainforest agreements. The environmental groups involved in the process—Sierra Club BC, Greenpeace, and Stand.earth (formerly ForestEthics)—won two prestigious awards, the US Sierra Club's Earthcare Award and the Buckminster Fuller Institute's Buckminster Fuller Challenge Prize, for the precedent-setting and innovative collaboration. It was described as a "paradigm shift" in being able to respect Indigenous rights while also conserving forests for future generations. That same year, in the course of a royal visit from Prince William and Catherine, the Duchess of Cambridge, the Great Bear Rainforest was included in the Queen's Commonwealth Canopy Initiative, launched in 2015 as a means of promoting the protection and use of best practices in forests throughout the Commonwealth.

Merran Smith: Innovative Strategist

Merran Smith completed a degree in biology at the University of Victoria. Through her studies and volunteer work with organizations such as Society Promoting Environmental Conservation, she came to realize it is not a lack of science but rather a lack of political will that is preventing the world from making necessary changes. This new understanding prodded her to join Sierra Club BC while she was at university.

After completing her degree, she travelled to Central America where she and her partner at the time, Mike Simpson, made videos for agencies such as CUSO and Oxfam that did not have the capacity to make their own. While there, she was able to see first-

Merran Smith. *Courtesy of Clean Energy Canada*

hand "the impacts of this aggression and the arms trade and the US foreign policy which was leading to these wars, Nicaragua, El Salvador, Guatemala, just brutal wars and torture. And just saw how, as North Americans, how much impact we could have by publicizing this." Smith said she did this work "until my heart just couldn't take it anymore."

Through her work in El Salvador, she met Ricardo Navarro, who ran the Salvadoran Centre for Appropriate Technology (CESTA was its Spanish acronym), which was trying to build an environmentally sound and just world using simple, sustainable technology such as pedal power and composting toilets. "It was just a very positive, optimistic project. People in the face of extreme poverty and such harsh conditions were doing fantastic things and working to make people's lives better."

When Navarro was brought to Canada by a group of Jesuits for a speaking tour, Smith joined him. She found him to be very inspiring. "His country is in disastrous shape and trying to work with a war going on . . . He wore a bullet-proof vest for months at a time, depending on whether his name was on the list of the people to eliminate. And he just had such a sense of humour." Navarro's optimistic, positive approach encouraged Smith and Simpson to form a partnership through Sierra Club with CESTA to create the GAIA Project (see chapter 3).

When Smith became involved with the Great Bear Rainforest, she found it to be unique and one of the few places like it left in the world. She contrasted Canada with Central America and thought, "We have a democratic society. There's no war; we are so rich. If we can't protect this, who can? We have every ability to protect this," adding, "that really drove me. I just felt that if we can't succeed here, how can you expect them to succeed in the Amazon rainforest or Madagascar or these places that we think are also so important. They've got poverty and war and corruption, things like that to deal with. We've got to figure out how right here." She hoped that perhaps they could create a model that could be emulated in other places in the world. She now realizes that this prospect was idealistic but it was that idea that started her on the decade of working to protect the Great Bear Rainforest.

In 2006, Smith ended her role with the GBR after the signing of the land use agreements and received the Wilburforce Foundation Conservation Leadership Award for her work. Smith felt her time was done and took time off to start her family. She finally had time to read the stack of books by her bedside, some of which led her to become concerned about the dangers of climate change and to make a decision about what she needed to work on next.

In our interview, Smith discussed the recent formal announcement of the 2016 Great Bear Rainforest agreements, twenty years after the negotiations had first begun, and what a compelling lesson that is for how long it can take to get things done. It was another story of the power of having both a vision and optimism. However, Smith does not think there is the same kind of time available for dealing with climate change. She believes that environmentalists need to start figuring out the solutions and building relationships now so that they are poised to proceed when the time is ripe. This idea motivated her to start her organization, Clean Energy Canada, a climate and energy think tank based at Simon Fraser University that works on advancing clean energy and climate solutions, such as renewable energy, clean electricity, clean transportation, and carbon pricing. In

2014, she received the Clean 16 award for leadership in clean capitalism. At the time of writing, she was co-chair of the NDP government's Climate Solutions and Clean Growth Advisory Council.

Smith tries to be relentlessly optimistic. The tactics and the leverage required are different from that used in an environmental campaign concerning a particular place. She pointed out that a huge piece has to do with economics. For example, solar and wind prices have dropped, making these options more price competitive. As well, China has become a big player. Such factors are the drivers for clean energy. Electric vehicles, as well, are going to become more prevalent as prices drop and the technology improves. Smith indicated that, although the climate campaign is different in many ways, there is still the same need for a vision and that in the last year or two, there has been a lot of progress. Hopefully, her pragmatism, creativity, and optimism will continue to get results. ▲

Lisa Matthaus: Environmental Economist

Lisa Matthaus grew up in the small BC coastal town of Sechelt and worked in Toronto after obtaining a commerce degree majoring in finance. She quit her job to go travelling. A trip to Africa in 1990 improved her understanding of the environment's role in society and the economy. While working in a bank in London, England, she found out about a relatively new program at University College London. She applied, and was accepted, for a master's degree in environmental and resource economics. After graduating in 1995, she returned to Sechelt to work on a project for the Federation of BC Naturalists, now Nature BC, helping her get a handle on coastal environmental issues.

She began her job at Sierra Club BC a month before Bill Wareham became the first executive director. "At that time, Vicky was still a driving force behind what was happening and there was good media access as well as access to the government." Shortly after Matthaus started, a brown envelope was dropped off at the office. It contained information related to the Vancouver Island Land Use

Plan and showed that the government intended to compensate MacMillan Bloedel for turning some of their tree farm licences into parks, even though this was public land and they did not own the trees. Worse, the government was going to privatize other public land and use that as the compensation!

With the help of Will Horter from Sierra Legal Defence (now Ecojustice) and Jessica Clogg from West Coast Environmental Law, Sierra Club BC wrote a press release and broke the story. At that point, Matthaus had not yet had any media training and, in fact, had previously said that she did not want to be involved with the media. She changed her mind because she was so mad.

This led to the major BC Land is Not for Sale campaign. At public meetings, they were able to embarrass the NDP government of the day with publicity about its plan to give away public land to logging companies. The NDP called for a public process and hearings were held around the province with hundreds of people declaring their stand against the idea. In the end, the government compensated MacMillan Bloedel monetarily. Matthaus was still angry but at least they had not lost the land.

Matthaus, along with some other environmental groups, worked on another large issue, the softwood lumber dispute between Canada and the US. The Canadian softwood industry had managed trade deals with the US in 1986 and 1996, and the one in 2006 was the third. "We took the perspective that BC *does* subsidize its logging, at least in part. This is largely because of the kinds of policies that we have that do not require strong, good environmental practices, which makes it cheaper to log. So, in a way, this is a subsidy. Also, there is the way that we set stumpage through a negotiation between the companies and government rather than a market-set price."

The Liberal government, headed by Gordon Campbell, had campaigned with a platform of cutting subsidies. Sierra Club BC published a report authored by Matthaus and Tom Green, an ecological economist, called *Cutting Subsidies or Subsidized Cutting*, in 2001. It discussed the various ways that forestry in BC is subsidized and the policy changes needed to get rid of those subsidies.

Lisa Matthaus speaks with the media after the announcement of the Great Bear Rainforest agreements, February 7, 2006. *Photo by Jeremiah Armstrong. © Moresby Consulting Ltd.*

Sierra Club BC and several other environmental groups tried to talk to both the BC government and the Canadian government negotiators about the various policy changes that would help solve the problem with the American logging industry and give BC a healthier industry. "We would have more log markets; it would be more market driven; and it would have a lot more space for value-added industries rather than just being the afterthought on the side, which is what it has always been in BC." The Canadian negotiators refused to talk to Matthaus and her colleagues; however, the Americans were interested in listening to their arguments.

After the negotiations ended and a softwood lumber deal was finally written up, Matthaus was fascinated to see that it contained some of the environmental groups' key suggested policy changes. Although the government did not go as far as they wanted, there was a 20 percent tenure take-back, the biggest take-back since the tenure system had been set up. As well, there would be something more akin to a market price to which stumpage would be attached. The province established more licences, giving some to communities and First Nations. Nevertheless, companies were again compensated for the tenure, which is a form of subsidization.

In 2001, Matthaus took over Merran Smith's role with the Great Bear Rainforest negotiations. Matthaus described Smith as a highly motivating force as well as very strategically nimble, and she found Rainforest Solutions Project to be an effective and supportive team. Matthaus credited two Sierra Club BC staff members, GIS mapper Dave Leversee and Claire Hutton, who had started working with the First Nations, as being key to SCBC's role in the GBR. In addition, Matthaus found that the faith of the funders helped to sustain them.

After five years of hard work, the GBR land use agreements were finalized in 2006. "There was a signing ceremony in Vancouver with Gordon Campbell on stage with RSP [the three environmental groups] representatives and First Nations, along with the logging companies and other table reps." Media, including international journalists, were present. "I got my name misspelled in *Pravda*, the Russian newspaper." Matthaus received the Wilburforce Foundation Award for Outstanding Conservation Achievement and, in 2007, the Sierra Club of Canada Gary Gallon Award.

When Matthaus returned after a break, she found that Sierra Club BC had started to focus on addressing climate change, an issue that was also starting to be recognized by the BC government. It was as if, as she put it, Gordon Campbell had "discovered climate change." She became involved with Sierra Club BC's climate change campaign and, in particular, she advocated for a carbon tax. In addition to the Great Bear Rainforest outcome, Gordon Campbell's announcement of a carbon tax was a significant highlight for her.

Two weeks later, in 2006, Matthaus left Sierra Club BC to travel to India for a year. Upon her return, she began working for a non-profit group called Organizing for Change. The organization started in the early 2000s as a project of several environmental groups, including SCBC, to demonstrate that strong environmental values exist across BC's political spectrum and that British Columbians expect elected officials of all political stripes to deliver credible and effective environmental policy. ♠

Claire Hutton: First Nations Outreach

Claire Hutton's educational background in biology and environmental science, along with significant experience with community development, was welcomed at Sierra Club BC in 2003. She became their First Nations outreach coordinator and, for six years, she was involved with organizing much of Sierra Club BC's practical, hands-on, innovative work with First Nations communities in the Great Bear Rainforest at a time when negotiations between the BC and First Nations governments and industry were moving forward.

Hutton was born in Australia, and moved to Vancouver when she was six. She grew up in an environmentally conscious family, spent a lot of time outdoors when she was young, and went to an alternative high school. She took a program in comparative development studies, focused on international community development, at Trent University in Peterborough, Ontario. The program included a year of work experience at a biological research station in Ecuador and, upon her return, she changed faculties, graduating with a degree in biology and environmental science. Following graduation, Hutton returned to BC where she worked for two years with the Ministry of Environment, travelling around the province providing day-long environmental programs, focused on ecology and consumer habits, for children in grades 4 to 7. In 1999, she enrolled in the Resource and Environmental Management Program at Simon Fraser University. She had a strong desire for her research to be practical and useful, and because of her interests in community-based forestry and monitoring, her thesis advisor suggested working with the Cowichan Tribes on Vancouver Island to develop a community-based forestry policy. Her work in community development, combined with her environmental science and biology background, served her well. During the project, over 150 Cowichan people were interviewed about their values related to forests to try to capture what a forest policy for the Cowichan Tribes should entail.

This type of information, never gathered previously, was very innovative. Conversations with such a large number of First Nations people in one location had not been done before. Topics included how forests are used, why community members value forests, important things that should be considered, and how the Cowichan people wanted their forests managed. This work would eventually become the focus of Hutton's thesis.

Hutton worked with the Cowichan Tribes as a forestry and environmental advisor for about three years. Jill Thompson, having met Hutton previously and been impressed by her skills and background, encouraged Hutton to have an interview at Sierra Club BC when she found out that Hutton was leaving the Cowichan Tribes. The job description intrigued Hutton and she accepted the offer. Hutton soon had an opportunity to join a trip with some of the Great Bear Rainforest negotiators who were travelling there by boat. It was an amazing introduction to a beautiful area.

Afterwards, Hutton went to Bella Bella on her own and in Klemtu she introduced herself to people in the community by arranging meetings and, in some cases, knocking on people's doors. She came away realizing how complex the situation was and wondering what she had gotten herself into. Some people she met were not interested in speaking with someone from an environmental organization. One person said to her, "You think that you can just put our people behind a fence. We're not animals. You can't cage us up in your 'parks.' We have already agreed to put aside [a portion] of our territory." Although she was taken aback by this reaction, she realized it was best to just listen to understand more fully what people's experiences were and where they were coming from.

After synthesizing the conversations, she found that two themes emerged from these initial community visits. The first involved the importance of engaging youth, and the second centred around the Guardian Watchmen programs that were just beginning.

Sierra Club BC had an education initiative delivering programs in schools, and Hutton wondered whether it was possible to adapt some of these programs for First Nations communities in the GBR. They received some funding to adapt the curriculum to make it more relevant for the First Nations' schools. Bella Bella had a fairly big school where they did some workshops with teachers and piloted lessons with students. That later led to developing a teachers' guide to non-timber forest products and the value of these products in the First Nation communities.

Hutton played a role in the development of the Coastal Guardian Watchmen Network and eventually, she decided that the network needed her full-time attention. She left Sierra Club to devote her energy to the project. It had switched over to being run by the Coastal First Nations, although the Sierra Club continued to be a partner. Caitlyn Vernon took over Hutton's job with Sierra Club BC.

Claire Hutton. *Photo © Melody Charlie*

Hutton said she felt really grateful to meet and work with many First Nations practitioners and community members during her time at Sierra Club BC and beyond. Many of the young people Hutton had met when she first started have over time taken on key roles in their communities. "They were always amazing and as the years have passed, just seeing them come into their own, in terms of leadership in their communities, their knowledge, clarity and incredible commitment . . . These young people are in leadership roles now."

For a number of years, Hutton coordinated the Coastal Guardian Watchmen Network, which expanded into an entity called the Coastal Stewardship Network. In 2013, she left to work for TNC Canada (now known as Nature United) as their community conservation and leadership advisor, supporting First Nations as they assert their authority to manage and steward their lands and waters. "So my job now is certainly still very linked to the work that I did at the Sierra Club. I feel like I have been so lucky to work with and learn from the communities that I've worked with. It's an evolving continuum and an exciting time as First Nations assume their rightful role in stewarding their territories." ♠

We envisage a world in which people live and prosper in a way that protects, restores, and heals the natural systems of our planet.
                                    —Colin Campbell

11

The Use of a Climate Change Lens

AS SIERRA CLUB BC ENTERED THE TWENTY-FIRST CENTURY, IT WAS transitioning from a volunteer-run agency to one employing a full complement of professional staff able to run well-coordinated, complex campaigns. Finding adequate funding to support these staff and campaigns was an ongoing challenge. Kathryn Molloy became the club's second executive director in 2003, at a time when the club had overextended itself and was having difficulty finding adequate funding to cover expenditures. Despite that fact, she and the club achieved some notable successes.

For ten years prior to taking on this position, Molloy had worked in a variety of ways to advocate for the need to address climate change. She continued to do so when she joined SCBC. She was surprised to find that none of the environmental groups she worked with had a significant climate change program in place. Sierra Club BC did have the GAIA Project with its Sustainable Living Bus and a small volunteer committee led by Bo Martin, but she thought there needed to be more. She remembered saying at an Organizing for Change meeting,

"I think this is the most pressing issue of our day and none of us is talking about it and none of us have it on our campaign programs, not for the future, not now."

Efforts to Educate the Public about Global Warming

ALTHOUGH SCBC DID NOT HAVE A FULL-ON CLIMATE CHANGE CAMpaign, it was one of the first environmental groups in BC to try to understand and address the effects of global warming thanks to one of its volunteers, Bo Martin, who worked to steadily highlight the issue throughout the 1990s and into the mid-2000s.

In 1988, Martin had become very concerned about global warming and decided he needed to learn more about the issue. He took two years of coursework in climatology at the University of Victoria, leading to a master's degree. Once he achieved his objective, Martin decided there was no point spending further time doing a thesis and left without a formal degree. He was able to use this expertise not only in his volunteer work with the Sierra Club but also with various task groups and committees set up by the Capital Regional District and the province. Under the auspices of Sierra Club BC, Martin participated in Capital Regional District planning sessions, contributed to various provincial committees, attended BC Hydro hearings, and generally worked hard to promote public awareness.

In a series of articles produced for the *Sierra Report* in 1997, Martin predicted changes that we are now experiencing: "winters will be wetter, while summers will get drier and warmer temperatures will increase evaporation making the key growing season even drier. The natural variation in year-to-year weather superimposed on top of the change will make winter/spring floods, summer droughts, and heat waves that much worse during some years. It is predicted that both the frequency and intensity of winter storms will increase, as will summer thunderstorms with accompanying lightning, wind and hail . . . With more precipitation during winter and spring, floods will become worse, snow melt will occur earlier and storms will be more intense."[159]

An Expanded Climate Change Program

KATHRYN MOLLOY, ALONG WITH A DEDICATED BOARD MEMBER, Patricia Lane, worked with the Sierra Club BC board and staff to build upon this promising beginning to develop a climate change agenda and embed it throughout the Sierra Club BC strategic plan. By the mid-2000s, Sierra Club BC began to frame conservation and environmental issues with a "climate change lens." This meant, practically, that it would address the effects of climate change directly through lobbying and public education, while also ensuring that all Sierra Club BC campaigns involved the promotion of strategies to mitigate damage caused by climate change. The wording of Sierra Club BC's mission statement was altered to read that it would "protect, conserve, and educate the public about BC's wilderness, species, and ecosystems, within the context of climate change impacts."

Moreover, the club's understanding of the environment was evolving to also include those who inhabit the environment, especially those who rely on resource harvesting for their livelihood and the First Nations who require that land use plans take socio-economic and cultural factors into account. A vision statement was revamped to read: "An ecologically sustainable province, which integrates human and economic activity, while conserving the province's wilderness and biodiversity values."

In 2006, Sierra Club BC prepared a detailed scientific background paper with a map showing the Lower Mainland areas that would be under water if sea levels rose by six metres, which was predicted on the basis of a two-degree increase in annual temperature. Sierra Club BC used the map for a postcard campaign, asking people to sign the cards and send them to the provincial government. Molloy and Colin Campbell went to a Richmond press conference with umbrellas and a paddle—the top of the paddle showing how high the water would reach. They were able to attract a lot of media, including Chinese-language media in Richmond.

A similar map of the Greater Victoria region was also generated. These two maps caused a great deal of discussion in the media, especially the map showing the effect of a twenty-five-metre rise in sea level in the metropolitan area of Victoria, which last happened when the earth experienced a two- to three-degree rise in annual temperature during the Pliocene era about three million years ago.[160] Public reaction was mixed, with some feeling that such a prediction was overstated and verged on scare-mongering, but Lisa Matthaus emphasized that "this is what we are heading for if we continue with 'business as usual' levels of greenhouse gas emissions."[161]

Many considered 2007 to be a tipping point, with public awareness of the need to acknowledge and confront climate change becoming widespread. Davis Guggenheim's Academy Award–winning documentary, *An Inconvenient Truth*, about Al Gore's climate change education campaign, received so much international acclaim that it resulted in Gore (and the Intergovernmental Panel on Climate Change) winning the Nobel Peace Prize that year. In a message from its executive committee, Sierra Club BC emphasized that "as almost everyone now agrees . . . global warming is the most urgent issue of our time."[162] In 2007, Sierra Club BC co-sponsored Al Gore's visit to Victoria for a public event that generated much local publicity. The club also instigated Sierra House-Cooling Parties and Sierra CERCles (Carbon Emission Reduction Clubs) to encourage networking, discussion, and lifestyle changes.[163]

Molloy thought that Sierra Club BC and Organizing for Change played a part in convincing then premier Gordon Campbell to bring a climate change agenda to BC: "Patricia Lane, once I turned her on to the whole climate change thing, she would just inhale books about it to the point that I couldn't keep up with her education on it anymore. So, she would write me book reports, which I would then send to Gordon Campbell, with the book." A close friend told Lane that "the best thing that ever happened . . . was when Campbell went to Hawaii and had a wake-up moment when he read Tim Flannery's book" *The Weather Makers*, and asked her to thank whoever sent it to him.

Molloy was thrilled when Gordon Campbell's Liberal government brought in a climate change agenda in 2007. In past years, it was not always easy to obtain a seat in the legislature's bleachers for the Throne Speech, but this time she was invited by Gordon Campbell's office, through Environment Minister Barry Penner, to be present on the floor. "I was seated behind the NDP caucus so I was looking right at the Liberal caucus, watching as the speech was being made, and I remember thinking to myself I could have written parts of the speech . . . I never felt so validated . . . I also noticed I was being watched, particularly by Barry Penner, the minister of environment, on how I was reacting. I mean, I was beaming . . . Although Gordon Campbell may have done a lot of things that I would not agree with, that was, in my view, his shining star that he gets to take away, the legacy that he left on the climate change agenda in British Columbia. Hence every municipality, every official community plan in this province has to have a climate action plan in it. And that was part of his legacy and I'm delighted with that."

In the Throne Speech, Campbell's government pledged to reduce BC's greenhouse gas emissions by at least 33 percent below current levels (10 percent below 1990 levels) by 2020.[164] A Climate Action Team would be established to identify ways to make the government of British Columbia carbon neutral by 2010. A new energy plan would be developed to enable British Columbia to become electricity self-sufficient by 2016 and reduce greenhouse gas emissions from the oil and gas industry to 2000 levels by 2016. Zero flaring would be allowed at producing wells and production facilities. At least 90 percent of electricity would come from clean, renewable sources and British Columbia would become the first jurisdiction in North America to require 100 percent carbon sequestration for any coal-fired project. It went on to discuss improvements in transportation and automobile standards, methods to encourage alternatives to fossil fuel use and other climate action strategies.

Promoting the Idea of a Carbon Tax

ALTHOUGH THE GOVERNMENT HAD ANNOUNCED A RANGE OF intentions to reduce greenhouse gas emissions in the 2007 Throne Speech, there was no budget to back that up. This did not happen until 2008, the following year. Lisa Matthaus recalled that two or three months prior to the budget announcement, Carole Taylor, the finance minister at the time, had mused on the radio about the possibility of a carbon tax. Matthaus thought it would be helpful for a person with an economics background to speak about it with some degree of knowledge. "It was really exciting to be one of the leading voices to say this was a good idea and it would be good for BC and good for the economy. If it is done in a revenue-neutral way, it is not a tax grab and it is not a cash grab." She volunteered to speak to the media in the lead-up to the budget. During a 7:00 a.m. interview on the CBC Vancouver morning show the day of the budget announcement, she said, "I recall debating someone from the Fraser Institute on CBC and while I was feeling so grounded in why a carbon tax made sense for BC, the Fraser Institute guy didn't seem that well prepared. I think they probably did not believe it would actually happen."

Later that day, Matthaus was included in the budget lock-up. Sierra Club BC was given only one invitation so she did not have a media person with her. As she recalled, "You get there at 9:00 in the morning and you open up the package with the press release that they are going to put out and then all the detailed stuff. I just remember reading the press release and—Oh my god—a carbon tax!"

Under the rules of the budget lock-up, no external communications are allowed—no phones, no Wi-Fi— until the budget is introduced in the legislature mid-afternoon. Attendees use that time to review budget documents, ask questions of government officials, prepare media releases, and, at the very end, stakeholders (like SCBC) and media come together for a free-for-all.

Matthaus wrote what would be the only environmental media release in the lock-up, including her own quotes. As she described it, "The wall separating stakeholders and media is rolled away and I am there holding up the Sierra Club logo as I walk out—Oh my god, I have the full scrum . . . They are asking all these questions and I have my talking points and my press release. I am madly trying to hand that out and trying to keep my talking points straight. At the same time, I am trying not to cry. I was so excited. Canada's first carbon tax! So, as an economist, it is not surprising how attached I am to that." Matthaus said she was almost in tears as she spoke on camera.

"And apparently, the BC government loved that; they used the media clip for years."

Seven years later, Clare Demerse of Clean Energy Canada interviewed several of the people involved with implementing the carbon tax, including Gordon Campbell and Carole Taylor. Those interviewed agreed that "the provincial economy enjoys stronger economic performance than the Canadian average. Carbon pollution is down, and so is per capita fuel consumption."[165] Many of the people interviewed gave Gordon Campbell credit for having the strength and conviction to implement the carbon tax. It was his decision to ensure that it was revenue-neutral. Carole Taylor told the interviewer, "I wouldn't pretend that everybody in the party thought it was a good idea. But there was strong leadership from the premier and myself—so they didn't love it, but they accepted it."[166]

In 2018, the BC government's implementation and Sierra Club BC's support for a carbon tax was endorsed when economist William Nordhaus became the co-recipient of the Nobel Prize for economics. As a result of his work concerning the interaction between climate and the economy, Nordhaus became a proponent of a carbon tax as being the most efficient way to reduce damages caused by climate change.[167]

The Notion of a Carbon Budget

COLIN CAMPBELL WROTE WELL-RESPECTED PAPERS DEALING WITH climate change issues during his time at Sierra Club BC. "Cliff Stainsby and I did a paper on climate projections for BC.[168] Andrew [Weaver] helped enormously by doing various runs of UVic's climate model for us. And it became, as Jens said at my retirement party, one of the first public presentations of carbon budgets. This is how much carbon you can actually use if you do not want such and such to happen." Previously people had discussed it in terms of reducing carbon emissions by a particular percentage by a certain time (e.g., 40 percent by 2030). "Instead you can say that it is permissible to release, say, 800 million tons, and you have a century to use it."

Campbell continued: "Basically, what Cliff and I worked out was that if you want to limit global warming to two degrees, and if carbon is allotted equally to all living humans so we all have the same amount every year to use, it takes BC less than ten years to use up a century allotment at present rates of emission . . . We discussed the idea to partner with a jurisdiction, like Namibia, where they do not use much carbon. Then we could amalgamate our carbon budgets but the obligation to them would be the same as it would be to ourselves: to develop and share a low carbon technology and economy. It is a very idealistic notion but BC could share its carbon budget and that would bring their per capita allotment up and bring ours down. But at the same time, for that favour, we would have to bring them fully modern technology." This important paper was published by the Canadian Centre for Policy Alternatives. The last time Campbell had checked a few years ago, it had been downloaded more than 25,000 times.

BC Government's Climate Action Plan

ON DECEMBER, 5, 2018, THE BC GOVERNMENT RELEASED ITS CLIMATE action plan, which introduced a host of measures including increasing the carbon tax along with incentives to encourage a shift to a low-carbon economy. The plan is to cut 19 million tonnes of greenhouse gas emissions by the year 2030. The building code will be revised to ensure more energy-efficient structures and support for zero-emission vehicles will be provided. In a press release, Caitlyn Vernon from Sierra Club BC called the plan "an excellent step towards defending our communities from climate impacts and building a strong clean energy economy that works for everyone"[169] although she continued to decry the government's commitment to LNG development. The release went on to say, "The Clean BC plan details exactly how 75 per cent of B.C.'s 2030 carbon reduction target will be achieved, and sets out a timeline for detailing how the remaining 25 per cent reduction will be met in the next two years. There is no mention of how we will meet our future (2050) pollution reduction targets."

The government followed through by presenting a budget in February 2019 that provided the necessary funding—$902 million over the following three years—to implement many of the proposals in the action plan. The remaining reductions in greenhouse gas emissions required to achieve BC's long-term climate change target will require further initiatives that are still to be outlined by the government.

Sierra Club BC remains committed to doing all it can to advocate about the pressing need to address climate change. In the past decade, it has lobbied diligently for the need to keep fossil fuels in the ground (see chapter 8 for discussions about oil and gas issues) and the need to conserve old-growth forests as carbon sinks (see chapter 12). Climate change provides the context and motivation for the club's work, and the board and staff believe it remains the defining issue of our time. The club continues to be hopeful that we can make the changes that are necessary. Its website home page has the words, "Inspiring generations to defend nature and confront climate change, so families, communities and the natural world can prosper together."

Bo Martin: Our Global Warming Expert

Bo Martin grew up in Stockholm, Sweden, and lived there until he was nineteen. He moved to Canada with some reluctance when his father was transferred to Toronto in the late 1960s. After completing an undergraduate degree at the University of Toronto, he trained at UBC to be a town planner and obtained a job in Victoria with the Department of Municipal Affairs. Here he met and married Sharon Chow, who would also be involved with Sierra Club BC for many years in a variety of capacities, including serving as chair of both the Victoria group and the SCBC Chapter, followed by a paid position managing the chapter office.

Martin recalled the club having a strong outdoor activity and hiking component in the 1970s and '80s, with newsletters listing an extensive schedule of outings for each month. He especially enjoyed leading hikes to the Mount Washington and Mount Albert Edward area for three-day expeditions, where he introduced

Bo Martin (in the back) hiked in the mountains near Cream Lake in Strathcona Park in 1986 with (left to right) Leslie Gordon, Sharon Chow, Martin Davis, and Mike Dempsey. *Photo by Bo Martin*

"newbies" to their first winter camping experiences. His photography skills were a welcome asset to the West Coast Strip campaign, which eventually resulted in the formation of the highly popular Juan de Fuca Provincial Park. The club explored and flagged the trail while Martin documented it all with his camera. He had a big binder filled with slides, which he provided to the Capital Regional District (CRD) Parks Branch when they took over promoting the idea of a park.

He next became involved with energy issues, and one of his first concerns was a proposed oil port across the strait in Washington state. The club, with Martin's help, along with that of Greg Dharms, made a submission for the hearings. Martin and Dharms were very interested in learning about how the process worked.

Martin's interest in the structure and process of hearings also led him to volunteer to attend BC Hydro rate hearings that were addressing Hydro's use of declining block rates. "The more you used, the cheaper it was . . . We thought that was really wrong and that it should really be the other way around . . . I always remember at the

Sierra Club BC members rally to encourage Canada to ratify the Kyoto Protocol on Climate Change in 2002. *Photo by Bo Martin*

time how we were often not really taken seriously. There was a lot of condescension about the public coming in, a sense of 'You don't know how things are done.' And we didn't get very far but eventually it seeped through. First we had a flat rate and now it's an increasing rate, which is exactly what we wanted." The hearings required Martin to sift through huge masses of information. Some Hydro submissions consisted of five to seven volumes, sent to him by courier. "We often thought that that's part of the tactics—throw all these masses of paper—because we were all just volunteers."

Bo was particularly proud of his work with a CRD task group that resulted in the 1992 report called *CRD Healthy Atmosphere 2000*, with over one hundred recommendations for addressing climate change. One of the group's more controversial recommendations was a significant increase in gas tax, which unfortunately overshadowed everything else. Although the report resulted in little official recognition from the municipalities or the CRD, Martin thought it helped to raise awareness and influenced some politicians and staff, particularly in the planning department.

In the early 1980s, Martin became Sierra Club BC's representative on the BC Energy Coalition, which consisted of various groups from across the province. With Martin's help, the coalition developed various policies as well as an alternative energy plan for BC. The Sierra Club BC Climate Change Committee—often just Martin on his own—was quite active. It organized a few workshops, provided public talks to various groups in the community, helped BC Transit develop its green policies, and was also involved with the Victoria Car-Share Co-op.

From 1994 to 1995, Martin was a member of the BC Energy Council, which produced a provincial energy plan—it was progressive, but it was never implemented. In 1997 to 1998, he participated in the province's Greenhouse Gas Forum, which was made up of many of the major stakeholders in the province. The forum provided advice to the provincial government on climate change policies during the period leading up to the Kyoto agreement.

In the late 1990s and early 2000s, Sierra Club BC campaigned for ratification of the Kyoto Protocol. Sierra Club BC held a demonstration down by the Inner Harbour near where the environment ministers were meeting. "We trucked in a huge pile of snow to get visibility for it," said Martin. Eventually the Kyoto Protocol was ratified; however, Martin was disappointed by the lack of concrete changes agreed upon.

After three decades of service, this disappointment contributed to Martin losing interest in being an active member. Martin believes that climate change is not a grassroots, local issue but rather one that has to be dealt with at the global level. A carbon tax, for example, needs to be instigated across multiple districts to be effective. Martin has been a strong proponent of a carbon tax for a long time, and reflected, "At least now it's pretty well accepted and we have it here." ▲

Kathryn Molloy: Climate Change Champion

Kathryn Molloy, raised in Toronto as the eighth of nine children, did not become involved in environmental causes until she was in her early thirties. She started off working in accounting and began a degree in education, but she left it uncompleted when she was

Kathryn Molloy (in front on right with purse) joins Sierra Club BC staff (from left to right) Jenn Hoffman, Elizabeth Matthews, Ali Donnelly, Hannah Hermanek, Erin Destautels (in bear suit), Lisa Matthaus, Gagan Leekha, Pharis Patenaude, Colin Campbell, Ana Simeon, J Scott, Lindsay Hill, Kerri Lanaway, Jill Thompson, Micki Stirling, and Claire Hutton outdoors in 2005. *Courtesy of Peter Campbell*

headhunted to work for a small environmental organization called the EcoCity Society, begun by Tooker Gomberg and Angela Bichoff in Edmonton. They were attracted by Molloy's community activism in her neighbourhood.

This was 1993, and EcoCity Society was concerned about climate change, at that time more widely known as "global warming." One of her first tasks was to give a presentation on that topic at the next city council meeting. When she said that she knew nothing about global warming, they gave her a stack of publications she estimated was about 30 centimetres thick and told her that for the next week her job was to read them. "I became passionate about it. I don't even remember who the authors were at that time but I was very heavily influenced in my beliefs around what I would call now climate change because of my relationship with Tooker and Angela. So, that's how I started working in the environmental field."

At the time, Molloy was young with a lot of energy and really wanted to make a difference. She tried to understand as much as she could about the environment and the impact of climate change on ecosystems, food security, and international issues. After her presentation to Edmonton's city council, one of the councillors told her that he looked forward to global warming as "it's so bloody cold here all the time." More than two decades later, Molloy lamented, "It feels like everybody has got the climate change jargon in their language and it's discouraging for me that it's taken this long to get here, when now the language needs to be about adaptation."

Part of her contract with EcoCity Society involved setting up a green community in Edmonton, which linked her with Green Communities Canada. Guided by a diverse, multi-stakeholder steering community, she wrote a business case for Edmonton's Green Community Centre, which opened after she left for Victoria in 1995. She later sat on the board for Green Communities Canada and took on a leadership role for City Green in Victoria to get it off the ground. Her first job in Victoria was with the Coast Waste Management Association, where she dealt with wood waste and emissions related to the slash-burning after forests were logged, and the use of beehive burners.

At the same time, Molloy began to volunteer with the GAIA Project at Sierra Club BC and continued with the project for eight years. She went to El Salvador in 1999 with Mike Simpson (co-founder of the GAIA Project), Sandra Thomson (manager of the GAIA Project), and other climate leaders. The group helped write the International Declaration of Interdependence for Climate Change, which emphasized the need to work internationally and interdependently in order to solve the climate change problem.

Molloy constantly looked for opportunities where she could advocate for the need to address climate change and sustainability. When some federal funds became available for climate change issues, she applied for funding for a project called Youth in Media. In conjunction with the film and television production company Gumboot Productions, she ran two programs with sixteen youth from across BC to create television commercials on climate change's causes, effects and solutions. The commercials were an international success. They were aired on CBC as well as by other broadcasters and won international awards.

Molloy was involved in a number of other environmental projects. Her consulting company became the go-to company for organizing a conference that used environmentally sustainable measures, which led her to be chosen as the project manager for the International Children's Conference on the Environment held at the University of Victoria in 2002. Coro Strandberg and Molloy started Victoria's Values-Based Business Network, with the help of Brian Pinch, to try to get environmental and social values woven into the business sector. In 1996, she also volunteered with Guy Dauncey, Todd Litman, and Bo Martin to start the Victoria Car Share Co-op, and later became its first paid manager. The co-op still exists although its name has changed to Modo.

Following the departure of Bill Wareham, Sierra Club BC's first executive director, two staff members approached Molloy and asked her to apply. She was reluctant at first as there were significant management issues, but with further encouragement from Lisa Matthaus and Jenn Hoffman, she agreed, thinking it would be a great opportunity to work with these women—both intelligent, dedicated, and passionate about their work. She started in September 2003.

Molloy and Patricia Lane, who was on the board at that time, tried hard to make others aware of climate change concerns. As Molloy recalled, "Climate change itself is hardly a tangible concept. You can't taste it. You can't see it. It's not like dying marmots. It's not fuzzy and cute and it's not beautiful, pristine, iconic forests and mountains. It's climate change and it was really a tough sell."

Lane, a great moral and educational support to Molloy, met with her every week: "She was just such a hard worker. I could just give her things to do, tangible things that I couldn't get done in terms of educating and awareness. So, it was very, very valuable." Molloy was also convinced that Lane had been instrumental in convincing Carl Pope, the executive director of the US Sierra Club, to take on the climate change agenda. Molloy and Lane had

attended the Sierra Club Canada–us joint meeting outside of Halifax where they met with both Pope and the head of campaigns. "I
believe that Patricia's appeal to them was powerful enough that
they had to go look into it. Because of that . . . there's a multi-mil-
lion-dollar endowment now. They got it. And they might have got
it eventually but I really think it was Patricia that not only planted
that seed, but kind of hammered it in."

Because of her role at Sierra Club BC, Molloy was appointed
to the Board Advisory Committee on environmental sustainability issues for the 2010 Vancouver Winter Olympics. She believed
her presence was influential. Molloy recalled asking the sponsors
how they planned to offset the travel emissions associated with
attending meetings and the Games. "I'll never forget the guy from
Teck Cominco pulling out his calculator and coming back and saying, 'That's going to cost us this much money.' And I said, 'Yeah these
things cost money.'" Nevertheless, she was able to convince the various sponsors—Bell, Teck, Rona, and others—to make the commitment to offset their emissions.

After a six-year stint as executive director, Molloy left Sierra Club.
It had been a challenging time. Funders were having to pull back
because of the economic crisis and the climate change agenda was
still very difficult to fund. The federal Conservatives were in power
under Stephen Harper and Sierra Club BC was being audited regularly by the Canada Revenue Agency. She realized that stress was
exacerbating her health issues. "So I retired from Sierra Club and it
was a hard decision, hard to go. But it was a good decision, I think.
Probably I should have left earlier but I didn't want to leave when
things were in a precarious position and what do you do? But for my
own personal health reasons I had to leave." Soon afterwards, her
husband was diagnosed with cancer and she was glad not to have
that job stress in addition to caring for him.

Molloy returned to work for four years as the executive director
of People for a Healthy Community, a small social service agency on
Gabriola Island, and received the Queen's Diamond Jubilee Medal
for her work there. Then she became the executive director of Heritage BC, a charitable not-for-profit agency supporting heritage

conservation across the province. As with anything Molloy becomes involved in, she worked hard to incorporate sustainability and climate change into the goals of Heritage BC. Following her husband's death, Molloy retired and has been travelling around the world to new places as well as revisiting ones she shared with her husband in past years. ♠

Patricia Lane: Board Member Extraordinaire

Patricia Lane was born in Tanzania to Irish-born parents who were working for the British colonial civil service. When she was ten, they moved to Ontario, where she lived until her early twenties. She followed her father into law and did her degree at Osgoode Hall Law School in Toronto.

After moving to BC, Lane's roots in the labour movement led her to become the director of research at the BC Federation of Labour. Lane said she did not believe in the historic divide between the labour movement advocates and environmentalists—which suggested that a person could not be both, even if they thought the environment was really important—as she was not brought up that way.

Lane went to work for the Yukon government, negotiating the first framework agreement with twelve Indigenous groups in the territory. She returned to Ontario to work for the provincial government's Fair Tax Commission, "which was a public policy consultation . . . a gigantic mediation is what we were doing, with 100,000 people on the database. We were one of the first groups to use crowd-sourcing to build consensus, and we were certainly one of the first groups to use email as an organizing method." For the past twenty-five years, Lane has had a private practice as a mediator and arbitrator in Victoria. This combination of experience and skills was beneficial in her volunteer role with Sierra Club BC.

In 2006, Al Gore's climate change movie, *An Inconvenient Truth*, galvanized Lane's family. "It was really clear that we couldn't lead an ethical life and pretend that business as usual is still an option.

And so, we started talking about what we should do and one of the things we decided was that if we were going to start proselytizing then we better walk the talk." They were able to reduce their carbon footprint to almost zero except for their flying, which they ended up offsetting at above-market rates.

Lane recalled, "We did it by buying our way into low-carbon living." They replaced both their old cars with a Prius, which at the time was the lowest carbon emitting option, and began using their bikes much more. They

Patricia Lane and her husband, Malcolm Maclure, stand on their roof to display their solar panel.
Photo by Diane Pinch

made a deal with their son that they would give him a portion of the money saved from not using the car to put towards new bike clothes. They replaced the brand-new oil tank they had just installed in their home with two large heat pumps, along with solar panels on the roof. Unfortunately, they purchased the first wave of solar panels from a dishonest company and they did not work! "We had to buy new ones, so we paid for those solar panels twice . . . One of the take-homes from that for me was that the rich were going to be able to buy their way out of the climate crisis and the poor are going to be hooped."

Their son complained bitterly about having to bike to school with all his gear in the rain. One day he pointed out that if his mother gave him a ride not a single polar bear was going to live a day longer. Lane began thinking about the delusion of individual action and the imperative of system change. She became concerned that Sierra Club BC was not doing anything about climate change except for what was happening with the GAIA Project. She and Kathryn Molloy discussed it and decided that the club needed to put a "climate lens" on everything. Molloy took this idea to the board for approval.

"It wasn't a hard sell. And from that point on the club started shifting more towards addressing climate change."

Lane's son, Liam, also became involved with climate change education at Sierra Club BC. Borrowing an idea from George Monbiot, he and his mother created a PowerPoint presentation to tell the story of climate change and started giving presentations in their home, which they called Sierra CERcles. The idea was to bring together groups of friends, colleagues, or neighbours so they could be given information and a venue for conversation, along with the tools and support needed to reduce their carbon footprint. "You know we had one hundred people through our house. We had deputy ministers, ADMs, and doctors and lawyers and nurses and social workers and teenagers, and we tried to make it multi-generational. And I know doctors went out and bought different cars the next day. I know that teachers changed their curriculum and I know that deputy ministers took it back into government. It was quite a powerful model. It didn't take that much work." She found it to be a recipe that worked well. "I think that's always been a strength of Sierra's, to invite people together to learn something. And they just work, those kinds of events really work, so that was our own little version of it."

Lane had joined Kathryn Molloy in the legislature to watch the Throne Speech in which the government announced its list of intentions to address climate change. "[Inviting SCBC] might have just been a PR stand, like 'Oh look, we've got the Sierra Club on our side,' but I don't think so." She thinks it is because Sierra Club BC had played an important role in making Campbell aware of the need to take action on climate change. ♠

If there is something you can do, or dream you can, begin it. Boldness has genius, power, and magic in it.

—Goethe

12

Continued Need for Passion and Persistence

THE PREVIOUS DECADE HAD ENDED ON A HIGH NOTE WITH THE announcement of a climate change agenda and a carbon tax by the BC government. However, the years since 2009 required Sierra Club BC to draw deep upon its heritage of persevering despite setbacks, and on the knowledge that every two steps forward is followed by one step back. The world economic crisis of 2008 and the change in the Liberal government leadership from Gordon Campbell to Christy Clark in 2011 led to the government shifting its priorities from climate change to the economy and jobs. Instead of the clean energy projects that had been promoted, such as the run-of-the-river initiatives, Clark embraced the idea of building LNG ports, thus reverting to fossil fuels as a major source of energy. Clark's government also stopped further carbon tax increases and BC has failed to achieve the lofty goals proposed in the 2007 Throne Speech to deal with climate change.[170]

In the meantime, the club persisted with campaigns that have been described in previous chapters—trying to conserve important places such as the Great Bear Rainforest and the Flathead and the Peace river valleys; lobbying against unsustainable and destructive mining and forestry practices; and advocating for a movement away from fossil fuel use. Although there were important successes to relish such as signing the GBR agreements, stopping the Enbridge pipeline, ending mining in the Flathead and protecting Fish Lake, there continued to be substantial concerns with the onset of new fossil fuel projects and major disasters such as the Mount Polley tailings pond breach.

George Heyman replaced Kathryn Molloy as executive director in 2009, not long after the global economic crisis of 2008, and on his first day on the job, he had thoughts of quitting. During the meeting with the foundation board, he was informed that the foundation was in debt for a large sum. It was now up to Heyman, as the executive director, to turn the situation around.

He was able to stave off a snowball effect of funders pulling back on their support because of concern over Sierra Club BC's ability to survive. He spent a day with the funders explaining his background and how he planned to solve the problem. They decided to continue the club's funding but required quarterly reports. "One of the highlights for me was a year later when I was able to show a surplus and show some steps I'd taken to get debt relief. I managed to negotiate our way out of one of our debts and make some progress on another."

Under Heyman's direction, the SCBC board continued to endorse using a "climate lens" to focus campaigns. Campaigns advocated for alternative energy and sustainable forestry methods, and focused on protecting endangered species.[171] Greater biodiversity allows plants and animals to be more resilient when facing climate change impacts. For nearly a decade, SCBC had worked with Sierra Club Canada on a campaign advocating for a federal Species at Risk Act (SARA). Canada was obligated to take action eventually as a signatory to the multilateral Convention on Biological Diversity in 1992, and with prodding from Sierra Club and others, SARA finally became law ten years later, in 2002, and came into full effect in 2004.

The basic purposes of SARA are to prevent wildlife and other species from becoming endangered or extinct, and to provide for their recovery if they are threatened. It is important to be able to identify and protect critical habitat that a species needs to survive and recover, before it becomes too late. The federal government has exclusive jurisdiction for what are considered "federal species" (aquatic species and migratory birds) and for all listed species on federal lands (First Nations reserves, national parks, national defence property, etc.).[72] Heyman was able to announce in the 2009 annual report that in response to pressure from the Sierra Club, as well as a lawsuit launched by Ecojustice on behalf of the club and other environmental organizations, the federal government had issued an "unprecedented Order in Council that will provide legal protection for the orcas' habitat."

Even so, there were delays in enacting the legislation, to the extent that further legal action was taken. The Species at Risk Act provided the framework for contesting these delays, and court action was filed by Ecojustice for another case, representing Sierra Club BC and eight other agencies, in 2010 in federal court against the Department of Fisheries and Oceans (DFO) for failing to adequately protect critical habitat of BC's resident orca whales. In 2012, a landmark decision from the appeal court upheld the ruling that the federal government is legally bound to protect orca whales, thereby helping to ensure stronger legal protection for Canada's endangered marine species. Campaign Director Susan Howatt considered this win one of her highlights. "We went to court and we won. The federal court compelled the government to implement protection plans for orca whales. And our work is not done. The orca whales are still endangered. But I think we took a big step forward in really demonstrating that the public really wants this. I think there is a lot of identity around whales in British Columbia and our coastline."

The federal government continued to drag its feet in following through on its commitments, so Ecojustice launched another lawsuit in 2014 on behalf of Sierra Club BC and several other groups, claiming that the federal government's continued failure to implement the Species at Risk Act threatened the endangered southern mountain caribou, Pacific humpback whale, Nechako white sturgeon, and marbled murrelet along the proposed Northern Gateway pipeline and shipping route. The result was successful, with the judge describing the case as "just the tip of the iceberg" of an "enormous systemic problem" within the federal government, citing the fact that more than 160 species at risk across Canada were still awaiting overdue recovery strategies.

Provincial Species at Risk Legislation

IN 2007, SIERRA CLUB BC PRODUCED THE *ENDANGERED SPECIES TOOLkit* with a forward by Margaret Atwood, which provided a comprehensive look at the situation in British Columbia.[173] It outlined the nature of the protection available at that time, identified species that were at risk, and provided guidelines for the ways in which individuals could take action. The publication stressed that, although there was a federal Species at Risk Act, the act was only effective, where it was effective at all, in areas that were under federal jurisdiction. It pointed out that, although SARA could be extended to provincially controlled lands, this would only occur at the discretion of the federal environment minister. This had never happened, despite repeated requests from conservation groups—until May 2018, when Environment Minister Catherine McKenna declared there to be an "imminent threat" to the mountain caribou's recovery. It was the first step in forcing the provincial government to develop a conservation plan before the federal government stepped in.[174]

In the absence of stand-alone endangered species legislation in BC, many species continue to be at risk. As of 2018, there remained only the 1996 BC Wildlife Act, which recognizes only four species as endangered or threatened: the Vancouver Island marmot, the American white pelican, the sea otter, and the burrowing owl. The Wildlife Act is weak as it does not provide a mechanism for developing a recovery plan to protect habitats or counteract what is causing the species to decline.

Bob Peart receives the 2016 EarthCare Award from Sierra Club US on behalf of Sierra Club BC, one of the recipients, along with the other participants involved in passing the Great Bear Rainforest agreements. LEFT TO RIGHT: Michael Brune (executive director, Sierra Club US), Kelly Russ (chair, Coastal First Nations), Bob Peart, Aaron Mair (board president, Sierra Club US). *Courtesy of Sierra Club Awards Committee, Sierra Club US*

Despite not having provincial legislation to provide a legal means for the club to propel further protection, Sierra Club BC under Heyman's helm continued to pressure the provincial government. Campaigners advocated for the government to end the grizzly hunt and they worked with mayors and councillors around the province to gain municipal support for developing a strong law to protect species and ecosystems.

In November 2017, Green Party MLA Andrew Weaver introduced a private member's bill proposing a BC Endangered Species Act. The bill drew upon Ontario legislation with further development by the Wilderness Committee and Ecojustice. Although the bill died when the 2017 provincial election was called, the NDP government has promised to support this legislation and has launched a three-part series of public consultations.[175] In September 2018, as part of this process, Sierra Club BC and eight other environmental and animal welfare organizations sent a letter to the minister of environment and climate change strategy—now George Heyman—along with a comprehensive set of comments regarding the purpose of the law, guiding principles, recovery strategy, enforcement, and stewardship on private land. Advocating for the protection of biodiversity and endangered species remains one of Sierra Club BC's ongoing campaigns.

After Heyman left in 2012, Sarah Cox fulfilled his duties until Bob Peart was hired to replace him a year later. Peart was in this role from 2013 to 2017. Due to his extensive administrative experience within government and agencies such as the Canadian Parks and Wilderness Society, Outdoor Recreation Council of BC, and the Royal BC Museum, Peart realized that the club required a strategic plan to determine how to maximize its efforts. The club's board and staff continued to be committed to a climate lens to focus campaigns and with this in mind, a three-year set of strategic directions was laid out. The Great Bear Rainforest remained a core campaign and in 2016, Peart was able to herald the agreements as a major achievement for Sierra Club BC.

The completion of the GBR campaign allowed forestry campaigner Jens Wieting to advocate even more intensely about the strong link between poor forestry practices and climate change. He warned that, in a typical year, BC produces more than sixty million tons of carbon dioxide emissions, primarily from burning fossil fuels, and another fifty million tons through destructive logging practices that include slash-burning and clearcutting carbon-rich old-growth forests. A significant advantage of old-growth forests is their ability to store carbon much more effectively than younger trees.[176] Throughout the period of working on the GBR, Wieting had managed occasionally to carve out time to help raise awareness about climate change, the indispensable role of BC's forests in the fight against global warming, and the massive lack of conservation for intact forest ecosystems on Vancouver Island and in other parts of the province.

In 2009, Wieting and Sierra Club BC's mapper Dave Leversee produced a report on the state of BC's coastal rainforest[177] with detailed old-growth mapping and data. With his colleague Colin Campbell, he wrote the 2012 report *Emissions Impossible*, highlighting the full extent of BC's greenhouse-gas emissions when emissions that are often uncounted are also considered—burning BC fossil fuels abroad and destructive logging and slash-burning practices. His research showed that while beetle outbreaks and fires caused increasing harm to provincial forests, destructive logging remained the single biggest cause for forest degradation in BC from 2003 to 2012. These and other reports, press releases, and opinion articles garnered solid media coverage.

Wieting considers the ongoing clearcutting of old-growth rainforest on Vancouver Island, the south coast, and inland temperate rainforests to be an ecological emergency. The loss of these ancient giants has continued relentlessly on Vancouver Island at a rate of about 10,000 hectares per year in 2016 and 2017 (approximately two soccer fields per hour). The vast majority of productive old-growth rainforest on the island has been logged and replaced by young forest. A 2018 Sierra Club BC map entitled "State of Vancouver Island's Coastal Temperate Rainforest"[178] showed the scarcity of remaining old-growth rainforest ecosystems and recent old-growth destruction. With so little left, Wieting warned that it is only a matter of time before the logging industry runs out of old-growth trees to harvest and fully transitions to logging second-growth. Communities are facing hard choices as the forest ecosystems change alongside the climate. Revenue from forestry and job numbers from logging are both declining. At the same time, intact forests are becoming increasingly important for defending communities from climate impacts such as flooding, drought, and fire. They can also help diversify the economy and provide clean air, water, and habitat for species.

Wieting, together with SCBC's allies the Wilderness Committee and the Ancient Forest Alliance, has convinced more voices to speak up for better forestry practices and the protection of endangered rainforest. In 2016, British Columbia's Chamber of Commerce voted to protect old-growth trees in locations where they have greater economic value for communities if left standing. That same year, the majority of delegates at the Union of BC Municipalities convention voted to protect all of Vancouver Island's remaining old-growth forests on public land. Just weeks before the 2017 provincial election, twenty-five international environmental groups called on the next BC government to preserve all of BC's endangered old-growth rainforests.

Sierra Club BC was hopeful for change after the election because of the NDP's campaign promise to use the evidence-based approach of the Great Bear Rainforest as a model for managing the rest of BC's old-growth rainforest. Sierra Club BC and their allies quickly met with the new forest minister, Doug Donaldson, to share their thoughts and recommendations. They advocated that comprehensive steps for conservation and improved forest management for Vancouver Island must respect First Nations' rights and interests, enable a transition to sustainable second-growth forestry, support diverse economic activities such as tourism, and reduce carbon emissions. A year later no meaningful steps had been taken and in June 2018, 223 forest scientists wrote Premier Horgan urging him to follow through on the NDP's election promise.

Wieting also advocates about the importance of preserving intact coastal rainforests for large species such as wolves, bears, and cougars, which need vast areas to roam and maintain a healthy population through genetic exchange. Other coastal species such as marbled murrelets also depend on large, connected habitats to avoid becoming isolated. Climate change can affect salmon migration patterns and spawning cycles as summer and fall temperatures increase and drought lowers water levels in streams. For such reasons, it becomes even more important to maintain intact watersheds and forests to help mitigate the effects of climate change.

Addressing climate change was also at the top of Executive Director Bob Peart's agenda. He was especially proud of finding funds to enable Colin Campbell to produce his final legacy document, *The Future Is Here*, prior to his retirement. That document provided a strategic blueprint for Sierra Club BC's campaigns, allowing campaigners to frame conversations about pipelines and other projects in terms of why they are not the best option, what are better alternatives, and what we as a society should be doing instead. A condensed version of *The Future Is Here* is included at the end of this book.

Also during this period, the board realized that in order for Sierra Club BC to work more effectively it had to be better positioned to work with First Nations. At the end of 2014, Rob Mitchell, a Sierra Club BC board member, approached Hannah Askew, a lawyer with West Coast Environmental Law, to join the board. She had come to their attention because of her expertise with Indigenous law and the relationships she had been able to develop with various First Nations. The board asked Askew to join the Nominations Committee with the idea that she would be able to help bring some diversity to the board.

Askew was able to convince two people to join—Darcy Lindberg, a mixed-rooted Nehiyaw (Plains Cree) doctoral law student from Alberta, along with Valine Crist, a member of the Haida First Nation who was involved in protecting her territory from oil and gas super-tankers and helping it shift to clean energy. With Askew and these two new board members, the board formed an Indigenous Solidarity Committee.

Thanks to staff members such as Claire Hutton and Caitlyn Vernon, the club had already been learning about the effects of colonization. The new committee began to draft a framework for a learning process for board members and staff to examine how to incorporate consideration of Indigenous rights and how this adjustment would impact campaigns, communications, and the overall way Sierra Club BC approaches its work. The recommendations of the federal government's Truth and Reconciliation Commission, released in 2015, were also an inspiration for the committee's work.

The board directed Sierra Club BC staff to not only filter its work through a climate change lens, but also to add an "Indigenous lens." Askew explained that this means the club has committed itself to learning about different aspects of Indigenous laws and governance while recognizing that it is not a uniform system. In fact, there is much diversity among Indigenous nations within BC. However, when, for example, a campaign is operating on a particular territory, the club and the campaigners have an obligation to gain understanding about that particular territory's governance system—not just the band council, but also its hereditary leadership. As well, they need to research how best to communicate with the people of that particular territory and to consider the implications of whatever the club may be asking the people to agree to. It is important to take into account the 2007 UN Declaration on the Rights of Indigenous Peoples, fully supported by Canada in 2016, and the provisions around free, prior and informed consent for any kind of development and resource decision-making that is proposed for a territory. All of this has implications for how Sierra Club BC does its advocacy work with the provincial and federal levels of government.

The club realizes that Indigenous peoples have lived on their territories for thousands of years and have developed a rich body of knowledge about their particular lands, including the species that live there, seasonal changes, fluctuations in predator/prey numbers and so on. The club would like to combine that Indigenous ecological knowledge with scientific knowledge to better inform its work.

Board member Valine Crist has held workshops for board and staff members to increase their knowledge about the history of colonization and its effects on Indigenous people. Board and staff members will continue to participate in these workshops, and this learning process will be open-ended. Internal work is also taking place to try to reduce any barriers and to create a more supportive and welcoming environment for Indigenous colleagues.

As Askew grew more familiar with Sierra Club BC and its activities, her admiration increased and she became passionate about what was happening within the organization. When the executive director position opened up, she decided to apply. Her expertise with environmental and Indigenous law was welcomed and she took on the executive director role in June 2018. One of her first goals was to help the club clarify its focus for the next two to three years. With the support of an organization called Innoweave (an initiative launched by the McConnell Foundation to improve the effectiveness of community sector organizations), the club embarked on a six-month process to develop a new strategic plan. Askew pointed out that the fiftieth anniversary in 2019 seemed like an appropriate time to look back and reflect on the club's successes and weaknesses. She noted that it would be a critical time given the 2018 publication of an Intergovernmental Panel on Climate Change report that provides clear guidance about what needs to be done to address climate change. She sees the role of Sierra Club BC as an important one at this crucial juncture. "We want to make sure we are as well positioned as possible to be a really strong voice for our ecological future and protecting the rights of future generations."

Askew had previously worked for the Tsleil-Waututh Nation, one of the nations that would be affected by the Trans Mountain pipeline expansion. Sierra Club BC had been instrumental in creating the Pull Together campaign, which raised over $650,000 to fund the court case against the project. As executive director of SCBC, Askew was honoured to celebrate with the Tsleil-Waututh and accept the appreciation from various nations for the help they had received from the club.

Askew indicated that she was especially proud when the court decision regarding the Trans Mountain pipeline was announced, emphasizing that Indigenous nations along the pipeline had not been adequately consulted, nor had the concerns about marine shipping traffic been properly assessed. She said, "I think the timing of that, with the mother orca whale that we saw in the news this summer carrying her dead calf for an unprecedented seventeen days, was influential. The global attention that was brought to that, but especially to those of us who are on the coast, showed that all is not well with what is happening under the water and those orcas are struggling."

Askew acknowledged that it takes courage to speak out against large resource projects. These conversations are difficult, as altering the existing economic system results in implications for many people. The 2018 announcement about the LNG investment in Kitimat was a challenge for Askew. "For me, it was the first controversial issue that I had to really come out on representing our organizational stance." There are First Nations in support of the project and although Askew emphasized that the club "recognizes and respects the jurisdictional authority of all the nations," she and Sierra Club BC felt compelled to speak out against the LNG project and let all levels of government— provincial, federal, and Indigenous—know their stance.

Askew ended our interview by discussing a new initiative that the club will be starting in 2019: a pilot outings program in partnership with Charlene George from the T'Sou-ke First Nation. It will involve trips in dugout canoes on the T'Sou-ke territory where participants will learn about being on the land from a T'Sou-ke perspective. Askew said that reconnecting people with nature has been an important part of Sierra Club's history. "Our educational program focuses on that a lot with elementary school-aged children, but I think that older kids and adults really need that as well . . . When people love and have that connection to woods and lakes and birds, they are more likely to be mobilized to do the work that needs to be done to protect them."

The environmental movement is said to have advanced in four waves, or stages. The first wave focused on conservation and the protection of special places; the second, on confronting pollution and the impact of human activity on the environment; the third, on developing professionalism and a willingness to work with corporate culture to find solutions; and the fourth, on raising awareness about and forestalling climate change.[79]

Over the past fifty years, Sierra Club BC has followed a similar sequence of stages. It is now entering a fifth stage in which relationships with First Nations have become important not just because they permit solutions of mutual benefit to be found, but because it is the right and just thing to do. The club has a statement on its website acknowledging Indigenous title and rights, which states: "In the Victoria area, our staff work and live in the lands of the Tsawout, Tsartlip, Pauquachin, Tseycum, Kwsepsum (Esquimalt), Songhees, Malahat, Scia'new and T'Sou-ke First Nations." It goes on to say that when attempting to protect various wild places around the province, the club recognizes that lands are not separate from people. The club is committed to working towards reconciliation and "recognizes that land in B.C. is subject to Aboriginal title and rights, much of it unceded, and that land use decisions cannot occur on First Nations territory without free, prior and informed consent."

Increasing the diversity of Sierra Club BC can only make it a stronger organization, and one ready to meet the challenges of the next fifty years.

George Heyman: Effective Leader

George Heyman had recently stepped down after serving three terms as president of the BC Government and Services Employees' Union (BCGEU), and although he suspected he was not everyone's idea of a good fit for the job, he was hired to be Sierra Club BC's executive director in 2009. He assumed that "my administrative abilities coupled with my history and my passion for trying to build some bridges around different groups in society, working together to make a difference and fighting climate change and providing alternatives, won board members over."

Heyman was born and raised in Vancouver, and during the late 1960s, when he was in his late teens and early twenties, he was intro-duced to hiking and camping. One of his first trips was to the west coast of Vancouver Island. There he met an older wanderer from California who told him about an old life-saving trail that went from Bamfield to Port Renfrew, which was later to become known as the West Coast Trail and part of Pacific Rim National Park. The two of them decided to hike the route. They went down the coast from the Alberni Inlet and decided to hike it back again as they did not have a vehicle for the return trip. "It was a fabulous trip. This was before it was a park, as I said, and before the trail had been rehabilitated in any way."

They hiked on the beaches and sandstone reefs where they could. Otherwise, they followed the old telegraph line and "there were places where the salal was a good two to three feet over our heads and we just had to keep our hands on that wire or we would have been completely lost. I remember there were a couple of places where we just didn't know how to get out of the brush." At one point, Heyman almost burst through what was left of a little bridge into the ravine below.

They went for days without seeing anyone else. The only food they had with them was brown rice, powdered milk, oatmeal, and a bit of sugar, and they ate mussels they found on the beach. About halfway along, they wandered up to the Carmanah Point Light

Station. "The lighthouse keeper and his wife welcomed us with open arms; they were obviously starved for human company. They insisted we stay for dinner and fed us salmon and ice cream, which almost made us sick because we were eating such a spartan diet at the time. They told us to our surprise, because we stopped in later on the way back, that they hadn't seen anyone in the fifteen or more years that they'd been there who'd actually completed the entire trail, let alone come back." Heyman had a great feeling of accomplishment at the end of the trip.

Heyman lived on the central coast of BC, in Terrace, Kitimat, and the Douglas Channel area, for about fifteen years. He worked in logging and construction, ending up with the Ministry of Forests as a log scaler. On the coast, there are about ten different grades of timber according to end use and this person grades the logs to determine the quantity (volume) and quality of the timber to ensure that the wood is being used appropriately, and its worth.

Heyman recalled it being contentious at times when he was working for the Ministry of Forests in Haida Gwaii, before the area had been protected. He thought this experience made him a stronger environmentalist. He was once asked to work in a logging camp in a very controversial area that is now part of the Gwaii Haanas National Park, but he told his supervisor that he did not support the logging taking place there and did not want to be associated with it. He expected to be fired but fortunately the supervisor, who was also an outdoors person, respected his wishes.

Heyman has always considered himself an environmentalist, if not always an active one. Much of his life was spent as a volunteer activist while having a career in the labour movement as a negotiator. He noted that the BCGEU supported environmental groups and took positions on environmental issues. Climate change was an important one that came to the forefront of people's minds by around 2005. With Heyman's help, the union started to do educational courses for staff and developed ideas to both raise awareness and lessen the organization's carbon footprint. Heyman wanted to find a way to bridge some of the misunderstandings between environmental activists—and social activists in general—and labour activists. The climate change issue seemed to offer a means of having those discussions. After leaving the BCGEU, Heyman wanted to find a way to continue this work. The position at Sierra Club BC offered him that chance.

Heyman was the executive director of Sierra Club BC for four years, although he was on leave for the last few months when he was campaigning to become the MLA for Vancouver–Fairview. In our interview, he summarized his accomplishments: "I think I was able to fill some structural gaps

George Heyman helps with a cleanup of Vancouver beaches.
Courtesy of George Heyman

for Sierra Club at a time when I think Sierra Club was at a bit of a crossroads about surviving or not surviving . . . financially. [It] just needed some new systems, better fundraising, and more attention to fiscal detail, all of which I'd had a chance to learn running a large organization. I thoroughly enjoyed the opportunity to be a public spokesperson on environmental issues for Sierra Club . . . I learned so much and it's made me who I am today."

When asked about the highlights during his tenure Heyman was effusive about his trip north. "One of the most amazing trips that I've had in recent years was when I was invited by the Gitga'at to go to Hartley Bay and the Great Bear Rainforest in my last months with Sierra Club. They invited me to come and see and learn and attend a feast and it was quite amazing, being there, speaking to them, going out on the boat with them, seeing whales, looking for bears and seeing first-hand what's at stake with the issue of tankers."

He ended the interview with some final words about his experience at Sierra Club BC: "It was very energizing and very refreshing and it taught me a lot . . . It energized me because it put me in touch with some new ideas, some new ways of doing things, with a freshness of attitude and mostly an absence of cynicism. And as I said earlier, I'd always considered myself an environmentalist. At Sierra Club, I learned how much I had to learn about some of the details of the issues and what could be done and what had real meaning and how to make a commitment."

Heyman was elected as MLA of Vancouver–Fairview in 2013 and served as opposition spokesperson for environment, green economy and technology until the change in government in May 2017, when he was appointed the NDP minister of environment and climate change strategy. ▲

Jens Wieting: Old-Growth Advocate

Jens Wieting grew up close to the coast of the North Sea in northern Germany, craving "wild places," as he called them, and he started travelling at a young age in search of them. After high school, he spent three months travelling in Ecuador along the coast and in parts of the Andes and around the Amazon River. He studied land use planning at the Technical University of Berlin and worked for the German Development Corporation protecting tropical rainforests in Nicaragua, and later for the German environmental advocacy organization Robin Wood as a tropical rainforest campaigner.

Wieting moved to Canada in 2006 when his wife accepted a position as a climate scientist at the University of Victoria. He determined that working with Sierra Club BC, with its science-based activism, would dovetail well with his academic background and conservation interests. He was interviewed by Lisa Matthaus and Claire Hutton and was well aware that they had to think carefully about hiring a relatively new immigrant as a forest campaigner—someone much less familiar with BC's political and environmental circumstances. Nevertheless, he was able to convince them to offer him the job and was excited to have the opportunity.

Wieting described having both "moments of joy and many moments of frustration" during his years of working towards the implementation of the Great Bear Rainforest agreements. The team had not anticipated at the beginning how very time consuming,

Jens Wieting (on the right) joins other members of the Rainforest Solutions Project team to receive the Buckminster Fuller Challenge Prize in New York. LEFT TO RIGHT: Eduardo Sousa (Greenpeace), Val Langer (Stand.earth), and Jody Holmes (Rainforest Solutions Project). *Photo by Nikolas Van Egten, courtesy of the Buckminster Fuller Institute*

tiring, and painful the process would be. "There were times when we almost lost faith and hope, but we got there." He said that they never gave up because they knew "the Great Bear Rainforest is a global treasure larger than Switzerland" and that whether or not they could achieve agreement details such as 1 percent more or less of the region being protected could result in a difference of tens of thousands of hectares of rainforest.

With the full implementation of the GBR agreements in February 2016, Wieting's forest and climate work shifted to different priorities. Later that year he travelled with his colleagues from the Rainforest Solutions Project to New York to receive the Buckminster Fuller Challenge Prize, an award from the Buckminster Fuller Institute, which acknowledged the team's innovative approach in achieving a victory for conservation, social justice, and Indigenous rights.

Wieting clearly loves the work he does, especially when it allows him to get out into the "wild places" he is helping to protect. He described the Koeye watershed in the Great Bear Rainforest as "one of the most beautiful places" he has visited. This area in Heiltsuk territory is very remote, with a beautiful estuary and snow-capped mountains on the horizon. He recalled a vivid memory of canoeing early one sunny October morning—he watched a grizzly bear, glimpsed a wolf in the fog, and was surrounded by spawning salmon, all within the same hour. He especially appreciated the idea that a person could travel great distances without encountering any evidence of industrial activity or environmental damage. Experiences such as this inspire Wieting to continue his environmental work. ♠

Hannah Askew: Justice Proponent

Hannah Askew was born in Toronto and lived there until she was twelve. She returned to the Shuswap and Okanagan area of BC every summer to visit extended family and enjoy the lake and outdoors. Her great-grandfather started Askew's Foods in 1929, initially a butcher shop that grew into a supermarket and now has several outlets in the Shuswap. Her family continues to operate the enterprise. Askew recalls travelling around the Shuswap in the summer with her grandfather as he sourced produce and meat from the local farmers and meat suppliers.

Eventually her family decided to move back to BC, first to Nelson and then to Vancouver, where she went to high school and later the University of British Columbia for an undergraduate degree in history. After completing a master's degree in history at the University of Toronto, she returned to work with the family business, liaising with the local farmers. This work inspired her to complete a second master's degree at McGill University related to agricultural issues, which became her entry into environmental issues connected to food sustainability.

Askew recalled that at that time in the early 2000s, many small farmers were struggling, and she became interested in investigating the broader systems that were making it difficult for them. Askew was impressed by the detailed knowledge the farmers had about their land. They knew which crops grew best given particular soil conditions and temperatures. Many of them bred their own seeds to take advantage of specific micro-conditions. Often the farmers had inherited their land and hoped to pass it on to their children, so they were motivated to ensure that it remained healthy for future generations.

Hannah Askew. *Photo by Craig Paskin*

She conducted her research through McGill's Anthropology Department and, as a result, took some courses about Indigenous issues. As well, through her field research with small farmers she met several First Nations people who had connections with the farmers. She came to appreciate that Indigenous peoples also thought like the farmers. They often lived on the same piece of land over generations, had a similarly intimate knowledge of their territory, and were invested in ensuring that the land remained healthy and flourishing for future generations.

Following graduation, Askew returned to Vancouver where she taught part-time at the Native Education College, and ran some intensive courses through its satellite programs on different reserves. She recalled especially a time with the Osoyoos Indian Band when some of her students took her out on the desert and told her about their territory and the impacts of colonization, especially the water crisis resulting from the many orchards in the area. This struck home as, since childhood, Askew had thought of this area as an idyllic landscape, one connected to so many pleasant childhood memories. Hearing these stories provided a much different perspective. Askew eventually decided to return to university, this time to attend law school with the goal of specializing in the intersection of environmental and Indigenous law. Osgoode Hall Law School began offering an Intensive Program in Aboriginal

Lands, Resources and Governments in 1994. Part of it involved a full-semester placement in an Indigenous community. Askew was accepted into the program and through it travelled to Kenya, where she lived for several months.

Askew graduated in 2014 and on the day she was called to the bar, she was hired by West Coast Environmental Law. They had been impressed with her previous work with them as a summer student. Her first assignment was to travel to several communities in the North, gathering information from a broad spectrum of people about the effects of living where resource projects have been proposed or built. She began to realize how much psychic toll rural communities have to bear as a result of the rapid changes in landscape. People feel loss as forests are removed and amenities such as the only strip of beach to which people have access are lost. As well, tension can arise between those for and those against a development proposal. Although there are often benefits, such as increased employment opportunities, especially for young people who can remain in their home area thanks to the jobs, there may also be costs such as rising rental fees and increased violence against women as a result of an influx of male workers with excess money. Often there is no process to help the communities work through some of the controversy and friction.

The consultative process involved a discussion of people's values; which ones the respondents saw as resilient to industrial involvement and which were more vulnerable. People were also asked for their views regarding best-case and worst-case scenarios and for suggestions for supports that would help their community deal with development. The information that Askew and her colleagues gathered was put into a report that advocated for a more proactive approach to environmental assessment that dealt better with the cumulative effects of resource development. They called this approach Regional Strategic Environmental Assessment. Following the report's publication, Askew and her colleagues spoke with various levels of government to promote this new type of assessment system. The government responded positively and, as a result, a cumulative effects framework is being developed by the BC government.

In 2014, the Tsilhqot'in had just won a precedent-setting court case dealing with aboriginal title. One outcome of that decision was recognition from the Crown that the Tsilhqot'in had governance authority over their territory. As a result, they wanted to revitalize some of their traditional laws to use as a foundation for their governance system. Askew worked as part of a team with elders, linguists, and others, trying to understand how decisions should be made around environmental governance—in particular, how their traditional legal procedure addresses the question of consent when an industrial activity is proposed. The UN Declaration on the Rights of Indigenous Peoples is relevant to this work. After this project, Askew worked with other First Nations groups to help deal with freshwater governance issues.

Askew's experience and expertise led to her being asked to join the Sierra Club board in 2014. In 2018, as the new executive director, she stepped up to lead Sierra Club BC into its sixth decade. ♣

Those who take action have a disproportionate
impact. The power of one is to move many.
                                        —Elizabeth May

13

Local Groups

SIERRA CLUB BC IS BASED ON THE MODEL OF ITS PARENT ORGANIZA-
tion, the US Sierra Club, in which local groups form the backbone
of the organization. These rank-and-file, grassroots groups set Sierra
Club BC apart from many urban-based social action and environmental conservation organizations. They are "our gumboots on the
ground."[180] Typical activities of the entirely volunteer-led groups
include monitoring local watersheds, working on ecological restoration projects, hosting public events, inviting the public to join
group leaders on nature outings, and advising local governments on
environmental issues.

According to a strict US Sierra Club model, a minimum of twenty-five members is necessary to establish a "local group." Once that
is achieved, the chapter helps the group develop a set of bylaws, an
executive committee is formed, and a series of conservation goals and
objectives are outlined. The bylaws ensure the group is consistent
with Sierra Club policies, standards, and goals as well as providing a
framework designed to promote fairness, accountability, credibility,
and a democratic character. Sierra Club BC endeavours to follow this
protocol although at times, due to sparser populations in outlying
areas, it has had to be flexible about numbers.

Over the years, Sierra Club BC local groups have formed and flour-
ished, sometimes foundered and sometimes come to a natural end;
some have been resurrected as environmental challenges surfaced,

and some have merged with other groups. There is no question that, when active, these local groups mobilize quickly and accomplish a great deal. In his comprehensive review of the rise of "wilderness politics" in the province, Jeremy Wilson noted that, "after three decades of observing the manifestations of a robust forest environment movement, British Columbians perhaps take for granted the high level of volunteer commitment underlying this activity. It is easy to forget that proponents of similar causes elsewhere (and of equally noble causes in BC) often fail to galvanize and mobilize citizens."[181]

The following is a brief account of local groups within the BC Chapter that have been active over the years.

Lower Mainland

WHEN SIERRA CLUB BC FIRST INCORPORATED AS A SOCIETY IN 1969, IT operated as a "local group" within the Pacific Northwest Chapter of the US Sierra Club, initially as the Vancouver group. Three years later, in 1972, it was designated as a local group of the Sierra Club of Western Canada, the newly formed Canadian chapter of the US Sierra Club. Vancouver was the site of the chapter until the late 1970s when Sierra Club BC headquarters moved to Victoria, leaving Vancouver members to form what became known as the Lower Mainland group. (Early exploits of the group—Cypress Bowl, Skagit Valley, and the West Coast Trail—are discussed in chapter 1.)

In the 1970s, the group's members were concerned about a proposal to build a continuation of a seawall from Spanish Banks to Wreck Beach—the clothing-optional, beautiful, sandy beach near the University of British Columbia—with the ostensible purpose of providing access for pedestrians and ambulances on the roadway (which would be similar to that in Stanley Park), and protecting the beach from erosion. Natural history enthusiasts and UBC students, professors, and geologists were also against this proposal as they wanted the beach to remain in as much of a natural state as possible.

In 1974, Robert Franson, an associate professor of law and SCBC member, filed an action against the City of Vancouver and Board of

Parks and Public Relations over the proposed erosion-control project at Wreck Beach. The action was unsuccessful, with the judge declaring that the Parks Board had the power to proceed. However, in the end, no seawall was built after various geologists convinced people that it would not stop erosion of the clifftop.[182]

The members also lobbied against logging and development on the UBC Endowment Lands. SCBC member Tom Nichols was one of the stalwarts behind this campaign. Although a ninety-hectare park had been established in 1975, the rest of the lands were slated for residential development. People wanted to maintain the lush forest with its singular beauty and cultural attributes. It resulted in another long-fought campaign with several groups allied in the Endowment Lands Regional Park Committee writing letters, talking to politicians, and attending public meetings. In 1989, the sixteen-year campaign successfully resulted in the formation of Pacific Spirit Regional Park, an 874-hectare area, thereby protecting both Wreck Beach and the Endowment Lands.

In the early 1990s, the Lower Mainland group published its own newsletter, the *Sea and Mountain Sentinel*; took part in public debates about the risks posed by west coast tanker traffic; promoted the concept of marine sanctuaries; and worked to preserve the Boundary Bay wetlands, including making a submission to government hearings regarding the proposed expansion of the Vancouver Airport into these wetlands.

In 1995, this local group became the first Canadian Sierra Club organization to develop a website, and shortly after, under the able direction of members Sid Tan and Godwin Chan, it also helped the BC Chapter launch an online presence. As well, the group was involved in efforts to protect Meager Creek Hot Springs, after an outbreak of E. coli bacteria led to a 1995 health department order for removal of the rustic pools that had been built to accommodate the large flow of visitors.

The Lower Mainland group experienced a resurgence of membership in 2001 as new issues surfaced. Three campaigns included looking at how kitchen waste from soup kitchens in the Downtown Eastside could be composted with the hope to expand the idea to a

The Lower Mainland group rallies at the BC Legislature to advocate for the protection of Eagleridge Bluffs, located along the highway from Vancouver to Whistler Mountain that the BC government wanted to improve prior to the 2010 winter Olympics. *SCBC Photo Files*

larger region; finding ways in which the Lower Mainland could be made more sustainable and livable at the municipal and household level; and opposing the licensing of additional private moorage facilities at Bedwell Harbour, which would pose potential harm to the eelgrass meadows.[183]

In 2005, the Lower Mainland group took part in the widespread opposition to the province's plans to reroute Highway 99—a four-lane overland segment of the Sea to Sky Highway—in a way that would destroy the culturally and ecologically significant Eagleridge Bluffs. The group relaunched a newsletter in 2006, now called *Footprints*, and a GIS mapping project followed to identify stumps from old-growth trees that had been logged and removed from the UBC Endowment Lands to make way for development. The group also challenged the province's Gateway Project, which would twin the Port Mann Bridge by building a side-by-side bridge, and widen Highway 1 to ease traffic in the corridor between Vancouver and

Langley. The environmental challenge of more cars and the road brought with it concerns about decreased air quality.

In 2007, the group campaigned to ban cosmetic pesticides (non-essential pest control products used to improve the appearance of non-agricultural greenspaces), and helped with the campaign to protect the Flathead Valley ecosystem. In 2013, the group took a stand against the 2012 Fraser Surrey Docks proposal to build and operate a coal transfer facility in Surrey that would see thermal coal brought in by rail from the US, loaded onto barges, and shipped to the deep-sea port at Texada Island, from where it would be shipped to Asia. The public review also heard from a number of First Nations and other environmental organizations who opposed exporting "dirty" US thermal coal through Canada and expressed concerns about the effects of coal car cleaning and effluent in the Fraser River. The Lower Mainland group also contributed to the Sierra Club BC Pull Together campaign to aid First Nations with their court challenges regarding pipeline proposals on their lands.

Victoria

LIKE THE VANCOUVER GROUP, THE VICTORIA GROUP WAS ESTAB-lished in 1971 as a local group within the Pacific Northwest Chapter of the US Sierra Club. (The group's early successful campaign to protect the Nitinat Triangle is described in chapter 1.)

In 1973, the group initiated a campaign to protect the West Coast Strip (now known as the Juan de Fuca Trail), a rugged seaside band of coastal forest running behind a series of beaches for forty-seven kilometres, starting west of Sooke at China Beach and extending north to Botanical Beach near Port Renfrew. The group organized outings to the area to explore the whole trail and if there was not an actual trail, volunteers would build that portion. Sharon Chow recalled that in the early days Bruce Hardy had led the campaign to protect the land for the trail and she laughingly said calling it the "West Coast Strip" probably made it more difficult to mobilize the public "because it's such a blah name." In 1982, Botanical Beach, famous for its bountiful tide pools, was put up for sale by its owners. After hard lobbying, the Victoria group, along with the SCBC Chapter and the Nature Conservancy, was able to negotiate both the purchase of the beach and management by BC Parks. Soon after, it appeared that the area behind another beach in this "strip," Sombrio Beach, was to be logged. With the aid of their legal counsel, Larry Fast, the Victoria group filed a petition to have the cutting permit, which had been issued to Western Forest Products, declared null and void. Unfortunately, this action was unsuccessful and the logging proceeded.

However, after years of continued campaigning, the Capital Regional District finally protected the entire strip in 1996, creating Juan de Fuca Provincial Park and incorporating information provided by SCBC members into its plan. The last parcels of private land along the trail were bought by the province in spring 2017 and now provide a protected corridor along the trail as well as increased access to various portions of it.[184]

In late 1972, the Victoria group, along with other advocacy groups, began to promote the idea of repurposing the former Canadian National Railway line that once connected Victoria to Leechtown, now a mining ghost town, in the hills north of Sooke. The idea was to have the Capital Region District (CRD) of Victoria convert the ready-made fifty-five-kilometre right-of-way into a groomed cycle path, a proposal that was heavily promoted, complete with bumper stickers—with the slogan Bikeway, Peddle It—and the circulation of pamphlets. SCBC encouraged the public to write letters supporting this idea and reportedly the BC minister of recreation and conservation received seven thousand letters over the period of a few months. The popular and much-used Galloping Goose Regional Trail opened in 1987.[185]

On Earth Day in 1990, the Victoria group opened Ecology House in Market Square, which served as a public information centre, bookstore, gift shop, and as a meeting place for Sierra Club BC committees. It launched the *Spearhead*, a quarterly newsletter for the membership, and distributed the *Bridge*, an environmental newsletter for the public. The group fought hard to identify and protect old-growth forests and promote sustainable forestry practices. Public education initiatives to this end included excursions to the Carmanah Valley open to the public, and the development of a demonstration woodlot in Sooke with an exhibit featuring alternative harvesting methods.

In the early 1990s, the Victoria group initiated an important campaign to protect the regional watershed from commercial logging conducted by the Greater Victoria Water District. Brian Pinch described the campaign as "a very collaborative effort" with several groups involved. "If there was one person that deserves the biggest credit it would be Ray Zimmerman. And another person was Mehdi Najari, whose meticulous research discovered the fact that the Water Board didn't actually have the legal authority to do logging." Aided by West Coast Environmental Law, Sierra Club BC and the Wilderness Committee—represented by two lawyers from Sierra Legal Defence Fund—initiated litigation against the Greater Victoria Water District. After a four-year battle that went to the BC Supreme Court, logging in Victoria's watershed was ruled illegal in 1994.[186]

The Victoria group, along with a number of other organizations, lobbied for protection of the off-catchment lands in the Sooke Hills, buffering the Greater Victoria watershed, which eventually resulted in a public inquiry. Pinch made a presentation to the Special Commission on the Greater Victoria Water Supply, promoting the scenic values of the Sooke Hills areas, which provided the public with opportunities for hiking and enjoying nature. Using a tactic that has proven effective ever since the days of John Muir, the campaigners arranged for Commissioner David Perry—who was appointed to make recommendations to the BC government—to go hiking in the Sooke Hills. He brought his son and Pinch said that they had an "absolutely wonderful day." Pinch believes that the protection of the Sooke Hills was certain from that day on. As a result of the combined efforts of the Victoria group and the other coalition groups, the Sooke Hills Wilderness Regional Park was established in 2017. Not only is it a much-enjoyed large park at the western edge of Victoria but it also helps temper rapid urban growth in the area.

In 1996, the Victoria group began a series of educational evenings once a month and commissioned Peter Dixon, chair of the Victoria group, to attend a public input workshop on the CRD's Green/Blue

Spaces Strategy. The year before, CRD Parks and the Provincial Capital Commission had initiated a strategy to protect a variety of "green" and "blue" (i.e., land-based and water-based) spaces in the CRD. These spaces were to be "natural and semi-natural areas, both land and water, that are of ecological, scenic, renewable resource, outdoor recreation and/or greenway value. These areas . . . could include developed, partly developed or undeveloped public and private spaces."[187] Dixon was able to provide an environmental perspective to the committee responsible for developing the strategy, which later provided a foundation for the CRD's Regional Growth Strategy in 2003.[188]

In 1998, the Victoria group made a submission to the Environmental Appeal Board hearings with respect to Agriculture Canada's plan to aerially spray BtK to eradicate gypsy moths. Vigorous opposition put a halt to the spraying proposal. That same year, Peter Dixon received the Drinking Water Stewardship Award from the Capital Regional District in recognition of the stewardship initiative to protect Ayum Creek.

Between 2000 and 2014, the Victoria group continued to work hard to ensure that the Juan de Fuca forest would be protected by regional bylaws—so that it would maintain its role as an important carbon sink, and continue to provide a wilderness corridor to offset habitat fragmentation. The group also opposed the elaborate Silver Spray development proposal to build some 274 homes, a lodge, a golf course, and a marina on lands bordering Crown foreshore next to East Sooke Park. The land was eventually annexed to Sooke and modified development plans proceeded. After Peter Dixon was sued by the developer, the group campaigned to reinstate the anti-SLAPP law,[189] which had been passed in the last days of the NDP government but scrapped by the Liberal government under Gordon Campbell in 2001.

In the 2000s, the group, including volunteers such as Caspar Davis, Dean Murdoch, and Patricia Molchan, hosted regular community nights to bring local people together to focus on climate change issues, and generally to offer environmental education. Along the same lines, the group organized public forums to review environmentally sound sewage treatment options for the Capital Regional

District. It also published a regular newsletter highlighting important environmental issues specific to the Greater Victoria area. In 2007, the group was part of an initiative to have Greater Victoria join the Canadian grassroots Transition Towns movement to encourage whole communities to use less energy. The movement was initiated in response to two beliefs: that climate change is real and has potentially catastrophic consequences, and that there would be a decline in oil supply that would worsen year by year.[190] To promote the necessary changes, Transition Victoria sponsored a variety of projects, workshops, and events.

With lead campaigner Jean Wallace, the Victoria group was active in the Pesticide-Free CRD movement to mobilize the CRD and the public to attend to cancer-related substances concentrating in the soil and water. As part of the campaign to reduce the municipal and industrial use of non-essential cosmetic pesticides in urban gardens and green spaces, the Victoria group co-sponsored a high-profile "organic garden contest." It was instrumental in persuading the municipalities of Victoria, Esquimalt, and Oak Bay to ban pesticides.

Brian Pinch: Long-standing SCBC Supporter

From an early age, Brian Pinch was drawn to the outdoors. His first backpacking trip was a Sierra Club BC outing organized by the club's chair at the time, John Willow. It was a fall trip to the Forbidden Plateau area of Strathcona Park. Pinch was smitten. Backpacking became a passion and when interviewed he estimated that he had backpacked over eight thousand kilometres, much of it with his wife, the author of this book.

Pinch was active in the University of Victoria Outdoors Club, ultimately serving as its president. He also met Ric Careless and was impressed with the campaign for the Nitinat Triangle. Pinch earned a master's degree in public administration, specializing in economic analysis and decision-making, especially with respect to large natural resource projects.

Brian Pinch on the West Coast Trail. *Photo by Diane Pinch*

Pinch described himself as "a child of the '60s" and, like many of his generation, he sought a career in government "to help make the world a better place. How times have changed!"

He worked with the provincial government at summer jobs including being one of the first two park rangers at the newly formed Cape Scott Park in 1973. Over the next decade he held positions with the Environmental Land Use Committee Secretariat, the Ministry of Environment, and Treasury Board.

He eventually became very disillusioned with working for the government. In his words, "I felt more like a bureaucrat and an apologist for the government than someone who was doing good for the environment." In 1985, he left to become a financial advisor where he could "run his own business and be measured on results." From the beginning, he had a special interest in environmental investing and this broadened to ethical and socially responsible investing (SRI). "Once you accept the idea that you want to bring in non-financial factors to your investments, then you start thinking about human rights and gender equality and nuclear energy and you go for the whole nine yards." He thrived in his second career, becoming nationally recognized as a pioneer in SRI and managing over $100 million for his clients prior to his retirement in 2008.

Pinch's early work in the club included the Cream Silver Mine campaign and the Victoria group's submission to the Pearse Commission (see chapter 5). Pinch recalled Eve Howden as a key person in the Victoria group, describing her as "an amazing lady, probably about twenty, thirty years older than me . . . The first time I ever used an ice axe, I borrowed it from her . . . She had a lot of meetings in her house." His final campaign, as chair of the Victoria group of Sierra Club BC, was for the protection of the Sooke Hills and Victoria's watershed from logging.

Pinch was actively involved in Sierra Club boards for much of his tenure with the club "at all levels and in all positions . . . likely I was on one Sierra board or another about half the time from the mid-1970s until about 2010." His roles on Sierra Club boards became increasingly senior, culminating with the role of chair of the Sierra Club BC Foundation for four years, from 2005 to 2009. He was also on the Sierra Club Canada board for several years.

Pinch is proud of his board work. "In the early years of the environmental movement, everything was run on a shoestring and was completely disorganized. This was widely accepted as 'just the way it is in the environmental movement.' I disagreed completely, countering that with 'this is just the way it is in ineffective organizations.'" Pinch focused on building effective boards, strong management teams, proper accounting, and accurate budgeting. "This was far from glorious work but I believe that it played an important role in the club's ultimate successes."

Pinch was a vocal opponent of environmentalists who had hard left-wing views and were reflexively anti-business. "While no apologist for business, I recognized that most citizens of BC are middle of the road and more than a few are right-wing. Many of these people also care about the environment as this issue cuts across political and economic classes. To change the world, we needed to reach out to others, not vilify them." Pinch believed that the Sierra Club was well placed to do this as "it has traditionally been one of the more credible and mainstream environmental groups."

Pinch was disappointed when Sierra Club Canada separated from the Sierra Club in the us and became its own legal entity. "That was a Sierra Club Canada decision that I think was a big mistake. But it was done." He points out that the us Sierra Club is one of the biggest environmental groups in the world and has "done amazing stuff. For example, they had a lot to do with improving fuel efficiency standards for cars in the us, stopping coal-fired power plants and, of course, all sorts of wilderness campaigns. So, it was great being part of such a big, exciting organization."

Throughout his many years of Sierra Club involvement, Pinch was a stalwart advocate of having fun. He organized many outings and socials and, in later years, always ensured that board meetings had a bottle of wine. "Unless people enjoy being involved, an organization is not sustainable."

Pinch has had an over-forty-year commitment to Sierra Club BC. In 2009, he received Sierra Club BC's Jack Hemphill Exceptional Volunteer Service Award. Pinch is still a Sierra Club member and supporter but has been inactive since 2010 as he is "travelling too much." He remains an avid backpacker, hiker, and skier and has a keen interest in natural history and music. His last words in our interview were "Maybe I'll be back someday." ♠

Campbell River

THE CAMPBELL RIVER GROUP WAS ESTABLISHED IN 1972 AND WAS active through the 1970s. It included two professional foresters. The group was involved with the campaign to protect the Nitinat Triangle, and opposed the Weldwood company trucking coal through the town.[191] It was also a founding member of the Campbell River Environment Council.

In the early 1980s, the group actively opposed the Quinsam Coal proposal for a strip mine in the Quinsam River watershed. Prior to that, there had been no active coal mining on Vancouver Island since the 1950s. The community was adamant that such a mine would contaminate "staggering" amounts of water in a watershed that contained salmon spawning grounds, the same grounds that allowed the community to proclaim itself the "Salmon Capital of the World."[192] After twenty days of public hearings that were contentious, and despite a 4,600-name petition and demonstration at the legislature in Victoria, the commission recommended that mining permits be granted. The panel also suggested that an environmental technical committee be established to monitor the mine's construction and operation in order to ensure that water remained protected for fishing, recreation, and domestic use. The permits were granted in 1984 and the mine started its operation in 1987.

Not long after this, the Campbell River group was subsumed by the Cowichan group.

Cowichan

THE COWICHAN GROUP WAS ACTIVE FOR TWENTY YEARS, BETWEEN 1981 and 2001. Its first meeting was held in Duncan, prompted by an imminent threat to the habitat of the Vancouver Island marmot, considered critically endangered. Naturalists had been lobbying since 1975 for the protection of this marmot—locally known as the white-nosed marmot for its characteristic markings. It faced extinction on Vancouver Island due to hunting. As well, clearcut logging reduced an already small habitat range while also making the marmot easy prey when it emerged from its winter burrows hungry and in search of food. At best, the marmot's habitat on Vancouver Island is limited as it lives within small sub-alpine patches of meadow at an elevation of one thousand metres at the edge of the forest. Although subject to avalanches, these meadows are the first to clear of snow in the spring when the marmot emerges from hibernation ready to feed on the early grasses and sedges.[193]

In 1987, after many years of advocacy by the group, the Haley Lake Ecological Reserve was set aside, and the population (with help from the introduction of captivity-bred marmots) is now on the road to recovery. Sierra Club members Warrick and Jan Whitehead became the reserve's first wardens.

During its years in action, the group also campaigned to stop mining in Strathcona Park, and protect the old-growth forests of the Upper Walbran Valley and the adjoining forests of the Carmanah. Members participated in the movement to achieve protected status for Mount Arrowhead Massif, which includes the Old Arrowsmith Trail, the oldest intact trail on Vancouver Island, and campaigned for the formal recognition and park status of the area that includes Cowichan Valley Trail, now an integral part of the Trans Canada Great Trail route.

In 1996, the name was changed to the East Vancouver Islands group in recognition of the membership, which extended from the Malahat to Campbell River and the Gulf Islands. Over the years, the group published a newsletter three times a year, conducted regular work parties and weekly field trips, mounted education initiatives that promoted low-impact hiking and camping strategies, introduced people to trails, alpine areas, and parks, and showcased the ecological importance of specific areas. In 2000, the group launched a letter-writing campaign to initiate federal endangered species legislation. The membership had decreased, however, and the following year, the remaining members merged with the Victoria group.

West Kootenay/Nelson

IN THE LATE 1970S AND EARLY 1980S, A GROUP WAS ACTIVE IN THE West Kootenay/Nelson area. The chair at this time, Lawson Legate, joined Barry Auliffe, Claire Gardner, and other members in promoting the creation of the Akamina–Kishinena Provincial Park, which eventually was established in 1995 in the southeast corner of the province. The group was also concerned about mining in Kokanee Glacier Provincial Park, and a proposal that resurfaced several times to divert water from the Kootenay River into the Columbia, known as the Kootenay Diversion. Local people were against this idea as it would affect nearby communities and tourism with loss of transportation routes and important habitats for waterfowl, migrating birds, and mammals. It would also increase sedimentation in Columbia and Windermere Lakes and decrease water temperature in the southern part of Columbia Lake.

The group briefly re-emerged in 2003, with Alan Ashcroft as interim chair, to help combat the Jumbo Pass ski resort proposal. Other issues included a proposed Bugaboos National Park, sustainability of endangered mountain caribou herds in the area, and the proposed highway expansion in Grohman Narrows Provincial Park. The group did not continue for long as Wildsight and the West Kootenay EcoSociety attracted more members and remain the dominant active environmental groups in the region.

Salt Spring Island

A GROUP WAS INITIATED ON THE ISLAND IN 1988 TO ADDRESS LOGGING issues on the island. After about a year and a half, it merged with the Cowichan group.

Quadra Island

IN THE AUTUMN OF 1997, A DOZEN QUADRA ISLAND RESIDENTS MET to discuss their growing concern about a number of environmental issues related to the island. There was a strong desire to involve a greater number of people and it was decided that affiliating with Sierra Club BC would lend strength and credibility to their efforts to organize themselves. In their view, the combination of activism, lobbying, respectability, and longevity provided a good fit.

Sierra Club Quadra Island was established in 1998. The group proceeded with a push to have its two parks, Octopus Islands Provincial Park and Small Inlet Provincial Park—together one of the most popular marine wilderness destinations on BC's coast—connected by an additional parcel of land. Save the Heart of Quadra Parks was officially launched in 2012, although it had been an ongoing campaign for many years. The needed parcel of land was finally acquired in 2014. The group also campaigned with a number of other organizations to have BC's environment minister launch an environmental assessment of applications for water and land rights on at least forty streams in the Bute watershed on BC's central coast (bottled water licences and proposed power projects).

In 2001, the Quadra group launched a joint appeal to rescind the waste permit for the Island Cogenerational Project (ICP) at Elk Falls.[194] The ICP plant, a natural gas–fired cogeneration plant adjacent to the Elk Falls pulp mill, was designed to deliver processed steam power to the mill. The permit in question allowed ICP to discharge air contaminants that the appellants argued contributed to an already serious air pollution problem, and that insufficient controls were in place. At the hearing, the Quadra group amended the appeal to ask that the permit be varied to meet certain conditions, but the permit was upheld.

Species that are endangered, threatened, or of concern in BC are classified as red-listed, blue-listed, or yellow-listed. The BC red list includes any ecosystems or species that are considered endangered, threatened, or extirpated (eradicated).[195] The Quadra Island group worked to identify and protect a significant number of red-list ecosystems from logging activities. In 2006, the group participated in the Special Committee on Sustainable Aquaculture, appointed to look at the economic and environmental impact of the aquaculture industry in BC.[196] In recent years, the group has focused its energies on risks related to farmed Atlantic salmon. The outbreak of heart and skeletal muscle inflammation in farmed salmon has recently been linked to the piscine reo-virus; the concern is that the virus will spread from open-net pens to Pacific salmon swimming nearby.

In 2007, Sierra Quadra attracted local media attention with articles and a photo contest to the phenomenon of a "green power" gold rush—which likened investor fervour for public offerings of green companies to that of the rush to exploit the goldfields in the 1800s. Similarly, the *Georgia Straight* reported that world investment in green sector clean energy initiatives in 2006 was four times what it was only two years earlier.[197] The group also introduced a reusable shopping bag, the Q-bag, after Quadra became the first Gulf Island to go plastic bag free.

Currently the group continues to review forestry plans, host films and speakers as part of its ongoing acclaimed series focusing on sustainable living, and run the Sierra Club–sponsored Great Annual Beach Clean-up (ongoing for twenty years).

Geraldine Kenny: Ardent Quadra Island Activist

Geraldine Kenny was born in Dublin, and worked in Berlin after completing a degree in art history. In 1983, she hitchhiked her way through Canada where a man she would later marry gave her a lift in Lake Louise. After living in Newfoundland for a short while, she and her husband moved to the west coast where she said, "This island suits me better."

Exploring BC with her husband she "was absolutely horrified at the extent of the clearcut logging devastation not only on Vancouver Island but all over the province." When she flew north to Kitimat and Smithers, she recalled, "looking out of the plane and all I saw were these naked patches and it was absolutely horrific. And I came from Europe . . . and had never seen forests as extensive as these, particularly the forests on Vancouver Island, which are absolutely overwhelming in their majesty and their sense of ecological history."

The Kennys bought shares in MacMillan Bloedel, which allowed them to attend the shareholders' meetings. She remembered saying at one meeting, "You come to Europe and pay thousands of dollars to go to the Cologne Cathedral, to see Montmartre, to go to Crete and to see all these fantastic cultural heritage [sites] and here you are cutting down the cultural heritage of this province." In our interview, she went on, "I was absolutely passionately involved in protecting the old-growth forests on Vancouver Island. After I read *Monday* magazine and I heard about the Sierra Club and how they were trying to stop the logging in the Carmanah and the Walbran valleys, I marched up the stairs in View Street and bumped straight into Peter McAllister and he invited me to a party at his place the next evening. That is how I got involved with the Sierra Club. I met some great people, really great passionate, intelligent, strategic thinkers, well rounded educationally as well. Really a great bunch of people and they still are thirty-five years later. It has been a great journey."

The Kennys took on a new challenge when they bought a piece of rural property on Quadra Island in 1994. Without any real gardening or livestock experience, they established Bold Point Farmstay, sharing their love of nature and sustainable small-scale farming with families from all over the world. Upon arriving on Quadra Island, Kenny immediately got involved with the logging concerns on the island. "Of all the issues that the Sierra Club has dealt with and is dealing with, forestry is my true passion and has been since day one with the Walbran and the Carmanah." She joined a local Quadra Island group known as the Forest Resources Committee with three other intrepid anti-logging activists (Ray Grigg, Judy Leicester, and Noel Lax) battling against TimberWest. They were getting nowhere and Kenny told the others, "You know if we want to achieve something, we have got to join an organization that is well funded, that has respect, is known nationally and internationally, and when somebody hears the name Sierra Club they pick up their ears and listen." Because of her experience in Victoria, she was aware of the Sierra Club's commitment, strategic planning, and competence. Vicky Husband and Sharon Chow came to give a presentation and, in 1997, welcomed Quadra Island to the club.

Also at that time Will Horter, who was then with the Sierra Legal Defence Fund, gave a two day workshop, introducing the group to the Forest Watch network. They learned to read logging plans and "with information and education comes power . . . we had our tape measures with us and we measured the trees and their location. If an eight-hundred-year-old Douglas fir was right in the middle of a proposed logging road, it wasn't when we finished. It was on the side of the road. Saved!" These tools allowed them to became more proactive and successful in their pursuit of preserving old-growth forests on the island.

Not everyone in the community was happy with their anti-logging activism. To counter this, Noel Lax suggested launching a public education program with guest speakers informing the islanders about ecology and the environmental consequences of logging on various wildlife in the forests. Kenny recalled that the Great Bear Rainforest presentation made by Ian McAllister (Peter McAllister's son) had standing room only in the two-hundred-seat community centre, with people from as far away as Parksville and Port Hardy attending. Speakers have since included Alexandra Morton, Andrew Nikiforuk, Will Horter, and various people from the Sierra Club, including Colin Campbell, Ana Simeon, Bob Peart, and Sarah Cox.

The series has done very well over the last twenty years. The 2017–18 series, called "Slugs and Snails, Toads and Whales," included two entomologists from the Royal BC Museum talking about slugs, snails, and spiders; Joe Foy of the Wilderness Committee presenting the beautiful film *Toad People*, and Jackie Hildering, who Kenny calls "a fabulous marine researcher, photographer and whale expert."

The group also wanted another way of dealing with the divisiveness within the community. Kenny recalled, "Everybody knew that we were affiliated with the Sierra Club and thank goodness the Sierra Club has a truly [unblemished] history. It is a respected and well-run organization. We had to think of what we could do to bring the community together. We wanted to show that environmentalism isn't always, 'Stop logging. Stop pipelines. Stop development.' We wanted to be proactive and it was then that board member Ken Roxborough suggested organizing a beach clean-up, and ever since 1997 that has been our contribution to Quadra Island."

Kenny highlighted the dedication and commitment of Judy Leicester in trying to obtain the four hundred hectares between Small Inlet Marine Provincial Park and Octopus Islands, owned by the Merrill & Ring forestry company, and considered by many to be a fitting addition to the existing parks. For many years, on the first Wednesday of every month, the group met at Leicester's house, where she served delicious desserts. After discussing other Sierra Club issues, Leicester always took out her folder and said, "Now the newest on Merrill & Ring is . . ." Leicester never gave up; she was persistent. When the

Judy Leicester (on the right) receives Sierra Club BC's Rosemary Fox Conservation Achievement Award in 2009. Diane Pinch receives the Geraldine Irby Award for Volunteerism and Brian Pinch, the Jack Hemphill Exceptional Volunteer Service Award. *SCBC Photo Files*

group received notification from BC Parks that preserving this land was their number one priority, they realized the potential success of the campaign.

Kenny remarked, "Now if that doesn't put gas in your fuel tank, I don't know what does. If you've got BC and Marine Parks behind you, you can start to move. Luckily, we have a very proactive regional director here on Quadra, Jim Abram, who was the lighthouse keeper for twenty-three years at Cape Mudge. He is very supportive of such projects. In addition, we have found MLA Claire Trevena to be very supportive of the project. So, we began chipping away to achieve our goal to save four hundred hectares from industrial clearcut logging."

Kenny extolled Leicester's efforts: "Judy did amazing work." She was a major driver behind this campaign and although she died in 2012 before seeing it become reality, the group persisted with her dream. They wrote to the CEO of Merrill & Ring, and went to Victoria where they lobbied Environment Minister Mary Polak, as did BC Parks and BC Marine Parks. The logging company wanted

$6 million for the land. The Quadra Island group received notification from Polak that if Quadra Island really wanted the government to buy this land, the people of Quadra Island had to demonstrate their commitment by raising funds themselves. They had five months to raise $250,000.

The group started fundraising and had a large thermometer notice board at the community hub at Quathiaski Cove documenting their progress. It was now time to involve other islanders in the Save the Heart of Quadra Parks campaign. Long-time friend Susan Westren and local historian Jeanette Taylor joined the core group, with Westren eventually taking the lead in fundraising. The island, with its population of only 2,500, was eventually successful in raising the $250,000 by the deadline. They celebrated their success at Tsa-Kwa-Luten Lodge with Stephen Hume from the *Vancouver Sun* as the keynote speaker.

In 2013, Kenny received the Rosemary Fox Conservation Achievement Award. She reminisced about Vicky Husband being her inspiration in the Sierra Club. Like Husband, she remains committed. She pointed out an L-shaped segment on her map next to Main Lake Provincial Park that had recently come up for sale—perhaps the next campaign for Sierra Quadra? ♣

Coast Mountain

THE COAST MOUNTAIN GROUP WAS ACTIVE BETWEEN 1999 AND 2005. It emerged due to a discussion at a barbecue between long-time environmental activist Bruce Hill and Rob Brown. The two had worked together for a number of years to bring about changes in conservation measures through the Steelhead Society.

During the years it was active, the group provided a work crew to rebuild trails on Bornite Mountain (Terrace, Kleanza Creek Provincial Park), undertook a mapping project of Howe Creek, contributed to research investigating the effects of oil and gas exploration off Haida Gwaii, hosted training sessions for Forest Watch, and pushed to reduce the municipal and industrial use of pesticides. The group also constructed a trail for recreational use between the Exstew River and Exstew Falls, organized several kayaking and hiking trips, and participated in the North Coast Land and Resource Management Plan (LRMP), and the Kalum LRMP. It then turned its attention to the question of lifting the moratorium on the exploration of oil and gas off the west coast of BC. With time, it was realized that lifting the moratorium was an unlikely possibility. As well, the final recommendations for the North Coast LRMP were published in 2005. With no other active concern to replace these issues, and perhaps due to fatigue of the members, the group became dormant.

Haida Gwaii

SIERRA HAIDA GWAII CAME TOGETHER IN 1999, AN OCCASION celebrated with a wild-food potluck. Jacques Morin, a resident and long-standing Sierra Club member, helped get the organization off the ground and continued to lead it until 2011. Over the years, the group initiated a Forest Watch program; opposed the proposal to lift the moratorium on the exploration of oil and gas off Haida Gwaii; advocated for legislation to protect marine areas; looked at alternative and sustainable living options for residents; disseminated information about the impact of logging on local stream habitats; participated in the Tlell LRMP; and proposed measures to offset the effects of climate change by promoting sustainability, recycling, and waste management.

In 2006, the group responded to two forest harvesting plans that threatened to disrupt the habitat of the red-listed Queen Charlotte goshawk. It submitted a complaint to the Forest Practices Board and also brought attention to the hydrological impact of the proposed plans in the Rennell Sound Landscape Unit in question. The land use agreement of 2007 contained protection for nesting sites, but did not take into account a secure habitat for foraging needs. Board recommendations included measures for goshawk protection but in the meantime, it became apparent that the group had to focus its energies on pushing forward provincial endangered species legislation.

Jacques Morin was one of the founders of the Haida Gwaii group and acted as chair for several years. *scbc Photo Files*

The Haida Nation strongly opposed coastal tanker traffic and, in 2010, Sierra Haida Gwaii, in coalition with other grassroots groups on the islands, asked local councils to stand with their First Nations neighbours and sign on to a No Tankers declaration. The response was overwhelmingly positive in the community—in part due to the economic importance of shellfish aquaculture, fishing, and tourism. The No Tankers declaration was endorsed by all Haida Gwaii municipalities.

Sea to Sky

THE SEA TO SKY GROUP IN SQUAMISH STARTED IN 2002 AND WAS active for a short while with Spencer Fitschen as its interim chair. The region was undergoing a renewed land and resources management plan process and the group became part of an environmental coalition. The process included aerial surveys and assessments of remaining intact wilderness areas and specifically managed zones. The group was also concerned about a proposed incinerator to improve recycling and composting and wanted to ensure that environmental concerns were kept in mind.

Malaspina

THE MALASPINA GROUP WAS ESTABLISHED IN 2003 IN POWELL RIVER at a time when NorskeCanada's Powell River Mill put forward a plan to use tire-derived fuel to power the mill. Concerns about harmful emissions became the rallying point, along with the additional concern that the appetite for this alternative source of fuel would pose a serious threat to tire recycling companies.

Two of the group's first initiatives were to advance the proposal to protect Millennium Park, a 92-hectare green space in the middle of Powell River, and to develop the Willingdon Beach Trail interpretive route along a disused 1910 railway bed. The group undertook a successful campaign to stop the building of a highway that would have run through Millennium Park. It promoted a Smart Growth campaign, a widely recognized urban planning strategy that attempts to direct the inevitable growth of towns and cities in "smart" ways (for example, transit-oriented, walkable, bicycle friendly).

In 2005, the Malaspina group co-hosted an all-candidates meeting in Powell River where Sierra Club BC initiated its non-partisan Vote Environment program to raise the profile of the environment as a key issue to be addressed in any election campaign. The Malaspina group also monitored salmon fry in a local creek, and worked with other Sierra Club organizations to challenge proposals for industrial developments at Bute Inlet, including a plan that would divert water into a plant for producing bottled drinking water, and generating run-of-the-river power.

In 2011, the group joined its voice to the protest against the proposal by the Fraser Surrey Docks to build and operate a coal transfer facility in Surrey. In 2012, group members succeeded in persuading Powell River to turn down a proposal to build an incinerator intended for burning waste shipped from the Lower Mainland, given the prospect of toxic emissions and the implications for global warming.

The following year, the Malaspina group spoke against the expansion of BC's coastal coal corridor from Fraser Surrey Docks to the deep-sea coal port on Texada Island. In 2014, the group headed off an attempt to rezone the Willingdon Beach-Millennium Park area for a housing development—it responded with a "Parks are not banks" campaign, writing letters and making presentations that resulted in keeping the park intact. The area is now included in the official community plan.

The group also successfully challenged a similar proposal that sought to remove twelve hectares from the Agricultural Land Reserve in the Powell River Regional District—land, it was argued, that could be used to produce food given that the region currently imports 95 percent of its food in a time when climate change amplifies the necessity to protect fertile land. Members wrote letters to the Provincial Agricultural Land Commission asking that the land be kept within the ALR and their efforts were successful.

Sierra Malaspina remains intact but with a reduced membership and limited activities. The group continues to support efforts to control tanker traffic on the coast and to oppose the expansion of pipelines, and on a local level, remains involved with trail maintenance and generally keeping track of development initiatives and environmental concerns.

Comox Valley

THE COMOX VALLEY GROUP CAME INTO BEING IN 2009 WHEN PLANS surfaced to build a gas station in a high-risk earthquake area next to an estuary that had been designated as an Important Bird Area by the Canadian IBA organization. The group, chaired by Mike Bell, saw the Courtenay River estuary as "the heart of the Comox Valley," and a key element in the development of an eco-neighbourhood—described in a write-up about the group on the Sierra Club BC website as "a place where life flourishes and is protected . . . where people, fish, birds and a variety of animals and other life form a single community . . . [with] a common sense of place . . . and live together in harmony."[198] The group consolidated community support and initiated litigation to prevent the gas station from being built. An appeal was unsuccessful and the gas station was built. Nevertheless, the group continued its work at promoting sustainability for the entire Courtenay River watershed.

Members of the Comox Valley group and CoalWatch denounce the proposed Raven coal mine at the Comox 2012 Canada Day parade.
Photo by Vanessa Scott

In 2009, Compliance Energy, headquartered in Vancouver, proposed an underground coal mine operation in the Comox Valley at Fanny Bay, on the east coast of Vancouver Island. The Comox group joined CoalWatch Comox Valley to battle the proposed mine. CoalWatch was formed in 2009 to look at the mining proposal and to advocate for "robust public participation during the environmental assessment process."[199] The members of this coalition examined countless documents, commissioned expert studies, talked to neighbours, staged street theatre, and organized letter-writing campaigns. It played a significant role in bringing to light the potential impact on the watershed as the environmental review proceeded. They presented briefs emphasizing the environmental and economic risks to the drinking water, the fish-bearing streams, and the Baynes Sound shellfish industry.

The initial mine proposal was rejected by the province in 2013 on the grounds that it did not "contain the required information,"[200] prompting Compliance Energy to put forward a new application in 2014. The BC Environmental Assessment Office advised the company that there were "issues identified in their application"—lack of consultation with First Nations and failing to address environmental impacts on drinking water and air quality—and the application was withdrawn in 2015.[201] Compliance Energy subsequently dissolved the company associated with the mine in 2016; soon after, the federal and provincial environmental assessments for the project were terminated, and CoalWatch was able to dissolve the society.[202]

With the success of the effort to prevent the Raven Mine from coming into being, Sierra Comox Valley had accomplished a major goal of the group. The Comox group is currently dormant, as a result of their success and the aging of key members.

Nanaimo

SIERRA NANAIMO CAME TOGETHER IN 2012 AS CONCERNS COALESCED around the prospect of significant increases in crude oil tanker traffic through the Strait of Georgia. Around this time, it became apparent that the largest tankers leaving Vancouver, while not fully loaded (due to draft restrictions on how deep vessels were allowed to sit below the water line), were benefiting from a lessening of these restrictions and seeing an increase in allowed load levels. This, combined with proposals to increase the volume of barrels shipped per day, and the number of loaded tankers per year, caused widespread alarm along the coast. Crude oil is thicker and heavier than refined gasoline products and therefore poses a greater risk to marine environments. Sierra Nanaimo advocated for protecting Nanaimo's marine environment and promoted the alternative of sustainable economic development, especially tourism.

The group hosted movie nights to draw public attention to the threat of pipelines and tankers. In 2013, it also gathered together a coalition of diverse groups to oppose Metro Vancouver's proposal for a new waste-to-energy incinerator at Duke Point given the very real concerns about overall air quality, not to mention toxic emissions. The group planned to concentrate on these two issues throughout 2014 and 2015. In April 2014, the city of Nanaimo rejected the proposal to build the incineration plant after having received many letters and emails opposed to the project. The Enbridge pipeline was quashed in 2016.

The group became less active following the success of these two campaigns and is currently dormant.

Okanagan Valley

THE SIERRA CLUB HAD A PRESENCE IN THE OKANAGAN VALLEY AS early as the 1970s and 1980s on the basis of Katy Madsen's advocacy initiatives in Summerland, but a formal local group did not come about until later. In the meantime, Sierra Club BC worked with the Okanagan Similkameen Parks Society to address a variety of environmental issues.

In 1980, the South Interior group, later known as the North Columbia group, was formed by members from Kelowna and Penticton with Robert Miles as its chair. One issue that concerned the group was the water quality of the lake system. Forestry, agriculture, and septic tanks were contaminating the lakes with phosphorous, causing the Okanagan Basin to be labelled an Environmentally Sensitive Area by the provincial Ministry of Environment. Other issues included fisheries proposals for the Similkameen River, a proposal to build an open-pit gold mine near Hedley, and threats to Okanagan Mountain Park and Cathedral Lakes Park. The group later lapsed around 1989.

Subsequently, Sierra Okanagan was formed in Vernon in 2012 with Brad Foster as its chair. The group is focused on conservation issues in the Okanagan, Shuswap, and Similkameen areas: "preserving all remaining natural areas in and around our communities, inclusive of wetlands, grasslands, and forests."[203] Of particular concern is the protection of watershed areas from the incursions of real estate development and industrial resource harvesting. Similarly, the group is encouraging ranchers to take on sustainable management of the grasslands used for free-range grazing and is working collaboratively to protect what remains of the grasslands. To this end, Sierra Okanagan is working to establish a network of connected parks and protected areas to prevent further fragmentation of wildlife corridors.

An early project focused on intervening in imminent development plans for the south-facing slope of the Bella Vista Range, which members of the local group describe as the "largest intact semi-arid habitat remaining north of the Oliver/Osoyoos region."[204] Sierra Okanagan relied on the 2002 *Sensitive Ecosystems Inventory*—consisting of information about the flora and fauna of the region compiled from a variety of studies and used to support sustainable land management decisions—to argue in favour of protecting the area. The report identified the slope as vulnerable on the basis of its shallow soils, susceptibility to hydrological changes, erosion, presence of invasive species, and human disturbance.[205] Similarly, the natural grasslands of the Goose Lake Range were seen to be at risk of overdevelopment and the group worked collaboratively with the regional district to promote the creation of a continuous trail following the historic Grey Canal, in order to protect a "vast area of undeveloped grassland . . . [to] encompass all the remaining grasslands uphill from the trail to connect with Okanagan Indian Band land" and thereby prevent further uphill development.[206] Sierra Okanagan proposed to collaborate with First Nations and local and provincial governments to protect several areas in the North Okanagan, including the Bella Vista–Goose Lake Range, in an area identified as the North Okanagan Grasslands Heritage Site.

In 2013, Sierra Okanagan engaged local government and other stakeholders in the Okanagan Valley in a wetland reclamation and interpretive trail project for Lower BX Creek in Vernon. Again, the city's environmental management strategy was based in part on the *Sensitive Ecosystem Inventory*, which took into account the sensitive riparian (river) ecosystem that, in Vernon, offers a "lush oasis in an otherwise arid landscape"—an ecosystem formed in part by the sensitive and threatened black cottonwood and red osier dogwood trees, and provides a habitat for a number of at-risk species.[207]

In 2016, Sierra Okanagan partnered with high school students from the Students Without Borders Academy to examine the significance of natural systems in the greater Vernon area. This was an opportunity for students to understand the importance of local niche species, and to understand the ways in which modern development has altered the natural world. Sierra Okanagan and the academy intend to incorporate the findings from this initiative into policy recommendations to local, provincial, and federal governments.

The future depends on what you do today.
                    —Mahatma Gandhi

14

The Future
Is Here

IT IS FITTING TO END THIS BOOK WITH AN ABRIDGED VERSION OF Sierra Club BC's *The Future Is Here* document, which outlines the club's vision for the future and proposes changes to the way BC's waters, lands, and resources are managed to prepare for climate change and its accelerating impacts.

The initial document was written by Colin Campbell, the club's science advisor. Released in 2015 and subsequently updated in 2017, it drew on Campbell's vast experience and knowledge of science and conservation research.[208] The intention is for *The Future Is Here* to be a living document that guides Sierra Club BC's direction and actions going forward. The expectation is that it will be updated as required, particularly its detailed recommendations.

The following condensed adaptation excludes detailed recommendations, and due to differences in format and availability many of the photos have been changed. To see the original document—and the most up-to-date version—go to the club's website.[209] A photo of the document's cover is contained in the colour insert.

As SCBC concludes in the document, "No government will be able to implement the scope of change required once the costs of environmental crisis and climate impacts become unmanageable. As a wealthy industrialized country with a high carbon footprint we have the ability—and the responsibility—to pursue an alternative path."[210]

THE FUTURE IS HERE

An Urgent Call to Defend Nature, Stabilize the Climate and Transition to Post-carbon Prosperity[211]

Executive Summary

CLIMATE CHANGE IS THE DEFINING ISSUE OF OUR TIME. A RADIcal transformation of British Columbia's natural landscape and biodiversity is already underway and climate impacts will continue to accelerate if we cling to business as usual. By 2080, modelling suggests British Columbia will be almost unrecognizable, both in terms of its natural environment and its human communities.

Informed by the latest climate science, Sierra Club BC advocates a three-pronged approach to prepare for these changes and defend ourselves against worsening impacts.

We must act to:

1. Stabilize our climate, by leaving fossil fuels in the ground, reducing our emissions and increasing the price on carbon.
2. Defend intact nature to preserve biodiversity and natural carbon banks, and protect the ecosystem services on which human economies and health depend.
3. Rapidly transition to an equitable post-carbon economy that leaves no one behind.

British Columbia is well placed to confront the challenge of climate change and undertake a rapid and necessary transition to a post-carbon world. The future is here and it is time for climate action.

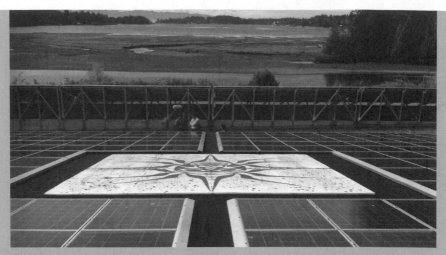

The T'Sou-ke First Nation became the first Indigenous solar community in the country in 2009 and is now a role model for other communities. *Photo by Caitlyn Vernon*

Introduction

BRITISH COLUMBIA'S BIODIVERSITY IS GLOBALLY SIGNIFICANT, HOME to three-quarters of Canada's mammal and bird species, 70 percent of freshwater fish, and thousands of other species.

Some, such as the Vancouver Island marmot, live nowhere else on earth. For others, such as grizzly bears and salmon, BC has become a vital refuge as their numbers decline.

Climate change, however, threatens BC's biodiversity. The well-being of species, ecosystems and biodiversity is intimately connected to human well-being. Resilient, diverse ecosystems deliver vital environmental services (such as filtering water and pollinating plants) on which human populations depend.

Greater protection for biodiversity provides the best chance for plants and animals to survive climate impacts. Human beings will have better prospects for survival.

Although large tracts of BC remain ecologically intact, our management of this abundance has often been short-sighted. BC has the highest number of species-at-risk of any province or territory.

Landscapes continue to be destroyed for short-term economic gain.

Mountain caribou numbers have been declining, especially in the Selkirk and Purcell mountain regions where they are at risk of extinction. They require unbroken tracts of old-growth forest for food and refuge from predators. *Photo by Dayn Craig*

Fossil fuel projects, logging practices and other carbon-intensive economic activities contribute to massive greenhouse gas emissions, often uncounted in provincial reporting.

Globally, we are in the midst of the "sixth extinction," with up to 50 percent of species expected to disappear by 2100. Business as usual will cause 3 to 5°C of warming within the lifetime of children born today, with catastrophic consequences.

British Columbians are already embracing climate-friendly solutions, including renewable energy systems, local food production and mass transit. We can still prepare ourselves and build resilience in light of climate change.

BC needs government leadership to mandate solutions and move boldly towards a post-carbon future.

By protecting biodiversity and shifting to a post-carbon economy in which families, communities and nature can prosper together, BC can become a world leader in confronting climate change. All we need is the political will.

The 2014 William decision granted full title over traditional land to the Tsilhqot'in Nation, the first time a court had done so. This hugely significant precedent was important for all First Nations including the Haida, whose regalia is pictured here, and has shifted the context for land and water use planning in BC. *Photo by Michael Ambach*

Acknowledging Title and Rights

MOST OF BRITISH COLUMBIA IS UNCEDED LAND, SUBJECT TO **Indigenous title and rights.**

Land use decisions cannot occur on First Nations territory without free, prior and informed consent. Working with Indigenous governments, BC should develop and expand land use designations that address title and respect cultural values and uses, conserving biodiversity as appropriate. Reconciliation for historical wrongs is necessary and important and any plan for our common future must recognize and address our painful shared history.

Although many glaciers were gradually receding prior to the early 1900s, over the last century climate change has greatly hastened their retreat. The contrast from 1917 to 2011 in the Athabaska Glacier can be seen clearly in these two photos. TOP PHOTO: *Courtesy of Library and Archives Canada/Bibliotheque et Archive Canada and the Mountain Legacy Project.* BOTTOM PHOTO: *Courtesy of the Mountain Legacy Project.*

Climate Change Impacts

CLIMATE CHANGE IS ALREADY AFFECTING BRITISH COLUMBIA. Over the last 120 years, average temperatures have risen 0.6°C on the coast, 1.1°C in the central and southern interior, and 1.7°C in the north.

Since the mid-twentieth century, coastal ocean surface temperatures increased. In 2015, temperatures off the west coast were 3°C higher than normal, threatening marine life, seabirds and salmon stocks.

Recently, BC has experienced lower winter snowpack, increased early river flows, and warmer summer stream temperatures. Spring is arriving earlier, as are many species of migratory birds.

Modelling predicts that by 2080, ecological zones will shift 900 to 1,500 metres higher in elevation and 450 to 750 kilometres north. Some species are already expanding their ranges northward or upwards, disrupting migration, breeding or flowering events. For many species, climatic changes are happening faster than they can move.

Overall, BC will see significant growth in the driest ecosystems. Grasslands and steppes will grow hugely at the expense of trees. The western red cedar may disappear. Some tree species will push upslope into alpine habitats.

Wetter ecosystems will be less abundant. Wetlands, essential for purifying our freshwater, will be most impacted, especially in southern forests.

Glaciers and snow pack on mountains will continue to disappear. The melting of northern permafrost will accelerate.

These changes, over the course of a single lifetime, will threaten water, food supplies and our health. They will destabilize the social and economic patterns that, for most people, make our lives orderly and predictable.

Carbon Accounting

CLIMATE CHANGE IS ALL ABOUT CARBON. THE BASIS OF ALL LIFE, carbon circulates among living animals and plants, the atmosphere, and the oceans. Carbon is also stored for long periods: as living forests (green carbon), in estuaries and marshes (blue carbon) and as fossil fuel deposits (black carbon).

The problem, simply put, is that less and less carbon is being stored long term, while more and more is in our atmosphere, as the greenhouse gas carbon dioxide, and dissolved in our oceans, contributing to acidification.

Slowdown in climate change allows nature a better chance to adapt

Reduced likelihood of dangerous, extreme and economy-disrupting events (flood, droughts etc.)

Healthy forests and other carbon banks help slow down climate change

STABLE CLIMATE
(success meeting emission reduction targets, carbon pricing, climate test for major projects and identified "unburnable" fossil fuel reserves)

Clean jobs and revenue allows phasing out of unsustainable jobs and revenue

DEFEND NATURE, STABILIZE THE CLIMATE AND TRANSITION TO POST-CARBON PROSPERITY

INTACT NATURE
(expanded protected areas & new land use designations with carbon and habitat as primary purpose, support for First Nations land use designations, restored environmental laws and protection from pollution)

POST-CARBON ECONOMY
(transition underway to renewable energy, clean high-tech, public transit, film and arts, tourism, sustainable forestry and agriculture)

Clean water and air, intact soils and landscapes support low carbon economy

Reduced pollution and overall impact allows better adaption to climate change

Earth's carbon stores are like banks, where we can deposit and withdraw carbon. Carbon is deposited when forests and other plant life remove carbon dioxide from the atmosphere. Carbon is withdrawn when we cut down forests, when we dredge up estuaries and marshes, and when we burn fossil fuels.

Since the industrial revolution, our withdrawals have increasingly exceeded our deposits, leading to an accumulation of carbon dioxide in the atmosphere, from 280 parts per million (ppm) in pre-industrial times to more than 400 ppm today.

The balance of payments has to change. We must increase carbon deposits and decrease our carbon withdrawals.

Effective Climate Action

STABILIZING THE CLIMATE

STABILIZING THE CLIMATE MEANS MANAGING CARBON RESPONSIBLY, minimizing the amount released into the atmosphere and preserving carbon banks.

Scientists have calculated our planet's carbon budget—the total amount of carbon we can pump into the world's atmosphere and stay under two degrees of warming—to be 1,000 gigatons. Two degrees of warming is widely considered the threshold beyond which climate change impacts become increasingly impossible to manage by humanity and ecosystems.

To date, humankind has emitted a little over 500 gigatons of carbon. At current rates, we will exceed the carbon budget in about 30 years. Scientists have calculated that to remain within budget, 80 percent of the world's fossil fuel deposits must remain in the ground.

DEFENDING NATURE

WITHOUT IMMEDIATE ACTION, BC'S GLOBALLY SIGNIFICANT BIODIversity is vulnerable to rapid deterioration, especially as a result of climate change.

Many scbc staff ride their bikes daily to reduce the use of fossil fuels, not just on World Car-Free Day. *scbc Photo Files*

Conservation biologists say about half of the land base should be protected or managed primarily to protect ecological values, in order to maintain ecosystems, biodiversity, and environmental services.

Managing 50 percent of bc's landscape to maintain ecological integrity and connectivity will give species and ecosystems a better chance to adapt to a changing climate, while protecting clean water and maintaining the soil base. bc has already made significant progress toward this goal. Protected areas comprise nearly 15 percent of the land base and another approximately 16 percent has development restrictions in place through designations such as the Agricultural Land Reserve and Wildlife Management Areas.

BLUE AND GREEN CARBON BANKS

WE CANNOT GROW OUR BLACK CARBON BANKS, BUT OUR GREEN AND blue carbon stores increase when we manage forests and shorelines sustainably.

Estuaries, such as this one in the Great Bear Rainforest, act as "blue carbon banks" capturing thousands of tons of carbon each year.
Photo by Daryl Spencer

BC's green carbon banks hold an estimated 18 billion tons of carbon in trees, roots and soils. Our forests can capture 30 million tons of carbon dioxide annually.

For a full decade, however, BC forests have been releasing dramatically more carbon than they have absorbed out of the atmosphere. While BC's forest carbon loss has been made worse by mountain pine beetles and major wildfire years, the biggest factor remains poor forest management.

Clearcut logging old-growth forests and replacing them with plantations releases large amounts of carbon pollution.

Natural intact forests adapt better to climate change. Each ecosystem develops complex and unique interrelationships of fungi, plants, and animals. Regions of BC unfragmented by human use are more productive, stable, and resilient to environmental disturbance.

BC's marine eelgrass meadows and estuarine salt marshes store at least 20 million tons of carbon and capture 180,000 tons annually. These blue carbon marine forests capture carbon at rates up to 90 times the uptake of terrestrial forests.

Marine protected areas comprise less than 2 percent of BC's ocean and have no connectivity. There is no protection for eelgrass. We must develop and implement a plan to identify and protect BC's blue carbon banks. This would involve mapping, education, partnerships with communities, First Nations and other environmental organizations, and advocacy.

SUPPORTING ECONOMIC TRANSITION

OUR ECONOMY DEPENDS ON CONTINUED, UNSUSTAINABLE WITH-drawals from the world's carbon banks, resulting in accelerating climate change and all that comes with it. We need to move quickly to a new kind of economy that respects nature's limits and sheds our dependence on fossil fuels.

It won't be easy, but with thoughtful planning and bold leadership, it can be done.

Critically, we must support workers, communities and businesses in the shift to a post-carbon economy.

The transition from resource-dependent industries to a diverse, post-carbon economy will be planned around clean technology, sustainable procurement policies, green infrastructure, and strong local economies. It will require making fossil fuels a scarce, increasingly expensive resource and encouraging behaviour change in individuals, governments, and businesses.

Workers leaving fossil fuel industries need secure and well-paid job opportunities, skills training, and a social safety net that ensures families are cared for along the way.

Solutions must also lighten, not perpetuate, the historical and ongoing burden on First Nations. First Nations must be full partners in the transition. We have an opportunity to build a new social contract: one that is inclusive, just, and leaves no one behind.

A post-carbon economy 'green jobs agenda' would:

- Be grounded in a fundamental respect for ecological limits.
- Ensure basic human needs for clean water and air.
- Promote reconciliation and economic certainty for First Nations.

- Allow individuals, families and communities to prosper and lead fulfilling lives.
- Provide workers with transition opportunities.
- Build vibrant local networks of exchange in contrast to current large-scale methods of production and distribution.

Funding to support this transition can begin with carbon tax revenue and from the elimination of fossil fuel subsidies. Given the scope and scale of the transition, a thorough review of government spending, revenue and tax structure and incentives will identify further mechanisms to promote this transition.

Warming temperatures will lead to lower crop yields and overall food production, according to the latest report by the Intergovernmental Panel on Climate Change.

Climate change calls into question the global food supply system, which is dependent on fossil fuels for transportation and monoculture farming.

We must preserve all potential agricultural land to maximize our self-sufficiency in the face of food shortages. Food-producing lands must be recognized as key to human survival and well-being in an era of climate change, and a critical strategic asset for the province and the nation.

A robust, small-scale agriculture sector, with processing and distribution hubs for added value and jobs, diversifies and strengthens regional economies.

Forestry will form an important part of a post-carbon economy, generating jobs and economic activity and supporting the long-term viability of communities.

But our forests will need to be managed in the context of two central factors: the need to defend and expand the role of forests as carbon banks and to manage 50 percent for nature.

BC requires a coherent forest action plan, with corresponding legislation, policy, and financial resources, taking into consideration the impact of climate change. The key components of this plan are described in the full version of the document.

Sierra Club BC's education program helps provide opportunities for children to connect with nature and improve their overall health.
Photo by C. Lyon

Reconnecting with Nature

CLIMATE CHANGE OFFERS A REVITALIZATION OF OUR UNDERstanding and concern for the natural world and our place in it.

In today's world, we see a worrying loss of connection to nature, especially among children. Eighty percent of children grow up in urban settings, spending 90 percent of their time indoors. Studies show a link between decreasing time spent outdoors and increasing symptoms of what has been dubbed "nature deficit disorder"—including poor academic achievement, health problems, and difficulties in social adjustment.

Many of today's children will live their lives in the midst of our efforts to confront the challenge of climate change. Building a healthy post-carbon society means creating opportunities for children and families to get outside and cultivate relationships with the natural world.

The Ten Steps to Transition

(See the full version of the document for further details.)

STABILIZE THE CLIMATE

1. Legislate a coherent 2030 BC emissions reduction target.
2. Increase and expand BC's carbon tax.
3. Establish a "climate test" for major fossil fuel projects and other proposals.
4. Develop a new land use designation for black carbon, setting aside "unburnable carbon."

DEFEND NATURE

5. Manage 50 percent of BC's land and sea with the primary purpose to conserve natural systems.
6. Ensure existing and new land use designations respect Indigenous title and rights.

TRANSITION TO A POST-CARBON ECONOMY

7. Redirect fossil fuel subsidies and carbon tax revenue to support transitions to a post-carbon economy and conservation of biodiversity.
8. Implement a forest action plan to restore forest health and create sustainable forestry jobs.
9. Create opportunities for children and families to reconnect with nature.
10. Develop an adaptation plan for BC to prepare the province for climate change.

Conclusion

CONFRONTING CLIMATE **change seems daunting, but here in BC we have the capacity and the natural assets to defend ourselves against further warming and prepare ourselves for the coming changes.**

The rapid progression of climate change demands we take steps now to stabilize the climate, preserve intact nature and ease our transition to an equitable post-carbon economy.

Changing the way we manage our lands and resources will require the joint efforts of many facets of BC society—communities, business, organized labour, the non-profit sector, faith groups—and the bold leadership of all levels of government, including First Nations governments.

The future is here, and science is helping to show us the way forward. Solutions that were once dreams of the future are now achievable and necessary.

In 2013, a variety of groups across the political spectrum joined forces in a National Day of Action rally to demand action on climate change and an end to fossil fuel expansion. *Photo by TJ Watt*

If we are successful, future generations will look back at the early-to-mid twenty-first century as the time when BC demonstrated true climate leadership by orchestrating a green industrial revolution that respected nature's limits.

Nature is not only our best ally in fighting climate change but may be our lifeline.

Sierra Club BC will lead on promoting these steps to transition, while bringing British Columbians together to make them a reality.

Sierra Club BC

SIERRA CLUB BC WORKS TO PROTECT, CONSERVE AND EDUCATE the public about BC's wilderness, species and ecosystems within the urgent context of climate change.

We will continue to build awareness about the impacts of a carbon-based economy, focus on place-based large landscape conservation to protect wild places and provide connectivity across the landscape, and work to increase understanding that our health and future is dependent on healthy ecosystems. We will act as allies to First Nations.

Sierra Club BC will adopt a leadership role advocating for this report's recommendations and raising awareness of the changing climate that makes them necessary. We will seek to build effective coalitions that can help make individual steps a reality.

Sam Bradd, Drawing Change

Acknowledgements

MANY PEOPLE HELPED ME WITH THE RESEARCH AND WRITING OF this book. I am especially appreciative of the people who generously shared their stories with me. Through these interviews I came to realize the amazing impact Sierra Club BC has had on our province. As well, I would like to thank the Sierra Club BC staff and volunteers (past and present)—Ana Simeon, Lynn Bakken, Tim Pearson, Elisabeth Hazell, Hannah Askew, Caspar Davis, Simone Cotterill, Bo Martin, Stephen Ruttan, Jens Wieting, Caitlyn Vernon, Lisa Matthaus, Ken Farquharson to name some of them—who assisted in so many ways by offering advice, reading early drafts, providing photos, and so on. Kat Zimmer's prowess with Photoshop and locating photos in SCBC's computer files was very valuable. I would like to thank Bob Peart in particular, who wholeheartedly supported me when I first suggested the idea of writing a history of the club.

I especially appreciated the feedback provided by three people—Ric Careless, Brian Pinch, and Terry Simmons—whose extensive knowledge of Sierra Club BC and the environmental movement in BC in general was valuable in ensuring that I had not made any obvious errors or left out something crucial. They very kindly read early drafts—not an easy feat. Nevertheless, I take responsibility for any omissions or details that may not fit with readers' recollections.

Several friends with writing experience also provided worthwhile advice about what to consider when attempting to write and publish a book. Thank you so much Rick Searle, Mary Rannie, Alan MacLeod, and Frances Backhouse. As well, I would also like to thank Vici Johnstone, who improved my understanding of the publishing business.

I would also like to acknowledge the three editors who greatly enhanced the organization and the readability of the book, and did so in such a diplomatic way. Claudia Haagen, Pam Robertson and Caroline Skelton, please accept my heartfelt thanks. As well, the staff at Harbour Publishing, including Anna O'Keeffe and Brianna Cerkiewicz, were a pleasure to work with and made this endeavour a much easier process.

I also thank my "virtual assistant," Terri Rothman who obtained the necessary permissions for many of the photos and quotations. As well, my sister-in-law, Darlene Pinch, volunteered many hours to type transcripts of quite a few of the interviews—a necessary but tedious chore.

In addition, I would like to thank the people who had the forethought to recognize the importance of preserving Sierra Club BC's files and other materials. First of all, there was board member Robert Miles, the primary push behind obtaining Simon Fraser University's 1978 agreement to be the initial depository. These materials were transferred to the University of Victoria Archives after the institution began to acquire items related to environmental studies in 1996. As well, I appreciate two dedicated archivists, Hugh Taylor in the mid- to late 1990s and Heather Chan in 2015, who decades apart, volunteered their time and expertise at Sierra Club BC to sort through an overwhelming storage closet full of materials prior to passing them on to the archives.

One of my first steps was to review these archived materials—a daunting task as there are stacks and stacks of boxes filled with reports, background notes, minutes, newsletters, photos, and other items going back over forty years. I would like to thank the director of the archives, Lara Wilson, the staff who retrieved multiple boxes for me from the storage rooms, and Lawrence Hong, who digitized slides and scanned photos for me.

Finally, I would like to acknowledge my husband's support. He became my best cheerleader whenever a step in the process of writing the book was achieved. It has been a learning experience for both of us and we look forward to celebrating the completion together.

Appendices

A

Founding Directors, Board Chairs, and Executive Directors

Founding Directors
1969–70
Terry Simmons (President)
William (Bill) Chalmers (VP)
Ken Farquharson
John Milne
James (Jim) Bohlen

Board Chairs

Sierra Club of BC Foundation (& local group of Pacific Northwest Region)
1970–72 Bill Chalmers
1971–72 Ken Farquharson

Sierra Club of Western Canada Chapter
1972-73 Jim Bohlen
1973-74 Bob Franson
1974-76 Pat Kariel
1977-80 Shirley Duncan
1980-83 Jim Bonfonti
1984-85 Sharon Chow
1985-86 Emlen Littell
1986-87 Robert Miles
1987-89 Peter McAllister
1990-91 Duncan Stewart
1991-94 Vicky Husband

Sierra Club of Western Canada Foundation
Previous years not found in archives; Likely a combination of Jack Hemphill & Emlen Littell for a number of years
1987-92 Jack Hemphill
1993-94 Emlen Littell

Sierra Club of BC Chapter
1994-95 Vicky Husband
1995-98 Pat Moss
1998-00 John Broadhead
2001-02 Michael Mascall
2002-03 Rob Hart/Paul Senez

Sierra Club of BC Foundation
1994-04 Tybring Hemphill
2005-10 Brian Pinch
2010-11 Jamie Biggar
2011-14 Doug McArthur
2015-17 Gail Riddell
2017-18 Jackie Larkin
2018- Valine Crist & Christine Leclerc

Executive Directors

1998-2002	Bill Wareham
2002-2003	Judy Lightwater (Interim Executive Director)
2003-2008	Kathryn Molloy
2008-2009	Susan Howatt (Interim Executive Director)
2009-2012	George Heyman
2012-2013	Sarah Cox (Interim Executive Director)
2013-2017	Bob Peart
2017-2018	(Interim Executive team: Caitlyn Vernon, Tim Pearson, Chantal Barchard)
2018-	Hannah Askew

B

Sierra Club BC's Publications

THE FOLLOWING IS AN INCOMPLETE LIST OF SCBC'S PUBLICATIONS THAT PRO-
vides an indication of the extent of the organization's research over the years.

West Coast National Park Life-Saving Trail: A Plea for Wider Boundaries, Sierra
   Club of British Columbia, prepared by Vancouver group, April 1971.
   An illustrated booklet documenting the reasons for including the Niti-
   nat area (later known as the Nitinat Triangle) in the new Pacific Rim
   National Park.

*The Nitinat Study: A Research Project Concerning the Nitinat Triangle on Van-
   couver Island*, prepared by Ric Careless, Karen McNaught, Gordon Price
   and Rod Gee of the Victoria group of the Sierra Club of British Columbia,
   1972. It provides a history of the area, a comprehensive inventory of its
   natural resources, a comparison of its recreation potential with that of
   Bowron Lakes, and a discussion of the recreation possibilities it would
   add to Vancouver Island.

The West Coast Trail and Nitinat Lakes, Douglas and McIntyre, Sierra Club of
   British Columbia, 1972. An authoritative guide to the West Coast Trail,
   reprinted numerous times over the years.

A Review of the [October, 1976] Report of the Royal Commission on Forest Resources,
   Peter H. Pearse, Commissioner; *Timber Rights and Forest Policy in British
   Columbia*, prepared by the Federation of British Columbia Naturalists and
   Sierra Club BC (Lower Mainland Group), January 1977.

Forest Energy Supply Feasibility Study, Home Heating Market, 1980. This study
   received the support of the Canadian Forestry Pacific Research Station
   and resulted in their publishing the report on Sierra Club BC's behalf.

Canada Community Development studies completed in 1981–82: *Feasibility of a Home Heating Fuelwood Industry* and *Feasibility of Small and Intermediate Scale Mariculture Industries.*

Feasibility Study of Mariculture Industry for Southern Vancouver Island, 1982. This study was well received by government and private aquaculture operators.

Nature Appreciation: A Resource with Market Potential for the Tourism Industry in Victoria, British Columbia, prepared by Josie Bannerman in association with Christina Mader for the Sierra Club of Western Canada, October 1984.

Victoria in a Knapsack, Susan Rogers and Anne Parkinson, Sierra Club of Western Canada, 1985. This book described a variety of areas in the region for hiking, nature appreciation, and beachcombing and included photos, maps, and descriptions of local history, flora, and fauna. The book had two printings of five thousand copies each, which was considered significant for a local book.

Nature Appreciation Market Survey, 1985. This tourism study provided evidence to support the need to preserve wilderness areas to promote tourism on Vancouver Island.

Background Data and Evaluation: Carmanah Creek Valley, submitted to the Sierra Club of Western Canada by Bruce K. Downie, PRP Parks: Research and Planning Inc., assisted by Shelagh Stiven, PRP Parks: Research and Planning, Inc., Chris Clements, Shearwater Mapping Ltd., and Ken Youds, J.K. Youds, Planning Consultant, February 1989.

Carmanah Creek Field Notes, January 23 to 24, 1990: Evaluation of a Proposed Hydrology Study for Carmanah Creek, prepared by E.J. Karanka and Associates for Sierra Club and Western Canada Wilderness Committee, February 1990.

The Case for Changing the Management Perspective: A Review of Forest Policy and Planning of the Greater Victoria Water Supply Area, 1924–1991, by O.R. Travers, prepared for Sierra Club of Western Canada (Victoria Group), November 21, 1991.

The GVWD: A House of Cards? A Critical Review of Logging Activity in Victoria's Municipal Watershed, 1924–1991, prepared by Mehdi Najari for the Sierra Club of Western Canada (Victoria Group), December 1991.

Economic Trends and Issues in the BC Forest Sector, prepared by Michael Mascall and Associates for Sierra Club of Western Canada, May 1993. Ray Travers, Vicky Husband, and Sharon Chow provided background information.

The Report on Compensation Issues Concerning Protected Areas, April 1993, prepared by Sierra Legal Defense fund for six environmental groups: Canadian Earthcare Society, Valhalla Society, B.C. Environmental Network, Forest Caucus, Earthlife Canada Foundation, Tatshenshini Wild, and Sierra Club of Western Canada. The report provided comprehensive legal analysis challenging corporate claims that forest licences and mining claims are private property rights.

Ancient Rainforests at Risk: Final Report of the Vancouver Island Mapping Project, by Brian Egan and Cameron Young, July 30, 1993.

"The Sierra Club of Western Canada and British Columbia Ministry of Forests Use of Multiple GIS Data Sources to Assess Logging Effects on Vancouver Island," Dave Leversee, *Earth Observation* magazine, July–August 1993.

An Analysis of the Economic Transition Issues Driving the Development of a New Forest Policy for British Columbia, prepared by Ray Travers for Sierra Club of Western Canada, November 15, 1993.

A Critical Review of the GVWD Long Term Water Supply Plan, prepared by Misty MacDuffee and Mehdi Najari for Sierra Club of Western Canada and Western Canada Wilderness Committee, January 1994.

A Review of the Ministry of Forests Strathcona Timber Supply Analysis Report: Recommendations for an Allowable Cut that will Help Protect Vulnerable Conservation Values, prepared by O.R. Travers and Bo Martin for B.C. Wild and the Sierra Club of BC, April 1995.

Conservation Areas of Interest on the Mainland Coast of BC, compiled and edited by Vicky Husband, Irene Mack, Ian McAllister, Peter McAllister, and John Nelson for Sierra Club BC and the Raincoast Conservation Society, May 20, 1996.

Compromising the Future: Overcutting in the Chilcotin–Cariboo, Ben Parfitt, November 1996.

Oweekeno Lake Reconnaissance Level Stream Inventory: Amback Creek, September 1996, prepared by M.A. Whelan and Associates and Sierra Club BC for Forest Renewal BC, the city of Campbell River, and the Ministry of Environment, Lands, and Parks, March 1997.

Beyond Timber Targets: A Balanced Vision for Vancouver Island, prepared by Darcy Riddell, Merran Smith, Tathra Street, and Jennifer Hoffman, June 1997.

Forestry Jobs and Timber: Vancouver Island Forestry Trends, 1991–1995, and their Implications for Forestry Policy, prepared by Sheldon Zakreski and Cory Waters for Sierra Club BC, June 1997.

Mid-Coast Cut & Run, Sierra Club BC, August 1997. This publication contains a map of the entire coast showing the areas harvested to date.

Reconnaissance (1:20,000) Fish and Fish Habitat Inventory of Owikeno Lake Tributaries (Reeve Creek, Sowick Creek, and Unnamed Tributary), prepared by M.A. Whelan and Associates for Sierra Club BC, February 1998.

Smokehouse Creek Fish and Fish Habitat, prepared by M.A. Whelan and Associates for Sierra Club BC, March 1998. This report provides summary information related to fish species characteristics, distributions, and relative abundance as well as stream reach and lake biophysical data for interpretation of habitat sensitivity and fish production capabilities.

Betraying Our Trust: A Citizen's Update on Environmental Rollbacks in British Columbia, 1996–1998, a combined effort of Sierra Legal Defence Fund, Greenpeace Canada, Sierra Club BC, and the BC Endangered Spaces Coalition, April 21, 1998.

Turning the Tide on Salmon, Summer 1998. This report discusses reasons for the serious decline in salmon numbers with habitat destruction being a prominent one. Sierra Club BC called on the provincial and federal governments to implement a wild salmon conservation policy.

Preliminary Bear Habitat and Ecological Assessment: Green, Khutze and Aaltanhash Valleys, Spirit Bear Conservancy Proposal, Central Coast, BC, prepared by Wayne McCrory for Sierra Club BC, August 31, 1998.

Central Coast Spring Adult Steelhead Inventory: Fish Distribution Overview, prepared by M.A. Whelan and Associates for Sierra Club BC, March 31, 1999.

The Sky Did Not Fall: The Pacific Northwest's Response to Logging Reductions, prepared by Ernie Niemi, Ed Whitelaw, and Andrew Johnston of ECONorthwest (Eugene, Oregon), April 1999.

Accounting for the Forests: A Methodological Critique of Price Waterhouse's Report: The Forest Industry in British Columbia 1997, prepared by Robert Gale, Fred Gale, and Tom Green of Ecological Economics for Sierra Club BC, produced in association with the Earthlife Canada Foundation, May 1999. The publication pinpointed six areas in which conventional accounting practices failed to identify the full social costs of industrial forest use.

Conservation Areas Design for the Central Coast of British Columbia, Canada, R.M. Jeo, M.A. Sanjayan, and D. Sizemore, prepared by Round River Conservation Studies for the Sierra Club of British Columbia, Greenpeace, the Forest Action Network and the Raincoast Conservation Society, 1999.

Out of Sight, Out of Mind and Almost Out of Time: Towards an Effective System of Marine Protected Areas of British Columbia, a brief prepared by Scott Wallace and David R. Boyd, April 2000. An overview of what Marine Protected Areas can and cannot do, outlining the challenges ahead.

Cutting for the Economy's Sake: Setting Timber Harvest Levels that are Good for BC's Economy: A Report on the Socio-economic Considerations Involved in Setting the Allowable Annual Cut in British Columbia, a working paper prepared by Tom Green for Sierra Club BC, April 2000.

Groundfish–A Case Study: The Conservation of Marine Biological Diversity and Species Abundance on Canada's West Coast–Institutional Impediments, prepared by Terry Glavin, March 2001. A report sounding the alarm about the state of groundfish and critical declines in Strait of Georgia lingcod and inshore rockfish.

Private Rights and Public Wrongs: The Case for Broader Regulation of B.C.'s Private Forestlands, Ben Parfitt, April 2001. This report highlighted the need for better environmental regulation of logging on private land in BC.

Cutting Subsidies, or Subsidized Cutting?: Subsidies to the BC Forest Industry and the BC Liberals' Commitment to End Them, a report prepared by Tom L. Green and Lisa Matthaus (Sierra Club BC) for the BC Coalition for Sustainable Forestry Solutions, July 12, 2001.

State of the Strait, prepared by Scott Wallace for Sierra Club BC, November 2002. A report describing the history and current condition of various

Strait of Georgia fisheries, as well as science-based strategies to halt and reverse negative trends.

The Right to be Responsible: A Framework for the Rebuilding and Conservation of Inshore Rockfish and Lingcod on the BC Coast, prepared by Terry Glavin, February 2002. A submission from Sierra Club BC, CPAWS, the David Suzuki Foundation, the World Wildlife Fund, and Watershed Watch.

Managing Environmental Volunteer Programs: A Conversation with Coordinators of Volunteers, a report resulting from the collaboration of five environmental organizations in Victoria: the GAIA Project/Sierra Club BC, Swan Lake Christmas Hill Nature Sanctuary, Capital Region District Parks, Life-Cycles, and the Greater Victoria Compost Education Centre, 2002. The report provides strategies and tips for creating an effective environmental volunteer program.

A Strategy for the Conservation of Pacific Salmon: Protecting the Public Interest in the Conservation of Wild Salmon in British Columbia, Terry Glavin, January 2003.

Strait of Georgia Roe Herring Fishery Report Card, Scott Wallace and Terry Glavin, April 2003.

On the Ground—Forest Certification: Green Stamp of Approval or Rubber Stamp of Destruction? A report commissioned by ForestEthics, Greenpeace, and the Sierra Club of Canada (BC Chapter), 2003. The report compares forest certification options.

Axing the Forest Service: How British Columbians are Losing their Eyes and Ears in the Forest, by Ben Parfitt and Kerri Garner, Sierra Club of Canada (BC Chapter), November 2004.

Independent Review of Nass River Sockeye Fishery Performance Measures, prepared for Sierra Club of Canada (BC Chapter) by David Levy, April 2005.

B.C. Sockeye Salmon Population Declines: Probable Causes and Recommended Strategies, prepared by David Levy, February 2006.

Nass River Salmon Fishery Report Card, prepared by David Levy, July 2006.

Blue Carbon—British Columbia: The Case for the Conservation and Enhancement of Estuarine Processes and Sediments in B.C., by Colin Campbell, Sierra Club BC, 2007.

Endangered Species Toolkit: The Citizen's Guide to Protecting Biodiversity in British Columbia (foreword by Margaret Atwood), by Jill Thompson, Elizabeth Farries, and Ana Simeon, 2007.

Greenhouse Gas Emission Reduction Scenarios for BC: Meeting the Twin Objectives of Temperature Stabilization and Global Equity, by Colin R. Campbell, Sierra Club BC, and Cliff Stainsby, BCGEU, under the auspices of the Canadian Centre for Policy Alternatives' Climate Justice Project, August 2008.

Defense for Climate and Species: Ecosystem-based management in the Great Bear Rainforest, prepared by R.F. Holt for ForestEthics, Greenpeace, and Sierra Club BC, February 2009. A report based on a review of potential climate change implications of the Great Bear Rainforest agreements.

State of British Columbia's Coastal Rainforest: Mapping the Gaps for Ecological Health and Climate Protection, Sierra Club BC, December 2009.

Managing BC's Forests for a Cooler Planet: Carbon Storage, Sustainable Jobs and Conservation, prepared by Ben Parfitt, January 2010. This report was part of the Climate Justice Project, a research alliance led by the Canadian Centre for Policy Alternatives (BC) and the University of British Columbia. Co-published by CCPA (BC); the BC Government and Services Employees' Union; the Communications, Energy and Paperworkers Union; the David Suzuki Foundation; Pulp, Paper and Woodworkers of Canada; Sierra Club BC; United Steelworkers District 3 (Western Canada); and the Western Canada Wilderness Committee.

Slipping Through the Cracks? The Fate of Focal Species in the Great Bear Rainforest, a report by Sierra Club BC, Greenpeace, and ForestEthics, 2010.

Axed: A Decade of Cuts to BC's Forest Service, by Ben Parfitt, published by Sierra Club BC and the Canadian Centre for Policy Alternatives, December 2010.

Restoring the Balance for Climate and Species, by Jens Wieting, with mapping analysis by Dave Leversee, Sierra Club BC, January 2011. This report shows that logging practices in BC's coastal rainforests are a significant source of uncounted greenhouse gas emissions.

Fair and Effective Carbon Pricing: Lessons from BC, prepared by Marc Lee for Sierra Club BC and the Canadian Centre for Policy Alternatives (BC), February 2011. Part of the Climate Justice Project, a five-year research project led by CCPA (BC) and the University of British Columbia.

Take It Taller: Great Bear Rainforest Overview, a report by ForestEthics, Greenpeace, and Sierra Club BC, February 2012.

Emissions Impossible? British Columbia's Uncounted Greenhouse Gas Emissions, by Jens Wieting and Colin R. Campbell, September 2012. This report discusses the concern that the BC government's climate policy had lost momentum and the provincial government was not building on its initial steps to fight global warming and reduce emissions in a coherent and adequate manner.

Carbon at Risk: BC's Unprotected Old Growth Rainforest, by Jens Wieting, with mapping analysis by Dave Leversee, Sierra Club BC, February 2013. This report raises concern that the province's full carbon footprint is actually much bigger than reported because of uncounted—and increasing—emissions from fossil fuels exported from British Columbia. In addition, emissions from BC's forest lands increased by 363 percent from 2000 to 2010.

B.C. Forests Carbon Meltdown: Backgrounder, Sierra Club BC, January 2014.

B.C. Forests Wake-up Call: Heavy Carbon Losses Hit 10-year Mark, by Jens Wieting, Sierra Club BC, June 2015. An analysis of the BC government forest carbon emissions data showing that for a full decade, BC forests had been releasing dramatically more carbon into the atmosphere than they had absorbed out of the atmosphere. BC's forests emitted 256 million tons of carbon dioxide during the period 2003–12. In contrast, BC's forests absorbed 441 million tons of carbon dioxide from 1993 to 2002.

Credibility Crisis: Major Flaws Threaten Credibility of NEB Assessment Process for Kinder Morgan Trans Mountain Pipeline and Tankers Proposal, Sierra Club BC, June 2015. The National Energy Board was widely criticized in its review of the Kinder Morgan pipeline expansion proposal for failures in process, for limiting participation, and for a lack of accountability and fairness. In this report, SCBC details the deficiencies in the process that gave rise to public criticism and dissatisfaction, causing some intervenors to withdraw.

Blind Spot: The Failure to Consider Climate in British Columbia's Environmental Assessments, by Erin Gray, with research assistance from Rosanna Adams, September 2015. A submission to the BC Climate Leadership Team, prepared by the Environmental Law Centre, University of Victoria, on behalf of Sierra Club BC.

The Future Is Here: An Urgent Call to Defend Nature, Stabilize the Climate and Transition to Post-Carbon Prosperity, Sierra Club BC, October 2015; updated June 2017. A forward-looking document aimed at providing guidelines for Sierra Club BC's future work, based on Colin Campbell's experience, scientific expertise, and knowledge of conservation research. Later updated by Caitlyn Vernon and others.

Vancouver Island's Last Stand, co-published by the Wilderness Committee and Sierra Club BC, Wilderness Committee Educational Report, Vol 35 (3), 2016, sierraclub.bc.ca/wp-content/uploads/2016/04/Vancouver-Islands-Last-Stand-newspaper_2016.pdf.

Vancouver Island and South Coast Rainforest at High Ecological Risk, by Jens Wieting, with mapping analysis by Dave Leversee, Sierra Club BC, March 2016.

Ajax Project Review—Review of Predicted Water Contamination, by Kevin A. Morin, with Minesite Drainage Assessment Group, prepared for Sierra Club of BC Foundation, March 2016.

Hydro Bill Madness: BC Government Goes For Broke With Your Money, prepared by lead author Caitlyn Vernon for Sierra Club BC, March 2017. Report along with a video that connected the dots between Site C, LNG, and increases to BC Hydro bills. The video garnered over 117,000 views and helped to make Site C an issue in the 2017 provincial election.

The Future Is Here: An Urgent Call to Defend Nature, Stabilize the Climate and Transition to Post-Carbon Prosperity, Sierra Club BC, June, 2017. The document outlines a vision and makes proposals for changing the way we manage BC's waters, lands, and resources in the face of climate change and its accelerating impacts.

Hidden, Ignored and Growing: BC's Forest Carbon Emissions, prepared by Jens Wieting, January 2019. Although the BC government's new climate action plan provides a number of good steps, one of its shortcomings is the lack of action for forests. This report discusses the need to take into account forest carbon emissions and advocates for a more transparent display of meaningful data that can inform forest management and logging practices.

C

Chronology of Sierra Club BC

1969
Sierra Club of BC, situated in Vancouver, becomes a local group of the Pacific Northwest Chapter of Sierra Club US with thirty-five dues-paying members; incorporated as a BC society on November 28, 1969; first major campaign is the threatened flooding of the Skagit River Valley.

1970
Sierra Club BC starts lobbying to ensure the life-saving trail (now the West Coast Trail) is included in Pacific Rim National Park on the west coast of Vancouver Island.

1971
Sierra Club of Victoria becomes a local group in February, and campaigns to include the Nitinat Triangle as part of Pacific Rim National Park; Don't Make a Wave Committee separates from Sierra Club BC and becomes Greenpeace; *Phyllis Cormack* sets sail for Amchitka; BC government passes resolution opposing tanker traffic on west coast.

1972
There are 500 dues-paying members in BC and Alberta, and 250 are required for chapter status; Sierra Club of BC becomes part of the new chapter—Sierra Club of Western Canada (SCWC), within Sierra Club US; campaign opposing a ski development on Brent Mountain (Penticton); Nitinat Triangle achieves protection; the campaign to protect Tsitika-Schoen is begun by SCWC, BC Wildlife Federation, and BC Federation of Naturalists; new NDP government forms Cypress Provincial Park; federal government places moratorium on tanker traffic on north coast and suspends offshore drilling; Campbell River group is formed.

1973

Concerns raised by SCWC include Mackenzie Highway, James Bay Project, Mackenzie Valley Pipeline; club opposes shipping oil in Juan de Fuca Strait, and participates in natural gas pricing hearings; Geraldine Irby begins editing the club's newsletter; campaign to protect West Coast Strip (now Juan de Fuca Trail) launches; Chilliwack Lake Provincial Park is formed.

1974

Part-time secretary Sharon Elliot is hired by the club; Vancouver group is formed; Haida Nation starts campaign against logging in South Moresby.

1975

SCWC is concerned about the oilsands question, Fraser River estuary, and 2, 4-D battle in the Okanagan; Spatsizi Provincial Park is established; SCWC submits and intervenes at the Royal Commission on Forest Resources, chaired by Dr. Peter Pearse; Katy Madsen discovers uranium claims in Okanagan and starts protest.

1976

Canadian entities start using the name Sierra Club of Western Canada (SCWC); Terry Simmons intervenes in Revelstoke Dam hearings; campaign to protect Cream Lake from mining.

1977

Save the Stein coalition formed; local group in Nelson formed; full-time conservation representative hired in Victoria (Bob Nixon from Winnipeg); SCWC becomes member of Fraser River coalition; SCWC becomes involved with South Moresby campaign; Schoen Lake Provincial Park is formed.

1978

Sierra Club of Western Canada is established under the Federal Companies Act and has 700 members; coalition to save Tsitika watershed is formed; SCWC takes over ownership of Talchako Lodge; Simon Fraser University agrees to archive SCBC's files.

1979

New club office at 536A Yates Street; SCWC instrumental in establishment of McCarthy Inquiry regarding the issuing of licences and certificates to guide outfitters in BC; submission to the Northern Pipeline Agency by SCWC member Leo Rutledge.

1980

Major campaign under the direction of George Wood to preserve the Robson Bight area; workshop held in Vancouver to develop strategies for protecting the Stikine; Friends of the Stikine is formed; First Nations oppose logging on Meares Island; BC government places seven-year moratorium on uranium mining; North Columbia group starts in the Okanagan.

1981
SCWC testifies at hearings held by the House of Commons Subcommittee on Acid Rain in Calgary; concerns include Site C, Hat Creek, Liard, South Moresby; 4,500-hectare Lower Tsitika ecological reserve park is proposed by SCWC; Khutzeymateen Ecological Reserve proposal brought to SCWC's attention; Cowichan group is formed.

1982
Discussions begin about setting up a national Sierra Club organization in Canada; Botanical Beach is put up for sale and a campaign to preserve it is launched; SCWC board decides to sell Talchako Lodge to its caretakers; Robson Bight Ecological Reserve is established; Site C Dam is rejected by BC Utilities Commission.

1983
SCWC has 1,100 members; Skagit Valley is finally saved after fourteen years; Valhalla Wilderness Society (in coalition with SCWC and other groups) wins its campaign for Valhalla Park after an eleven-year battle.

1984
Canadian and US governments sign the Skagit River Treaty; First Nations establish Meares Island as a tribal park and set up a blockade—the first significant event of the War in the Woods.

1985
Foundation's name changes to Sierra Club Foundation of Western Canada; SCWC publishes *Victoria in a Knapsack*; Haida set up blockade on Lyall Island.

1986
South Moresby train caravan travels from Newfoundland to Vancouver; agreement is reached between Canadian and US organizations to set up a national organization in Canada; SCWC becomes involved in the Height of the Rockies campaign, and becomes concerned about logging in the Kitlope Valley.

1987
Stein Valley is an active campaign; a new master plan for Strathcona Park is worked on; Haley Lake Ecological Reserve is secured as habitat for endangered white-nosed marmot thanks to the Sierra Cowichan local group; South Moresby National Park Reserve is established; boundaries of the third section of Pacific Rim National Park are established and the settlement price is agreed to; Nitinat Triangle is now officially part of the park; Galloping Goose bike path is established; 9,000-year-old glass sponge reefs are found off the west coast; Height of the Rockies is made into a Forest Service Recreation Area.

1988
Randy Stoltmann announces finding stands of tallest Sitka spruce in Canada in the Carmanah Valley and SCWC becomes involved; Wolf Working Group is established; Buy Good Wood campaign begins; Tahsish Ecological Reserve

is formed; local group is formed on Salt Spring Island; proposal for Windy Craggy Mine in area of Tatshenshini is announced; South Moresby Agreement is signed.

1989

Tatshenshini campaign is started; Elizabeth May becomes the club's national representative; Sierra Lower Mainland's sixteen-year campaign for the UBC Endowment Lands is successful and Pacific Spirit Park is formed.

1990

Carmanah Pacific Provincial Park is created; Sierra Club of Canada national office is set up in Ottawa; Sierra Legal Defence Fund is incorporated in Vancouver; Babine River Corridor Park is established; Peter McAllister sets sail for Great Bear Rainforest (GBR) to explore coastal valleys; Victoria group sets up Ecology House in Market Square.

1991

Referendum on whether there should be a BC Chapter or a West Coast Islands Chapter—decision is for a BC Chapter; SCBC's mapping study comparing 1954 to 1990 forests is released; twenty-five European politicians, scientists, and journalists visit BC logging sites; Koeye Valley in the GBR is set aside as a study area by the government.

1992

Vancouver Island Map Project's map is released with the interim report *Ancient Rainforests at Risk*; Kyuquot Sound/Brooks Peninsula campaign begins; Sierra Club of Canada becomes a legal entity with Elizabeth May as its first executive director; BC establishes the Commission on Resources and Environment (CORE); Canada signs the UN Convention on Biological Diversity.

1993

SCWC starts working with Salvadoran Centre for Appropriate Technology (CESTA in El Salvador), with GAIA Project, tree planting; final report of SCWC's mapping study of Vancouver Island is released, providing an inventory of remaining old-growth forest; Hearings regarding the Kemano Completion Project are set up and SCBC makes a submission; Gwaii Haanas Agreement is signed with 50 percent of Haida Gwaii to be protected; Britain's Channel 4 produced its *Battle for the Trees* documentary about the GBR; 850 people are arrested in Clayoquot Sound blockade; Clayoquot Sound Scientific Panel is set up; Forest Stewardship Council is formed to set standards on forest products; Tatshenshini-Alsek Park is established; Environmental Mining Council is formed with SCBC as a founding member.

1994

Khutzeymateen is declared a park on the eve of the Victoria-hosted Commonwealth Games; Ts'il-os Provincial Park (Chilko Lake) is created; Kitlope is protected; BC government adopts CORE recommendations for Vancouver Island's nearly intact watersheds, and adds Tahsish, Kwois, lower Tsitika, upper

Carmanah, and Walbran as protected areas; Premier Harcourt announces land use plan for Cariboo-Chilcotin that protects seventeen new areas. Sierra Club of Western Canada is disbanded and Sierra Club of BC (SCBC) is established as a separate chapter within Sierra Club of Canada; SCBC's Rainforest Bus starts running to inform the public about current environmental issues in the rainforest; Sierra Victoria's four-year battle to protect Victoria's watershed from logging is successful.

1995
Tatshenshini-Alsek Wilderness Park is declared a World Heritage Site; Kemano Completion project is declared dead by Premier Harcourt; Lower Mainland group is first Canadian entity to have a website; Height of the Rockies and Skagit Valley become provincial parks; Canadian Rainforest Network including SCBC, WWF, Greenpeace, Forest Action Network, and others join the campaign for the preservation of the entire coast from Knight Inlet to the Alaska Panhandle.

1996
Stein Valley a notable victory; SCBC is a founding member of the Wild Salmon Coalition; Juan de Fuca Provincial Park is established; proposal to build LNG plant at either Kitimat or Prince Rupert is opposed by SCBC; BC government enacts BC Wildlife Act.

1997
Environmental education kits for elementary and secondary classes are developed by Jenn Hoffmann; Cypress Provincial Park master plan is completed—SCBC had been a contributor.

1998
Bill Wareham becomes SCBC's first executive director; Sierra Club BC's environmental education program launches; Quadra Island group forms; SCBC calls for a moratorium on grizzly bear hunting; SCBC takes over coordination of Forest Watch; Victoria group makes a submission to the Environmental Appeal Board against spraying BtK for gypsy moths.

1999
SCBC moves to 576 Johnson Street; Rainforest Bus spends May driving 5,000 kilometres through twelve states on the US east coast with 4,000 people touring the bus, then starts a Canadian tour; Marine Campaign begins; Babine River Corridor Park is established; Coast Mountain and Haida Gwaii groups form; European publishers visit GBR and Joint Solutions Project is established; forming of the JSP and beginning of negotiations is *Time* magazine's best environmental story of 1999.

2000
Fisheries and Oceans Canada drafts Wild Salmon Policy; BC government increases conservation area in Muskwa-Kechika to 63,000 square kilometres; Clayoquot Sound becomes a UNESCO World Biosphere Reserve; SCWC and

partners seek to work collaboratively with First Nations towards lasting conservation solutions in Clayoquot Sound; Vicky Husband receives the Order of BC; campaign starts against proposal to build gas pipeline to Vancouver Island.

2001

Protection of 71,347 hectares surrounding Spruce Lake in Chilcotin is achieved; BC government accepts recommendations of SCBC and allies, coastal logging companies, First Nations, and local communities to protect 600,000 hectares of GBR and put another 896,000 hectares into deferral until informed land use decisions can be made; Stikine River Provincial Park and Cariboo-Chilcotin are formed and South Chilcotin Mountain is protected, later to become a park; 12 percent of BC's land base is now protected.

2002

SCBC and allies join the Marine Planning Caucus to campaign to ensure integrated planning commitment built into Oceans Act actually happens; Vicky Husband receives the Order of Canada; Clayoquot Sound becomes a UNESCO biosphere; Sea to Sky group forms in Squamish; federal Species At Risk Act is enacted.

2003

SCBC moves office to 733 Johnson Street; West Kootenay and Malaspina local groups start; Sierra Club Canada becomes a separate legal entity from the US organization; Turning Point Initiative, later known as Coastal First Nations, forms an alliance of several of the First Nations groups in the GBR; Kathryn Molloy becomes the new executive director.

2004

Land use planning process for southern portion of the GBR reaches consensus agreement; Shell Canada is granted a 400,000-hectare tenure for coal-bed methane; SCBC makes a submission to the Federal Panel on Offshore Oil and Gas; BC government and First Nations have first government-to-government deliberations about the GBR; BC Hydro halts proposal for a gas pipeline to Vancouver Island; GAIA Project ends.

2005

Sierra Malaspina celebrates victory in its campaign to stop a highway from being built through Millennium Park; Coastal Guardian Watchmen Network is founded; SCBC starts its Vote Environment campaign.

2006

Canada's Seafood Guide is available as a wallet card; SCBC helps launch SeaChoice; after a joint campaign, the provincial government protects 2.2 million hectares of mountain caribou habitat in northeastern BC; Elizabeth May resigns as executive director of Sierra Club Canada to become leader of the federal Green Party; proposal for open-pit coal mine in Flathead is announced; SCBC publishes flooding maps for the Lower Mainland and

Victoria that draw public attention to the potential impact of climate change on BC's coastal communities.

2007
Sierra CERCles (Carbon Emission Reduction Clubs) are initiated; SCBC's global warming campaign helps persuade the BC government to adopt world-class targets for carbon emission reductions; SCBC joins the Flathead campaign; Taseko Mines acquires property at Fish Lake; $120 million raised to support conservation management and economic diversification in the GBR; SCBC and other groups in the Rainforest Solutions Project receive the World Wildlife Fund's Gift to the World award for their GBR achievement; Al Gore visits Victoria; Gordon Campbell's government brings in a climate change agenda; *Endangered Species Toolkit* is published.

2008
Climate-friendly budget is announced by the BC government with the first significant carbon tax in North America; SCBC launches a new website; tenth anniversary of the education program in schools; SCBC joins other groups to launch a lawsuit against the Department of Fisheries and Oceans, alleging the DFO failed to protect critical orca whale habitat under the Species at Risk Act, the first lawsuit of its kind in Canada, filed by Ecojustice; a four-year moratorium is placed on oil and gas development in the Sacred Headwaters; the Kitlope area becomes a conservancy.

2009
Federal government issues an order making it illegal to destroy orca whales' critical habitat, but the definition is not strict enough so Ecojustice files a second suit; a new SCBC local group forms in the Comox Valley; the Lifetime Achievement Award is given to Ruth Master, founding member of Sierra Comox Valley; 2.1 million hectares of old-growth forest is protected through GBR agreements with legislation of ecosystem-based management in an additional 700,000 hectares of the GBR; George Heyman becomes executive director.

2010
SCBC expresses concern about the destruction of Fish Lake and tailings from Taseko's proposed Prosperity Mine, then Fish Lake is saved when the federal government overrides the BC government's approval of the project; SCBC becomes concerned about the Site C Dam proposal; SCBC and other groups convince the BC government to legislate a ban of mining and energy development in Flathead; South Chilcotin Mountain Park is formed; Enbridge applies to build the Northern Gateway pipeline from Edmonton to Kitimat; Tofino raises concern about mining on Catface Mountain.

2011
Juan de Fuca Provincial Park is saved from a proposed resort development after a three-day public hearing and years of SCBC campaigning for protection of the area; Heyman recommends eliminating SCBC's chapter status and

transferring its functions into the foundation; run-of-the-river project in Bute Inlet is stopped.

2012

Taseko Mines reveals a new plan for Fish Lake; Kinder Morgan announces plans to twin Trans Mountain pipeline and dredge Second Narrows channel to allow larger tankers; two new local groups form: Nanaimo and Okanagan Valley; courts decide that federal government is legally bound to protect orca whales; a permanent ban on oil and gas development in the Sacred Headwaters is announced.

2013

Bob Peart is the new SCBC executive director; the Youth Environmental Leadership Program (YELP) launches; Ecojustice launches a court challenge over water use and fracking in BC against BC Oil and Gas Commission, on behalf of a coalition of SCBC and other groups; Teck Resources sets aside blocks of land for conservation purposes in Flathead; Sierra Comox Valley celebrates as Raven coal mine proposal in Comox Valley is rejected due to lack of consultation with First Nations and concern about impacts on drinking water and air quality; SCBC board finalizes the decision to dissolve its chapter status, Sierra Club BC is now a separate organization from Sierra Club Canada.

2014

SCBC in coalition with other groups wins a court case against the federal government over the failure to protect, under the Species at Risk Act, four endangered species (Nechako white sturgeon, marbled murrelet, humpback whale, and mountain caribou) put at risk by the proposed Enbridge pipeline; the Pull Together campaign is launched with RAVEN Trust to raise funds for First Nations legal challenges against Enbridge; SCBC responds to Mount Polley spill—the worst mining waste disaster in Canadian history—making recommendations for independent review, which are adopted by the provincial government; Colin Campbell retires; Quadra Island achieves a new park, unofficially known as Heart of Quadra Parks; Fish Lake is saved once again after a heated campaign against Taseko's revised proposal for a Prosperity Mine with the federal review dismissing the revised application; Tsilhqot'in win the right of aboriginal title in court.

2015

Justin Trudeau announces that he will introduce legislation for a ban on north coast oil tankers; BC Hydro begins construction on Site C Dam; Colin Campbell produces *The Future Is Here*; Fourth Annual Bioblitz in Flathead; Raven Mine's revised proposal in Comox is withdrawn.

2016

First Nations win a major court challenge against Enbridge and the challenge is not repealed, marking a final victory for the Pull Together campaign that stops the Northern Gateway pipeline after a twelve-year battle; the federal government rejects the Enbridge Northern Gateway pipeline but approves the Kinder Morgan pipeline; Woodfibre LNG port is approved; the federal government approves Petronas fracked gas plant; final agreement for Great Bear Rainforest is announced, protecting 85 percent of region's rainforests after a twenty-year campaign; SCBC and its partners receive US Sierra Club's Earthcare Award and Buckminster Fuller Challenge Award.

2017
Ahousaht First Nation announces it is setting aside 80 percent of its territory in Clayoquot Sound as cultural and natural areas; UN concludes Canada is failing to protect Wood Buffalo National Park; both Petronas (Pacific North-West LNG) and Aurora LNG abandon the idea of building projects near Prince Rupert; federal government denies approval for Taseko mine at Fish Lake and Tsilhqot'in First Nation asks the court to overturn the BC government's drilling permit; NDP wins provincial election; BC government rejects Ajax Mine near Kamloops; BC government decides to proceed with Site C Dam; Pacific North Coast Integrated Management Area framework is endorsed by the federal government; BC government announces a moratorium on grizzly bear hunting; Sooke Hills Wilderness Regional Park is formed; last parcels are purchased along Juan de Fuca Trail; Andrew Weaver proposes a private member's bill for the BC Endangered Species Act, supported by new NDP government; BC government opposes Kinder Morgan pipeline and goes to court seeking jurisdiction to limit the transport of heavy oil, causing significant friction with Alberta and federal governments; federal government introduces the Oil Tanker Moratorium Act.

2018
Federal minister of the environment declares an imminent threat to mountain caribou, first step in requiring BC to develop a conservation plan; federal government, as a means of ensuring a pipeline to the west coast, purchases the project from Kinder Morgan; Pull Together campaign continues to raise funds for First Nations involved with court challenges—$639,000 as of the spring; Federal Court of Appeal overturns approval for Trans Mountain; Sierra Club BC's education program offers French language workshops and a teacher mentorship program with monthly meetings; Hannah Askew becomes executive director in July; federal government directs National Energy Board to reconsider the marine shipping aspect of the Trans Mountain Pipeline proposal and to consult with Indigenous communities affected by the proposed pipeline; BC government announces that an LNG pipeline will be built with a terminal at Kitimat; BC government announces its climate action plan in December.

2019
BC's minister of finance announces funds ($902 million over three years) for the climate action plan; National Energy Board releases its Reconsideration report for the Trans Mountain pipeline, endorsing its approval despite the likely "significant adverse" effects on orca whales and the environment; Sierra Club BC celebrates fifty years since its formation in 1969.

D

Alliances and Partnerships

A SAMPLING OF THE MULTITUDE OF ALLIANCES, COALITIONS, AND PARTNER-
ships that Sierra Club BC has participated in over the years. Many of these
coalitions or partnerships were created to address a particular issue and often
ended once the goals were achieved. Others remain active today.

Run Out Skagit Spoilers (ROSS) Committee: Prior to 1969. Included Sierra
  Club BC, Society Promoting Environmental Conservation (SPEC), Alpine
  Club of Canada, BC Wildlife Federation, Federation of Mountain Clubs,
  Vancouver Natural History Society, BC Federation of Fly Fishers, Dog-
  wood Canoe Club, and others opposed the flooding of Skagit Valley by the
  High Ross Dam.
Arctic International Wildlife Range Society: Sierra Club BC worked with other
  public groups in the 1970s and early 1980s towards the establishment of
  a park in the northern Yukon to protect the Porcupine caribou herd and
  other wildlife species in that area.
SPOILS (Stop Pollution from Oil Spills): In the 1970s, Sierra Club BC, with the
  BC Environmental Council, drew Canada-wide attention to the problem
  of supertanker accidents and sinkings along the coast.
Alliance against Uranium Mining: Formed with SPEC and the Federation
  of BC Naturalists in 1979 to participate jointly in an inquiry about uranium mining.
Public Advisory Committee to the Forest and Wildlife Ministries: This com-
  mittee was started by Bob Nixon of the Sierra Club in 1980, and included
  representatives from several environmental groups.
Fraser River Coalition: Formed in 1977 by Sierra Club BC, Federation of BC
  Naturalists, BC Wildlife Federation, SPEC, United Fishermen and Allied
  Workers Union, BC Steelhead Society, West Coast Environmental Law,

Vancouver Natural History Society, Richmond Anti-Pollution Association, and the Community Forum on Airport Development.

Rivers Defense Coalition: Formed to oppose the Kemano expansion and protect the Nechako River. Made up of Sierra Club BC and other environmental groups, fishers, citizens of the Bulkley and Nechako valleys, and First Nations including the Cheslatta Indian Band.

Kitimat Oil Coalition: In the early 1980s, Sierra Club BC and fifteen other groups opposed a proposed Kitimat oil port and pipeline running east to Edmonton to transport Alaskan oil to the southern states.

Peace Valley Environmental Association: Spearheaded by Leo Rutledge, a farmer and Sierra Club BC director, this group came together to oppose the Site C Dam in the 1980s.

Parks for Tomorrow Coalition: Included Alberta Wilderness Association, Canadian Nature Federation, Canadian Parks and Wilderness Society, Federation of Alberta Naturalists, Federation of Ontario Naturalists, and Sierra Club of Western Canada.

Coalition for Wildlife and Wilderness in B.C.: Late in 1986, Sierra Club BC was one of the founding members of this coalition, along with B.C. Wildlife Federation, Ducks Unlimited, Federation of BC Naturalists, Friends of Ecological Reserves, and Guide Outfitters Association of BC. Its purpose was to provide a common front on matters of common concern.

Northwest Conservation Act Coalition: Came together in 1987 to fight hydro exports to the US.

Lower Stikine Management Advisory Committee: Created in 1988 with SCBC and Friends of the Stikine as members. The committee nominated the Stikine to be a Canadian Heritage River in 1995. To date there are only three BC rivers with this designation (Kicking Horse, Fraser, and Cowichan).

Friends of Cypress Provincial Park: Since 1990, Sierra Club BC has been a member with other groups and individuals dedicated to protecting Cypress Park's natural environment and associated values.

Wild Salmon Coalition: Formed circa 1991 with SCBC mapping critical salmon streams and raising awareness.

Southwestern BC Wildlands Alliance: Formed circa 1990 by Canadian Parks and Wilderness Society, BC Spaces for Nature, Burke Mountain Naturalists, Federation of BC Mountain Clubs, BC Mountaineering Club, Alpine Club of Canada, Canadian Earthcare Society, and Sierra Club BC.

B.C. Environmental Network: A network of public interest, non-profit organizations in BC concerned with environmental integrity, formed in the early 1990s.

Campaign for the Northern Rockies: In 1993, Sierra Club BC joined Canadian Parks and Wilderness Society and Chetwynd Environmental Society in a twenty-organization coalition to protect this vast wilderness area.

Mapping Consortium: Set up in 1995 to produce maps, which became highly respected for their accuracy and impact. Included Sierra Club BC, BC Wild, Ecotrust Canada, and Interrain.

Canadian Rainforest Network: Established in 1996 and made up of twenty diverse groups, including Greenpeace Canada, Sierra Club BC, Sierra Legal Defence Fund, Steelhead Society of BC, Valhalla Wilderness Society, Bear Watch, and others, working to protect the ecological integrity of BC's ancient temperate rainforests.

Great Bear Rainforest Alliance: Formed in the 1990s by Sierra Club BC, Greenpeace, Forest Action Network, and Raincoast Conservation Society.

Forest Stewardship Council: Organization certifying wood products from properly managed forests and "ecolabelling" them. Sierra Club BC applied to join in 1996 and was granted a seat at the table.

BC Endangered Species Coalition: Formed in 2001 by Sierra Club BC, Ecojustice, David Suzuki Foundation, and Wilderness Committee.

Help MELP: Represented over sixty environmental- and recreation-oriented organizations that joined hands to advocate for increased environmental protection budgets. (The name refers to the former Ministry of Environment, Land and Parks.)

Georgia Strait Crossing Concerned Citizens Coalition (GSXCCC): Formed in 2000 to oppose the proposed natural gas pipeline and BC Hydro's plan to switch to fossil fuel–based electricity generation. Sierra Club BC volunteer Tom Hackney led the group.

Markets Initiative: Starting in 2000, a collaborative effort by Sierra Club BC, Friends of Clayoquot Sound, and Greenpeace strove to reform the purchasing practices of Canadian book and magazine publishers by encouraging a shift to ancient forest–free paper.

BCfacts.org: Launched in May 2003 by nine of BC's most prominent environmental organizations—including Sierra Club BC, the David Suzuki Foundation, the Western Canada Wilderness Committee, and West Coast Environmental Law—to document the BC Liberal government's environmental record.

BC Coalition for Sustainable Forestry Solutions: SCBC was a founding member of the group formed in 2002 in response to the BC government's sweeping rollbacks to environmental policy, launching community meetings to encourage discussion of environmentally and socially beneficial forestry practices.

Sustainable Campuses Project: Sierra Youth Coalition and Sierra Club BC. Sierra Youth Coalition was a national organization founded by Sierra Club Canada, and the BC Chapter provided staff with support and space.

Climate Change Teacher Training Programs: Partnership with Wild BC in schools across the province (2005-06).

Flathead Wild Coalition: Formed by Wildsight, the Canadian Parks and Wilderness Society (BC), Sierra Club BC, Yellowstone to Yukon (Y2Y) Conservation Initiative, Headwaters Montana, and the National Parks Conservation Association.

Coastal Guardian Watchmen Training Program: Partnership agreement between Northwest Community College, Qqs Project Society (Heiltsuk

Nation), and Sierra Club BC to enhance the economic well-being of the central and north coast First Nations communities in BC through training and skills development. Circa 2009, SCBC's active involvement was no longer needed.

Green Jobs BC: An alliance of labour and environmental groups with a shared vision of an inclusive, sustainable economy that provides good jobs, is socially just, protects the environment, and reduces carbon emissions.

Environmental Non-Governmental Organization (ENGO) Marine Planning Network: Circa late 2000s, Sierra Club BC joined with Living Oceans, David Suzuki Foundation, Canada Parks and Wilderness Society, and World Wildlife Fund to help develop a marine plan that implements ecosystem-based management and a network of marine protected areas throughout BC's North and Central Coast.

Campaign against Coal-fired Power Plants: Formed in 2006 by Sierra Club BC and eight other groups opposing the BC government's decision to build coal-fired plants at Tumbler Ridge and Princeton.

SeaChoice: A national program involving Sierra Club in collaboration with many allies, which produces a list of sustainably caught fish for consumers.

Species at Risk Coalition: Formed by Sierra Club BC, Ecojustice, David Suzuki Foundation, and Wilderness Committee.

Clayoquot Solutions Steering Committee: Formed by Sierra Club BC, Greenpeace, ForestEthics, Friends of Clayoquot Sound, Western Canada Wilderness Committee, and Natural Resources Defence Council.

Organizing for Change (OFC): Since 2003, Sierra Club BC and a number of environmental groups have been working collaboratively to develop policy priorities for the provincial government.

Site C Dam Campaign: Y to Y, Peace Valley Environment Association, SCBC, Raven Trust.

Clayoquot Sound Conservation Alliance: Greenpeace, Friends of Clayoquot Sound, Sierra Club BC, Stand.earth, and Wilderness Committee.

Coast to Coast Grizzly Bear Initiative: Formed by the Canadian Parks and Wilderness Society (BC), Conservation Northwest, Sierra Club BC, the St'át'imc Chiefs Council, AWARE Whistler, BC Nature, Pemberton Wildlife Association, Whistler Naturalists, Lillooet Naturalist Society, and BC Spaces for Nature.

Coalition of Groups Against Fracking: Formed in 2017 to call for the government "review" of the natural gas industry's fracking operations to be broadened to a full review. The groups included Canadian Centre for Policy Alternatives, Sierra Club BC, Union of BC Indian Chiefs, Canadian Association of Physicians for the Environment, David Suzuki Foundation, Wilderness Committee, West Coast Environmental Law, SkeenaWild Conservation Trust, Saanich Inlet Network, Public Health Association of BC, My Sea to Sky, Keepers of the Water, Friends of Wild Salmon Coalition, Douglas Channel Watch, Council of Canadians, Corporate Mapping Project, and BC Tap Water Alliance.

Selected Sources

History of the US Sierra Club

Brower, David, *For Earth's Sake: The Life and Times of David Brower*. Salt Lake City: Peregrine Smith Books, 1990.

Cohen, Michael P., *The History of the Sierra Club: 1892-1970*. San Francisco: Sierra Club Books, 1988.

Fox, Stephen, *John Muir and His Legacy: The American Conservation Movement*. Toronto: Little, Brown and Company, 1981.

McCloskey, Michael, *In the Thick of it: My life in the Sierra Club*. Washington: Island Press, 2005.

Muir, John, *The Yosemite*. New York: The Century Co., 1912. Republished by The Modern Library, 2003.

Turner, Tom, *Sierra Club: 100 Years of Protecting Nature*. New York: Henry N. Abrams, 1991.

Conservation in BC

Careless, Ric, *To Save the Wild Earth*. Vancouver: Raincoast Books, 1997.

Davis, Lynn, editor, *Alliances: Re-envisioning Indigenous/Non-indigenous Relationships*. Toronto: University of Toronto Press, 2010.

Friends of Ecological Reserves website ecoreserves.bc.ca/ecoreserves/about-eco reserves/.

Johnston, Moira, "Canada's Queen Charlotte Islands: Home of the Haida." *National Geographic*, Vol 172 (1), 1987, 102-127.

May, Elizabeth, *Paradise Won: The Struggle for South Moresby*. Toronto: McClelland & Stewart, 1990. Free download at: elizabethmaymp.ca/wp-content/uploads/Eliza beth_May_Paradise_Won.pdf.

Smith, Merran, *Place of Power: Lessons from the Great Bear Rainforest*. Vancouver: Tides Canada Foundation, 2010.

Vernon, Caitlyn, *Nowhere Else on Earth: Standing Tall for the Great Bear Rainforest*. Victoria: Orca Book Publishers, 2011.

Forestry Issues

Findley, Rowe, "Will We Save Our Own?" *National Geographic*, Vol 178 (3), 1990, 106-136.

Haddock, Mark, *Professional Reliance Review: The Final Report of the Review of Professional Reliance in Natural Resource Decision-Making*. BC Ministry of Environment and Climate Change Strategy, June 2018, engage.gov.bc.ca/app/uploads/sites/272/2018/06/Professional_Reliance_Review_Final_Report.pdf.

Penn, Briony, "New Calls for a Moratorium on Old-Growth Logging." *Focus Online*, July 2016, focusonline.ca/node/1113.

Penn, Briony, "Taking back control of resource extraction on public land," *Focus* magazine, September 6, 2018, focusonvictoria.ca/focus-magazine-septoct-2018/taking-back-control-of-resource-extraction-on-public-land-r9/.

Wilson, Jeremy, *Talk and Log: Wilderness Politics in British Columbia*. Vancouver: UBC Press, 1998.

Marine Issues

Campbell, Colin, *Blue Carbon—British Columbia: The Case for the Conservation and Enhancement of Estuarine Processes and Sediments in B.C.* Sierra Club BC, 2007, sierraclub.bc.ca/wp-content/uploads/2015/08/Blue-Carbon-British-Columbia-Report.pdf.

Mitchell, Alanna, *Sea Sick: The Global Ocean in Crisis*. Toronto: McClelland & Stewart, 2009.

Energy and Mining Issues

Cox, Sarah, *Breaching the Peace: The Site C Dam and a Valley's Stand Against Big Hydro*. Vancouver: On Point Press, an imprint of UBC Press, 2018.

Horne, Matt and Joshua MacNabb, *LNG and Climate Change: The Global Context*. Pacific Institute for Climate Solutions, University of Victoria, 2014, pics.uvic.ca/sites/default/files/uploads/publications/LNG%20Paper%202014%5B1%5D.pdf.

Thompson, Andrew, *West Coast Oil Ports Inquiry, Statement of Proceedings*. February 1978, www.empr.gov.bc.ca/Mining/Geoscience/MapPlace/thematicmaps/OffshoreMapGallery/Documents/West-Coast-Oil-Port-Inquiry-Statement-of-Proceedings.pdf.

Walters, Joshua, Shi-Ling Hsu, and Gareth Duncan, *Windy Craggy: Mining in British Columbia*. Vancouver: University of British Columbia Faculty of Law, 2007, www.allard.ubc.ca/sites/www.allard.ubc.ca/files/uploads/enlaw/pdfs/windy-craggy_05_15_09.pdf.

Climate Change and Biodiversity

Bloomberg, Michael R. and Carl Pope, *Climate of Hope: How Cities, Businesses, and Citizens Can Save the Planet*. New York: St. Martin's Press, 2017.

Ecojustice, "Legal Backgrounder, Species at Risk Act (2002)." www.ecojustice.ca/wp-content/uploads/2015/03/MAY-2012_FINAL_SARA-backgrounder.pdf.

Flannery, Tim, *The Weather Makers*. New York: Harper Collins Publishers Ltd., 2006.

Klein, Naomi, *This Changes Everything: Capitalism vs. The Climate*. Toronto: Vintage Canada, a division of Random House, 2015.

Underpinnings of *The Future Is Here* Document

Biodiversity BC, *Taking Nature's Pulse: The Status of Biodiversity in British Columbia*. 2008.

Holt, Rachel and Gregory Kehm, *Conservation and Adaptation in British Columbia: Strategic Opportunities in a Climate Changing World*. Veridian Ecological Consulting, 2014.

Lee, Marc and Amanda Card, *A Green Industrial Revolution: Climate Justice, Green Jobs and Sustainable Production in Canada*. Canadian Centre for Policy Alternatives, 2012.

Locke, Harvey, "Nature Needs Half: A Necessary and Hopeful New Agenda for Protected Areas." *Parks*, Vol 19 (2), 2013.

Peart, Bob, Sarah Patton, and Eva Riccius, *Climate Change, Biodiversity and the Benefit of Healthy Ecosystems*. Canadian Parks and Wilderness Society (BC), 2007.

Pojar, Jim, *A New Climate for Conservation: Nature, Carbon and Climate Change in British Columbia*. Commissioned by the Working Group on Biodiversity, Forests and Climate, 2010.

Wilson, Sara and Richard Hebda, *Mitigating and Adapting to Climate Change Through the Conservation of Nature*. The Land Trust Alliance of British Columbia, 2008.

Endnotes

Preface

1   Sierra Club of British Columbia (1969); Sierra Club of Western Canada (formed in 1972 but did not use name until 1976); Sierra Club of British Columbia name resumed (1994); Sierra Club of Canada, BC Chapter (until 2011); and it is now known officially as Sierra Club of British Columbia Foundation, but often shortened to Sierra Club BC (since 2013).

Chapter 1

2   John Muir, *A Thousand-Mile Walk to the Gulf*. New York: Houghton Mifflin, 1916, 1.

3   John Muir, "The Treasure of the Yosemite." *The Century* magazine. XL, no. 4, 1890. "Features of the Proposed National Park." *The Century* magazine. XL, no. 5, 1890.

4   Tom Turner, *Sierra Club: 100 Years of Protecting Nature*. New York: Henry N. Abrams, 1991, 24.

5   Anne Rowthorn, *The Wisdom of John Muir: 100+ Selections from the Letters, Journals, and Essays of the Great Naturalist*. Birmingham, AL: Wilderness Press, 2012, 1.

6   National Organization for Women, "The National Organization for Women's 1966 Statement of Purpose." The website notes: "This is a historic document adopted at NOW's first national conference in Washington, D.C., October 29, 1966." now.org/about/history/statement-of-purpose/.

7   "The 1960s," History of American Journalism website. Designed by students in Rick Musser's Journalism History class, University of Kansas, history.journalism.ku.edu/1960/1960.shtml.

8   Turner, *Sierra Club*, 197.

9   Michael Doherty, "An Angel on the Shoulder: The Political Influence of the Sierra Club in British Columbia." Master's thesis, University of Victoria, 1986.

10   Along with Sierra Club BC, the original Canadian contingent included the BC Wildlife Federation, the Alpine Club of Canada, the UBC Varsity Outdoor Club, the Society for Pollution and Environmental Control, the BC Mountaineering Club, and the Simon Fraser Outdoor Club.

11   Terry Simmons, "The Damnation of the Dam: The High Ross Dam Controversy." Master's thesis, Simon Fraser University, 1974.

12   Geraldine Irby, "The People, the Ideas, the Times: How the Sierra Club was born in Canada." *Sierra Report*, Vol 13 (4), Winter 1994/95, 4–5.

13   Jacqueline Kirn, "The Skagit River-High Ross Dam Controversy: A Case Study of a Canadian-U.S. Transboundary Conflict and Negotiated Resolution." Master's thesis, University of Washington, 1987, 68.

14   Concern about the Skagit River Valley was raised again in 2018 when conservation, recreation, and wildlife organizations became aware of logging at the headwaters of the Skagit River in what is known as the "Manning Park doughnut

hole," a small area where logging and mining is allowed in the park. People worried that it could lead to further industrialization in the form of a copper mine. They argued that it goes against the spirit of the treaty, if not actually breaching the treaty. See: Justine Hunter, "U.S. conservation groups decry B.C. logging in Skagit River system," *The Globe and Mail*, October 10, 2018.

15   Sierra Club of British Columbia, *West Coast National Park Life-Saving Trail: A Plea for Wider Boundaries.* April 1971.

16   Michael McCloskey, *In the Thick of It: My life in the Sierra Club.* Washington: Island Press, 2005.

17   Ric Careless, *To Save the Wild Earth.* Vancouver: Raincoast Books, 1997, 235.

Chapter 2

18   The first time civil disobedience was ever endorsed by the parent US Sierra Club—for a one-time-only event—was February 13, 2013, when forty-eight leaders from environmental, civil rights, and community organizations from across the US joined together for a peaceful protest at the White House with the expectation that they would face possible arrest. They demanded that President Obama put a halt to the Keystone XL tar sands pipeline and address the climate crisis. See: sierraclub.typepad.com/michaelbrune/2013/01/civil-disobedience.html.

19   Quote by a Sierra Club "chapter staffer," cited in Turner, *Sierra Club,* 258.

20   Bob Nixon, in an interview with Peter Grant for *ForesTalk Resource* magazine (Summer 1981). Nixon originally worked as a nuclear engineer on US submarines and studied forestry prior to becoming the first paid conservation chair for Sierra Club BC.

21   *Sierra Club of BC Foundation Annual Report.* 2000, 2.

22   A non-profit public interest organization that has provided free legal support to numerous local, national, and international environmental organizations. According to its website, Earthjustice.org: "Initially known as the *Sierra Club Legal Defense Fund*, we were always a separate entity from the *Sierra Club*. We changed our name to *Earthjustice* in 1997 to better reflect our role as a legal advocate for a diverse, and growing, group of clients" and "because the earth needs a good lawyer."

23   The case went all the way to the US Supreme Court, but unfortunately, the court ruled in favour of the Disney development proposal. In the end, due to a number of factors, Mineral King was not developed and instead the property was added to Sequoia National Park.

24   "Our Story," Ecojustice website, www.ecojustice.ca/about/our-story.

25   Elizabeth May, *Who We Are: Reflections on my Life and Canada.* Vancouver: Greystone Books, 2014.

Chapter 3

26   SCBC's educational website, which includes an Ecomap that provides information about the nine different ecosystems of the province, can be found at sierraclub.bc.ca/ecomap.

27   "Ricardo Navarro: 1995 Goldman prize winner, El Salvador." YouTube video published 2013, www.youtube.com/watch?v=i85m_7gh0ZM.

28   "Toilets, Trees and Transformation: Inspiration from El Salvador[1995]." YouTube video published 2013, www.youtube.com/watch?v=QhbTEyY1C9U.

Chapter 4

29 In a brochure from the 1930s. The original lodge was known as Stuie Lodge and offered big game hunting, fishing, hiking, and riding. It could be reached by a Union Steamship travelling "every Tuesday" from Vancouver to Bella Coola, www.tweedsmuirparklodge.com/assets/The-Lodge/Tweedsmuir-Park-Lodge-Brochure-cirac-1930s.pdf.

30 Careless, *Wild Earth*, 95–114.

31 Rosemary Fox, "The Spatsizi." *Sierra Report*, Vol 13 (4), Winter 1994/95, 4.

32 University of Victoria Archives, Rosemary Fox correspondence and reports (Box 96-087, Sierra Club 4/5, 04/04/74).

33 Susan Todd, "Designing Effective Negotiating Teams for Environmental Disputes: An Analysis of Three Wolf Management Plans." Doctoral dissertation, University of Michigan, 1995, 86.

34 "Moratorium on Grizzly Hunting Demanded." *Sierra Report*, Vol 17 (3), Autumn 1998, 4.

35 "Alcan Project: A Potentially Devastating Impact." *Sierra Report*, Vol 13 (2), Summer 1994, 1.

36 Rosemary Fox, "A Call for Wilderness Protection—The Stikine: A New Start in a Ten-Year Battle." *Sierra Report*, Vol 9 (1), Spring 1989, 3.

37 Mike Clarke, "Site C Dam: How We Got Here and What You Need to Know." CBC *News*, December 16, 2014, www.cbc.ca/news/canada/british-columbia/site-c-dam-how-we-got-here-and-what-you-need-to-know-1.2874998.

38 Ibid.

39 *Report of the Joint Review Panel—Site C Clean Energy Project*, BC Hydro and Power Authority. May 2014, www.ceaa-acee.gc.ca/050/documents/p63919/99173E.pdf.

40 Submission to the UNESCO World Heritage Centre/IUCN Mission to Wood Buffalo National Park and World Heritage Site, Sierra Club of British Columbia Foundation, May–June 2016, sierraclub.bc.ca/wp-content/uploads/2015/08/Site-C-Submission-to-Monitoring-Mission-Sierra-Club-BC.pdf.

41 The decision calls on Canada to make proven progress towards fully implementing all seventeen of the recommendations from the fall 2016 UNESCO mission to Wood Buffalo National Park, jfklaw.ca/unesco-directs-canada-protect-wood-buffalo-national-park-assess-site-c-dam.

42 Jeff Lewis, "Ottawa unveils action plan to protect ecology of Wood Buffalo National Park." *The Globe and Mail*, February 2, 2019, A15.

43 Wayne McCrory and Erica Mallam, "News from the Rain Forest Grizzly Valley, the Khutzeymateen, B.C." *Friends of Ecological Reserves* newsletter, July 1990, 11, ecoreserves.bc.ca/wp-content/uploads/2011/12/Log199007.pdf.

44 Also, Ksi X'anmaas (Kwinamass River) Conservancy, Khyex Conservancy, and the Kts'mkta'ani/Union Lake Conservancy, subject to constitutionally protected aboriginal rights and title interests.

Chapter 5

45 May, *Paradise Won*, 100.

46 Friends of Clayoquot Sound, focs.ca/about-us.

47 Wilderness Committee, "Clayoquot Sound Backgrounder," www.wildernesscommittee.org/clayoquot_sound_backgrounder.

48 Ron MacIsaac and Anne Champagne, *Clayoquot Mass Trials: Defending the Rainforest*. Gabriola Island: New Society Publishers, 1994.

49 Andrew Ross, "Clayoquot Sound Chronology," prepared for the Politics of Clayoquot Sound Research Project, October 1996.

50 Brian Sarwer-Foner, "Grass Roots Tactics to Save Big Trees: Clayoquot Protest Moves Across Canada." *McGill Daily*, November 8, 1993, archive.org/stream/ McGillLibrary-mcgill-daily-v83-n035-november-08-1993-13917/mcgill-daily-v83-n035-november-08-1993_djvu.txt.

51 Brian Pinch, *Environmental Interest Groups on Vancouver Island.* Unpublished paper, December 1974, 16.

52 Comment by Paul Spong, long-time orca researcher based near Robson Bight, as told to Martin Dunphy. "Sierra Club says Vancouver Island orca beaches threatened by proposed old-growth logging." *Georgia Straight*, April 12, 2018, www.straight.com/news/1057561/sierra-club-says-vancouver-island-orca-rubbing-beaches-threatened-proposed-old-growth.

53 A 1975 submission to the Royal Commission on Forest Resources chaired by Dr. Peter Pearse —the Victoria group's was written by Brian Pinch, Eve Howden, and Bruce Hardy, and the Vancouver group's was written by Jerry Fagerlund.

54 Jeremy Wilson, *Talk and Log: Wilderness Politics in British Columbia.* Vancouver, UBC Press, 1998, 152.

55 R. Schwindt, "The Pearse Commission and the Industrial Organization of the British Columbia Forest Industry." *BC Studies*, no. 41, 1979, 6.

56 Dave Leversee, "Cooperative Forest Management: The Sierra Club of Western Canada and British Columbia Ministry of Forests Use of Multiple GIS Data Sources to Assess Logging Effects on Vancouver Island." *Earth Observation* magazine, July/August 1993.

57 The Order of British Columbia website, orderofbc.gov.bc.ca/members/ obc-2000/2000-vicky-husband.

58 Pat Price, "Guardian of the Trees." *BC Woman*, November 1993, 24–27.

59 Karen Wilson, "Profile: Vicky Husband." *Everwild*, October/November 1992, 11.

60 Ibid.

61 Wilson, *Talk and Log*, 177.

62 Personal communication with Ric Careless: He was able to convince Stephen Owen, commissioner of CORE, to also include the Cariboo–Chilcotin as one of the land use planning tables by showing him that a major amount of top calibre wilderness could be preserved with limited impact on forestry. CORE's involvement with the Cariboo–Chilcotin region opened up the opportunity to preserve millions of acres of wilderness parks across the "Chilcotin Ark" and in the Caribou Mountains. BC Spaces for Nature led the efforts across the Ark; however, Sierra Club BC was especially involved in the South Chilcotin portion of the Ark and also contributed to the preservation effort in the Tsylos area. This laid the groundwork for Sierra Club BC's more recent efforts in the Fish Lake (Prosperity Mine) issues in the early 2000s.

63 Michael Mason, *Environmental Democracy: A Contextual Approach.* New York: Earthscan, 1999.

64 Wilson, *Talk and Log*, 281.

65 Ibid., 291.

66 *Vancouver Island Summary Land Use Plan.* British Columbia government, February 2000, 33. www2.gov.bc.ca/assets/gov/farming-natural-resources-and-industry/ natural-resource-use/land-water-use/crown-land/land-use-plans-and-objectives/westcoast-region/vancouverisland-rlup/vancouver_island_slup.pdf.

67   Ray Travers, *An Analysis of the Economic Transition Issues Driving the Development of a New Forest Policy for British Columbia.* Victoria: Sierra Club of Western Canada, 1993.

68   Ibid., 66.

69   Merran Smith, "Buy 'Good Wood' or it's Goodbye Forests." *Sierra Report*, Vol 17 (2), Summer 1998, 5.

70   Jill Thompson, "How Grassroots Became a Forest: Forest Watch BC Now a Free-standing Organisation." *Sierra Report*, Vol 20 (1), Spring 2002, 4–5.

71   Malcolm Curtis and Ian Dutton, "Environmental Activists Give Forestry Employees an Eyeful." *Times Colonist*, August 13, 2001.

72   Ben Parfitt and Kerri Garner, *Axing the Forest Service: How British Columbians are Losing their Eyes and Ears in the Forest*, Sierra Club of Canada (BC Chapter), November 2004.

73   United Steelworkers District 3 and USW Wood Council, *Campbell's Legacy of Mismanagement and Steelworkers' 10 Point Plan for the BC Forest Sector.* March 2008, usw2009.ca/docs/forestry%2010%20point%20plan.pdf.

74   Briony Penn, "Taking back control of resource extraction on public land." *Focus* magazine, September 6, 2018, focusonvictoria.ca/focus-magazine-septoct-2018/taking-back-control-of-resource-extraction-on-public-land-r9/.

75   Sierra Club BC's submission to the BC government's Professional Reliance Review, January 19, 2018, sierraclub.bc.ca/wp-content/uploads/Sierra-Club-BC-Professional-Reliance-Review-Submission.pdf.

76   Mark Haddock, *Professional Reliance Review: The Final Report of the Review of Professional Reliance in Natural Resource Decision-Making.* BC Ministry of Environment and Climate Change Strategy, June 2018. engage.gov.bc.ca/app/uploads/sites/272/2018/06/Professional_Reliance_Review_Final_Report.pdf.

77   *Vancouver Island's Last Stand.* Co-published by Wilderness Committee & Sierra Club BC, Wilderness Committee Educational Report, Vol 35 (3), 2016, sierraclub.bc.ca/wp-content/uploads/2016/04/Vancouver-Islands-Last-Stand-newspaper_2016.pdf.

78   According to a pamphlet in the SCBC archives, following Prime Minister of Norway Gro Bruntland's 1987 report to the UN, in March 1989 the Canadian federal government appointed members of the National Round Table on the Environment and the Economy, made up of "influential individuals from government, business, science, strategic policy, and the public interest sector" and representing diverse interests and viewpoints. In February 1990, Husband was invited, along with three other individuals, to present a twenty-minute speech and to answer members' questions about the Canadian Forest Sector.

79   May, *Paradise Won.*

80   Moira Johnston, "Canada's Queen Charlotte Islands: Home of the Haida," *National Geographic*, Vol 172 (1), 1987, 102–127.

Chapter 6

81   Wildland Consulting, *Valhalla Provincial Park Management Plan.* 2004, 3, www.env.gov.bc.ca/bcparks/explore/parkpgs/valhalla/valhalla_background_2005_new_maps.pdf?v=1526428800058.

82   The Land Conservancy, "Valhalla Mile," conservancy.bc.ca/valhalla-mile.

83   Careless, *Wild Earth*, 118.

84   BC Parks, *South Chilcotin Mountains Park and Big Creek Park Management Plan.* 2014, 7, www.env.gov.bc.ca/bcparks/planning/mgmtplns/lillooet/background-

documents/big-creek_south-chilcoltin/sc-mtns-big-crk-draft-mp.pdf?v=
1559580536078.

85   BC Ministry of Forests, *Annual Report of the Ministry of Forests 1993/94*, www.for.
gov.bc.ca/hfd/pubs/docs/mr/annual/ar_1993-94/ann1.htm#yg.

86   Sierra Club British Columbia, *Annual Report*. 2000, 7, sierraclub.bc.ca/wp-con-
tent/uploads/2015/03/ar_2000.pdf.

87   BC Parks, *South Chilcotin Mountains Park and Big Creek Park: Management Plan*. February
2014, 3, www.env.gov.bc.ca/bcparks/planning/mgmtplns/lillooet/background-
documents/big-creek_south-chilcoltin/sc-mtns-big-crk-draft-mp.pdf?v=
1559580536078.

88   Sierra Club BC, "Flathead River Valley." sierraclub.bc.ca/campaigns/flathead.

89   "Missing Piece Would Double Waterton Lakes National Park." *E-KNOW*, www.e-
know.ca/travel-tourism/missing-piece-double-waterton-lakes-national-park.

90   US Fish and Wildlife Service, National Wild and Scenic Rivers System, established
on the basis of the 1968 Wild & Scenic Rivers Act. See "The National Wild and
Scenic Rivers System: A Brief Overview" on the Congressional Research Service
website: nationalaglawcenter.org/wp-content/uploads/assets/crs/R42614.pdf.

91   "Fourth Flathead Bioblitz aims to catalogue species." *E-KNOW*, www.e-know.ca/
news/fourth-flathead-bioblitz-aims-to-catalogue-species.

92   Sierra Club BC website, sierraclub.bc.ca/campaigns/southern-rockies.

93   Sarah Cox, *Breaching the Peace: The Site C Dam and a Valley's Stand Against Big Hydro*.
Vancouver: On Point Press, an imprint of UBC Press, 2018, 176.

Chapter 7

94   Michael McPhie, *Prospects for Mining in British Columbia, a Report for the British
Columbia Business Council in Support of the Opportunity 2020 Project*. Mining Asso-
ciation of British Columbia, 2009, 1, www.bcbc.com/content/559/2020_200910_
McPhie.pdf.

95   Wilderness Committee, "Clean Up BC's Dirty Mining Industry." Vol 35 (1), 2016.
www.wildernesscommittee.org/sites/all/files/publications/2016_mining_paper_
web_final.pdf.

96   Ocean Watch, Howe Sound Edition website: oceanwatch.ca/howesound/clean-
water/britannia-mine-contamination.

97   Wilderness Committee, "Clean Up BC's Dirty Mining Industry."

98   This chronology is outlined in a newsletter entitled *Sold Out to Mining Interests*,
produced by Friends of Strathcona Park and Western Canada Wilderness Committee, Summer 1987, www.wildernesscommittee.org/sites/all/files/publica-
tions/1987%2008%20strathcona%20Park.pdf.

99   Nancy Brown, "Park Activists Go Free." *Times Colonist*, May 18, 1989,
beyondnootka.com/articles/strathcona_park/strathcona_9.html.

100 BC Ministry of Energy, Mines and Petroleum Resources, "Government Confirms
Position on Uranium Development," news release, April 24, 2008, archive.news.
gov.bc.ca/releases/news_releases_2005-2009/2008EMPR0029-000624.htm.

101 Joshua Walters, Shi-Ling Hsu, and Gareth Duncan, "Windy Craggy: Mining in
British Columbia," case study, University of British Columbia Faculty of Law,
2007, 5, www.allard.ubc.ca/sites/www.allard.ubc.ca/files/uploads/enlaw/pdfs/
windycraggy_05_15_09.pdf.

102 Ibid.

103 BC Spaces For Nature website: www.spacesfornature.org/campaign_tat.html.

104 According to a 2001 statement, the mission was "to help protect the long term eco-logical integrity of British Columbia and the Yukon from the impacts of mineral developments from exploration to abandonment. We work with communities, labour unions, government and industry toward the environmental reform of mining practices and regulation through research, education, dialogue and advocacy." See: thegreenpages.ca/2001/03/18/environmental_mining_council_0.

105 Sierra Club BC, *2011 Annual Report*, 7.

106 Federal Minister of the Environment, *Report of the Federal Review Panel, Prosperity Gold-Copper Mine Project, Taseko Mines Ltd., British Columbia*, July 2, 2010, www.ceaa.gc.ca/050/documents/46911/46911E.pdf.

107 Tyler Wilkinson-Ray, Colin Arisman, and Luke Kantola in partnership with Salmon Beyond Borders, *Chasing Wild: Journey into the Sacred Headwaters*. Film produced by Wild Confluence Media, US, 2017, www.youtube.com/watch?v=mA-c1-txocKw&feature=youtu.be.

108 MiningWatch Canada, "MiningWatch Canada Files Charges Against B.C. Government and Mount Polley for 2014 Tailings Pond Disaster." October 18, 2016, miningwatch.ca/news/2016/10/18/miningwatch-canada-files-charges-against-bc-government-and-mount-polley-mine-2014.

109 Sierra Club BC pamphlet, *BC Mineral Tenure Act*.

Chapter 8

110 Christine Mai-Duc, "The 1969 Santa Barbara Oil Spill that Changed Oil and Gas Exploration Forever." *Los Angeles Times*, May 20, 2015, www.latimes.com/local/lanow/la-me-ln-santa-barbara-oil-spill-1969-20150520-htmlstory.html.

111 "Exxon Valdez Oil Spill 1989," *Life: 100 Photographs that Changed the World*. Time Home Entertainment Inc., 2011.

112 Yereth Rosen, "Exxon Valdez Oil Spill Saga Reaches Anticlimactic End in Federal Court." *Anchorage Daily News*, October 15, 2015, www.adn.com/environment/article/exxon-valdez-saga-reaches-anticlimatic-end-federal-court/2015/10/16.

113 Will Koop, "Appendix A: Oil Pipeline Timeline," *Pushing the Tar Sands Envelope*. Submission to the National Energy Board, July 10, 2006, 23, www.bctwa.org/NEBSubmission-July10-06-AppA.pdf.

114 Ibid.

115 Rosemary Fox, "Kitimat and the Oil Supply Dilemma." Background article, Sierra Club BC files in the University of Victoria Archives.

116 "Chairman's Report, Kitimat—Oil on BC's Waters," *Sierra Club, Western Canada Chapter Quarterly Newsletter*, Vol 6 (4), December 1976.

117 Andrew Thompson, *West Coast Oil Ports Inquiry: Statement of Proceedings*, February 1978, 2, www.empr.gov.bc.ca/mining/geoscience/mapplace/thematicmaps/offshoremapgallery/documents/west-coast-oil-port-inquiry-statement-of-proceedings.pdf.

118 Heather Ramsay, "Offshore drilling divides B.C.'s North." *Tyee*, November 9, 2004, thetyee.ca/News/2004/11/09/OffshoreDrillDivideBC/print.html.

119 Roland Priddle, "Evaluation of the Views Expressed." *Report of the Public Review Panel on the Government of Canada's Moratorium on Offshore Oil and Gas Activities in the Queen Charlotte Region, British Columbia*, prepared for the Minister of Natural Resources Canada, October 29, 2004, ii, www.nrcan.gc.ca/sites/www.nrcan.gc.ca/files/energy/pdf/eneene/sources/offext/pdf/prpcep-eng.pdf.

120 Ibid., iii.

121 Cheryl Brooks, *Rights, Risks and Respect: A First Nations Perspective on the Lifting of the Federal Moratorium on Offshore Oil & Gas Exploration in the Queen Charlotte Basin of British Columbia*, prepared for the minister of natural resources, Ottawa, October 20, 2004, www.turtleisland.org/news/fnep.pdf.

122 RAVEN is an acronym for Respecting Aboriginal Values and Environmental Needs, raventrust.com.

123 Jas Johal and Peter Meisner, "Kinder Morgan Pipeline Expansion will Increase Tanker Traffic Nearly Seven-fold," *Global News*, October 15, 2013, globalnews.ca/news/900601/kinder-morgan-pipeline-expansion-will-increase-tanker-traffic-nearly-seven-fold.

124 Peter Erickson, "Global Impact of Oilsands Growth could Counteract Canada's Promised Carbon Cuts." *Analysis, Energy*, June 13, 2018, www.nationalobserver.com/2018/06/13/analysis/global-impact-oilsands-growth-could-counteract-canadas-promised-carbon-cuts.

125 "New Trans Mountain pipeline review to meet February deadline: NEB." *Global News*, October 12, 2018, globalnews.ca/news/4544258/trans-mountain-neb-hearing-schedule.

126 "BC files final argument to NEB against Trans Mountain Pipeline." *CBC News*, January 22, 2019, www.cbc.ca/news/canada/british-columbia/b-c-files-final-argument-on-trans-mountain-1.4988822.

127 National Energy Board News Release, "NEB releases Reconsideration report for Trans Mountain Expansion Project," February 22, 2019, www.neb-one.gc.ca/bts/nws/nr/2019/nr04-eng.html.

128 Sierra Club BC website, "Sierra Club BC Statement on National Energy Board Recommendation to Approve Trans Mountain." February 22, 2019, sierraclub.bc.ca/sierra-club-bc-statement-on-national-energy-board-recommendation-to-approve-trans-mountain.

129 Dylan Heerema and Maximilian Kniewasser, *Liquefied Natural Gas, Carbon Pollution, and British Columbia in 2017: An overview of B.C. LNG issues in the context of climate change.* Pembina Institute, August 2017, www.pembina.org/reports/lng-carbon-pollution-bc-2017.pdf.

130 Carol Linnitt, "NDP Offers Tax Breaks, Subsidies to Attract BC's Single Largest Carbon Polluter: LNG Canada." *Narwhal*, March 22, 2018, thenarwhal.ca/ndp-offers-tax-breaks-subsidies-attract-b-c-s-single-largest-carbon-polluter-lng-canada.

131 Sierra Club BC website, "UN climate science report shows new LNG terminals are a blueprint for climate disaster," sierraclub.bc.ca/tag/lng.

132 IPCC, "Summary for Policymakers of Special Report on Global Warming of 1.5°C Approved by Governments, Intergovernmental Panel on Climate Change," October 8, 2018, www.ipcc.ch/pdf/session48/pr_181008_P48_spm_en.pdf.

133 "What New Relationships? Taking Responsibility for Justice and Sustainability in British Columbia," *Alliances: Re-envisioning Indigenous/Non-indigenous Relationships*, edited by Lynne Davis. Toronto: University of Toronto Press, 2010.

134 Caitlyn Vernon, *Nowhere Else on Earth: Standing Tall for the Great Bear Rainforest*. Victoria: Orca Book Publishers, 2011.

Chapter 9

135 "Fish Inquiry Must Include Habitat, Groups Unite to tell Brian Tobin." *Sierra Report*, Vol 13 (3), Autumn 1994, 7.

136 Pinch, *Environmental Interest Groups*, 18.

137 John Fraser, "Executive Summary." *Fraser River Sockeye 1994: Problems and Discrepancies: Report of the Fraser River Sockeye Public Review Board*, Government of Canada, Department of Fisheries and Oceans, 1995.

138 Sierra Club BC, "Turning the Tide on the Salmon." *Salmon Report No. 1*, Summer 1998.

139 Department of Fisheries and Oceans, Government of Canada, *Canada's Policy for Conservation of Wild Pacific Salmon*, June 2005, www.pac.dfo-mpo.gc.ca/publications/pdfs/wsp-eng.pdf.

140 Bruce Hill, "Activist Guide to Seafood and Sushi." *Sierra Report*, Vol 18 (1), Spring 2000, 3.

141 Ross Crockford, "Seafood Guide Helps People Eat Ethically, Spot What's Fishy." *Georgia Straight*, February 12–19, 2004, 37.

142 According to the organization, "SeaChoice works throughout the seafood supply chain to drive continued improvements in the sustainability of seafood available to Canadians and exported to other markets." See: www.seachoice.org/our-work.

143 B. Lucas, S. Verrin, and R. Brown, eds., "Ecosystem Overview: Pacific North Coast Integrated Management Area (PNCIMA)," *Canadian Technical Report of Fisheries and Aquatic Sciences 2667*, Fisheries and Oceans Canada, 2007, x, www.pncima.org/media/documents/pdf/ecosystem-overview-pncima.pdf.

144 "BC's North Coast Ocean Under Threat," *Sierra Report*, Vol 25 (3), Spring 2008, 6.

145 Rhona Govender and Alexander Brown, "Sea of Glass—Protecting BC's Glass Sponge Reefs," *BCnature*, Winter 2015, 6, www.bcnature.ca/wp-content/uploads/2015/11/BCNature-winter-web.pdf.

146 Department of Fisheries and Oceans, "Pacific North Coast Integrated Management Area (PNCIMA)," www.dfo-mpo.gc.ca/oceans/management-gestion/pncima-zgicnp-eng.html.

147 Fisheries and Oceans Canada website, www.dfo-mpo.gc.ca/oceans/mpa-zpm/hecate-eng.html; www.marketwired.com/press-release/protecting-jurassic-period-glass-sponge-reefs-another-step-towards-canadas-marine-conservation-2196764.htm.

148 Colin Campbell, *Blue Carbon—British Columbia: The Case for the Conservation and Enhancement of Estuarine Processes and Sediments in B.C.* Sierra Club BC, 2007, 2, sierraclub.bc.ca/wp-content/uploads/2015/08/Blue-Carbon-British-Columbia-Report.pdf.

149 Spearheaded by Sierra Club BC science advisor Colin Campbell and writer Ana Simeon. See: sierraclubbc.scbc.webfactional.com/our-work/seafood-oceans/spotlights/code-blue.

150 Colin Campbell, "Counting our blessings: Reflections on working in the conservation movement." Sierra Club BC website, sierraclub.bc.ca/2810-2.

151 Campbell, *Blue Carbon–British Columbia*.

Chapter 10

152 *Huchsduwachsdu Nuyem Jees/Kitlope Heritage Conservancy Management Plan*, British Columbia, Haisla Nation, BC Parks, 2012, 12.

153 *A Brief History of British Columbia's Parks and Protected Areas*, www.bcauditor.com/sites/default/files/publications/2010/report3/files/oagbcconservationofecologica lintegritysupplementalinfohistory.pdf.

154 Coast Forest Conservation Initiative, "Joint Solutions Project," www.coastforestconservationinitiative.com/_About/joint_solutions.html.

155 Merran Smith, *Place of Power: Lessons from the Great Bear Rainforest*. Vancouver: Tides Canada Foundation, 2010, 23.

156 Smith, *Place of Power*, 30.

157 Deborah Curran, "'Legalizing' the Great Bear Rainforest: Colonial Adaptations Towards Conservation and Reconciliation." *McGill Law Journal*, Vol 62 (3), 2017, 837.

158 Smith, *Place of Power*, 31.

Chapter 11

159 Bo Martin, "Climate Change: How Will It Affect B.C.?" *Sierra Report*, Vol 16 (3), Autumn 1997, 5.

160 According to Stefan Rahmstorf, Potsdam Institute for Climate Impact Research, in the article "Modeling Sea Level Rise," *Nature Education Knowledge*, 2012, Vol 3 (10), 4, www.nature.com/scitable/knowledge/library/modeling-sea-level-rise-25857988.

161 Lisa Matthaus, "B.C.'s Capital Faces Flood Risk: Is Victoria Going Under?" *Sierra Report*, Vol 24 (3), Winter 2006, 6.

162 Martin Golder, "Message [from the] Chair of the Executive Committee," *Sierra Club BC Annual Report 2007*, 3, sierraclub.bc.ca/wp-content/uploads/2015/03/SIERRA CLUB BC_AnnualReport_2007.pdf.

163 Sierra Small Parties were described as "intimate get-togethers over drinks and snacks [where Sierra Club BC] provide[s] presentations and other resources that inspire commitment and action." For those who were ready to move to the next level, there were Sierra CERCles, "small groups [of people] who support each other in taking personal action to reduce their carbon footprints. CERCles provide people with easy to use tools for measuring their footprints and help them find ways to reduce their greenhouse emissions." *Sierra Report*, Vol 25 (2), Fall 2007, 2, 4.

164 "British Columbia Speech from the Throne," February 13, 2007, www.leg.bc.ca/content/legacy/web/38th3rd/Throne_Speech_2007.pdf.

165 Clare Demerse, *How to Adopt a Winning Carbon Price: Top Ten Takeaways from Interviews with the Architects of British Columbia's Carbon Tax*, Clean Energy Canada, February 2015, 6, cleanenergycanada.org/wp-content/uploads/2015/02/Clean-Energy-Canada-How-to-Adopt-a-Winning-Carbon-Price-2015.pdf.

166 Ibid., 11.

167 Dale Beugin and Chris Ragan, "To Avoid Catastrophic Climate Change, We Need Carbon Pricing," *The Globe and Mail*, October 10, 2018, 15.

168 Colin Campbell and Cliff Stainsby, *Greenhouse Gas Emission Reduction Scenarios for BC: Meeting the twin objectives of Temperature Stabilization and Global Equity*, Canadian Centre for Policy Alternatives, August 2008.

169 Sierra Club BC website, "Sierra Club BC hails Clean BC as important step forward," December 5, 2018, sierraclub.bc.ca/sierra-club-bc-hails-clean-bc-as-important-step-forward.

Chapter 12

170 Marc Lee, "The Rise and Fall of Climate Action in BC." Policy Note website, February 13, 2017, www.policynote.ca/the-rise-and-fall-of-climate-action-in-bc/.

171 Sierra Club BC, *Annual Report*. 2009, sierraclub.bc.ca/wp-content/uploads/2015/03/Annual-Report-2009.pdf.

172 Ecojustice, "Legal Backgrounder, Species at Risk Act (2002)." www.ecojustice.ca/wp-content/uploads/2015/03/MAY-2012_FINAL_SARA-backgrounder.pdf.

173 Sierra Club BC, *Endangered Species Toolkit: The Citizen's Guide to Protecting Biodiversity in British Columbia*. Victoria, www.sccp.ca/sites/default/files/species-habitat/documents/sar toolkit_sierra club bc.pdf.

174 Justine Hunter, "Ottawa Orders BC to Act to Protect Caribou Habitat." *The Globe and Mail*, May 7, 2018, 8.

175 Ibid.

176 Jens Wieting, "Preserve Old-Growth Forests to Keep Carbon Where it Belongs." *Tyee*, September 12, 2017, thetyee.ca/Opinion/2017/09/12/Preserve-Forests-Carbon-Belongs.

177 Jens Wieting with mapping analysis by Dave Leversee, "State of British Columbia's Coastal Rainforest, Mapping the Gaps for Ecological Health and Climate Protection." Sierra Club BC, December 2009, www.sierraclub.bc.ca/campaign-spotlights/coastal-rainforest-at-risk.

178 "White Rhino" map shows Vancouver Island's most endangered old-growth rainforests: sierraclub.bc.ca/white-rhino-map-shows-vancouver-islands-most-endangered-old-growth-rainforests.

179 "Environmental and Conservation Movements," *The Canadian Encyclopedia*, www.thecanadianencyclopedia.ca/en/article/environmental-and-conservation-movements.

Chapter 13

180 "Local Groups," Sierra Club BC website, sierraclub.bc.ca/about/local-groups.

181 Wilson, *Talk and Log*, 8.

182 My thanks to the recall of early members Ken Farquharson and Tom Perry. The latter recalled going to Parks Board meetings concerning this issue in 1969–70.

183 Louise Pedersen, "Lower Mainland Group Update, Vancouver Members Invited to Participate," *Sierra Report*, Vol 21 (3), Fall 2003, 6, sierraclubbc.scbc.webfactional.com/publications/newsletters/sierra-report/sr_22_3_fall03.pdf/at_download/file.

184 Sarah Petrescu, "B.C. to complete purchases of land along trail." *Times Colonist*, April 7, 2017, A4.

185 Pinch, *Environmental Interest Groups*, 39.

186 West Coast Environmental Law website: www.wcel.org/sites/default/files/publications/On%20The%20Ground.pdf.

187 Capital Regional District Parks, "Regional Green/Blue Spaces Strategy." October 1997, www.crd.bc.ca/docs/default-source/parks-pdf/greenblue_spaces_strategy.pdf?sfvrsn=0.

188 Capital Regional District, "Regional Growth Strategy," January 2018, 23, www.crd.bc.ca/docs/default source/crd-document-library/bylaws/regionalgrowthstrategy/4017--capital-regional-district-regional-growth-strategy-bylaw-no-1-2016.pdf?sfvrsn=ecb611ca_4.

189 SLAPP is the acronym for "strategic lawsuit against public participation;" a lawsuit that is intended to silence criticism by burdening the defendants with legal defence costs.

190 The movement was pioneered in Ireland in 2006 and spread rapidly to a number of other countries. John Barry and Stephen Quilley, "The Transition to Sustainability: Transition Towns and Sustainable Communities," in *The Transition to Sustainable Living and Practice*. Liam Leonard and John Barry, eds., Bingley, UK: Emerald Group, 2009, 1–28.

191 Weldwood of Canada Ltd. was primarily a forestry and lumber company but had mineral rights in the area and partnered with several mining companies to try to develop a coal mine on the Quinsam River near Campbell River. Despite public opposition, the Quinsam Coal mine finally opened in 1987. Graham Brazier, "Denman Opposes Coal: Fast Facts on the Raven Coal Project," denmanopposescoal.wordpress.com/about/publications-by-doc-members /development-of-mining-on-the-tsable-river/part-iii-exploration-sampling-and- maneuvering-1966-2010.

192 Graham Brazier, "Quinsam and Raven Coal Mines on Vancouver Island." *Weekend Sentinel*, February 9, 2011, watershedsentinel.ca/articles/quinsam-and-raven- coal-mines-on-vancouver-island.

193 "Animal Profile," The Marmot Recovery Foundation, marmots.org/ about-marmots/animal-profile.

194 Environmental Appeal Board, June 4–8, 2001, www.eab.gov.bc.ca/ waste/2000was028b_31b.pdf.

195 BC Environmental Protection and Sustainability, Conservation Data, www2.gov. bc.ca/gov/content/environment/plants-animals-ecosystems/conservation-data- centre/explore-cdc-data/red-blue-yellow-lists.

196 The Legislative Assembly of British Columbia, Special Committee on Sustainable Aquaculture, *Final Report, Volume 1,* May 2007, www.leg.bc.ca/content/legacy/ Web/cmt/38thParl/session-3/aquaculture/reports/PDF/Rpt-AQUACULTURE-38-3- Volume1-2007-MAY-16.pdf.

197 Jeannine Mitchell, "The Drive for Clean Energy Sparks a B.C. Gold Rush," *Georgia Straight*, November 28, 2007, www.straight.com/article-120347/ the-drive-for-clean-energy-sparks-a-b-c-gold-rush.

198 Sierra Club, "Estuary as Eco-Neighbourhood," 2009, sierraclubbc.scbc.webfactional.com/local-groups/comox-valley/estuary-as-eco-neighbourhood.

199 CoalWatch Comox Valley, "Final Update for the CoalWatch Comox Valley Society," October 11, 2016, www.coalwatch.ca/final-update-coalwatch-comox- valley-society.

200 *CBC News*, "Vancouver Island Coal Mine Application Rejected." May 17, 2013, www.cbc.ca/news/canada/british-columbia/vancouver-island-coal-mine- application-rejected-1.1378341.

201 *CBC News*, "Raven Coal Mine: Compliance Energy Withdraws Application," March 3, 2015, www.cbc.ca/news/canada/british-columbia/raven-coal-mine- compliance-energy-withdraws-application-1.2980134.

202 CoalWatch Comox Valley, "Final Update."

203 Sierra Club BC, "Local Groups, Sierra Okanagan," sierraclub.bc.ca/about/ local-groups/#toggle-id-3.

204 Sierra Club BC, "The North Okanagan," sierraclubbc.scbc.webfactional.com/ local-groups/okanagan/the-north-okanagan.

205 Kristi Iverson, *Sensitive Ecosystems Inventory: Bella Vista–Goose Lake Range: Volume 1: Methods, Ecological Descriptions, Results and Management Recommendations.* 2002, a100.gov.bc.ca/appsdata/acat/documents/r1306/sei_4198_rpt_1099611704566_ ef4bfe45e38244118b80cb542d44acdd.pdf.

206 Sierra Club, "The North Okanagan."

207 Alan Brooks Nature Centre, "BX Creek Wetlands Enhancement and Interpretation Project," abnc.ca/stewardship/bx-creek-wetlands-enhancement-and- interpretation-project.

Chapter 14

208 Many people, too numerous to mention, provided preliminary comments to Colin Campbell and Sierra Club BC, including Ben Parfitt, Dr. Rachel Holt, Dr. Richard Hebda, Dr. Jim Pojar, Dr. Phil Dearden, Mark Haddock, Dr. John Woods, Lisa Matthaus and Dr. Briony Penn. Detailed references and citations can be found at Sierra Club BC's website: sierraclub.bc.ca. The original document was made possible with support from the McLean Foundation and Tides Canada Foundation-Wild Salmon Ecosystem Fund. Sierra Club BC extends special thanks to Roger Handling of Terra Firma Digital Arts in the production of the complete document.

209 Sierra Club BC, *The Future is Here*. Updated June 2017, sierraclub.bc.ca/wp-content/uploads/SierraClubBC_Future_Is_Here.pdf.

210 Sierra Club BC, *The Future is Here for the New Government of British Columbia*. August 2017, sierraclub.bc.ca/tag/the-future-is-here/.

211 Chapter 14 is an abridged version of *The Future is Here*, used with permission of Sierra Club BC.

Index

Page numbers in **bold** refer to photographs within the text.